Ascend to Greatness

HOW TO BUILD AN ENDURING ELITE COMPANY

SALVATORE D. FAZZOLARI

iUniverse®

ASCEND TO GREATNESS
HOW TO BUILD AN ENDURING ELITE COMPANY

iUniverse books may be ordered through booksellers or by contacting:

iUniverse
1663 Liberty Drive
Bloomington, IN 47403
www.iuniverse.com
844-349-9409

ISBN: 978-1-6632-1966-4 (sc)
ISBN: 978-1-6632-3086-7 (hc)
ISBN: 978-1-6632-1965-7 (e)

Library of Congress Control Number: 2021917163

Print information available on the last page.

iUniverse rev. date: 11/05/2021

In loving memory of five of my eight siblings who have passed: Nunzia, Rita, Isabella, Vincenzo, and Giuseppe. Two of them passed much too early, at a very young age. They are now all together in their eternal resting place with our parents and grandparents.

CONTENTS

Leadership is having a compelling vision, a comprehensive plan, relentless implementation, and talented people working together.[1]

—ALAN MULALLY

ASCEND TO GREATNESS

The idea for *Ascend to Greatness* emanated from my lifelong quest to answer an elusive question that I believe does not get completely answered with total clarity in current business leadership books. The Holy Grail question is, What specifically makes a company elite, and importantly, how do you build and sustain such an exceptional organization? This has led me to write this book, *Ascend to Greatness: How to Build an Enduring Elite Company*, which I believe specifically spells out, in the form of an *elite enterprise model*, exactly what is required to ascend the summit of greatness.

The question of whether I have succeeded in creating the "Holy Grail" book I have been seeking for so long is, of course, up to my readers to determine. However, *Ascend to Greatness* does serve as what I believe is a strong contender for an inclusive, innovative, and comprehensive framework that will guide today's leaders toward answering the elusive question of what makes an enduring elite company.

As you will learn in the pages that follow, I believe extraordinary companies are built and sustained by following a clear and actionable blueprint that I call an *elite enterprise model*. My enterprise model is built on three foundational pillars of enduring greatness, all driven by seventeen core principles. The three foundational pillars that companies need to get consistently right at an elite level include *leadership, strategy,* and *execution*.

My belief in this innovative elite enterprise model is founded on approximately four and half decades of professional experience. My indispensable experiences include serving as CEO of a Fortune 1000 company; serving on the board of directors of both public and private enterprises; advising companies through my consulting practice; working with private equity firms; and doing extensive research on elite companies. Like many CEOs, I have managed through shocks, disruptions, and ever-increasing turbulence. I have seen and experienced the business world through three very different lenses: public companies, private equity-owned enterprises, and consulting private organizations. I was also blessed to have participated in three remarkable *Good to Great* dialogue sessions with the greatest business mind in the world, Jim Collins. Through all these indispensable experiences, I have seen what works and what doesn't. Cumulatively, these experiences have formed the foundation for my elite enterprise model.

A BLUEPRINT FOR NEWLY APPOINTED LEADERS

The elite enterprise model that is outlined in *Ascend to Greatness* is intended as a practical guide, a detailed road map focused on helping leaders build and sustain an elite enterprise. This book can be particularly helpful to a newly appointed leader of either an entire company or a business segment. I wrote *Ascend to Greatness* with my own experience specifically in mind. I would have been grateful to have a received a copy of this book when I was first promoted to president of the company, years before ascending to the CEO position. I believe that this book would have been indispensable to me. Thus, my hope is that all newly appointed leaders will have an opportunity to read this book early in their tenure, ideally before taking the helm.

The principal audience for *Ascend to Greatness* is leaders of small to medium-size businesses, not CEOs of large companies. However, this book could be used as a refresher for even some larger companies that are either striving to achieve elite status or struggling to sustain greatness. If you are a professional manager, a segment or group business leader, a newly appointed CEO of a family owned or privately owned company, or even an MBA student, this book is for you. Also, this book translates well to any type of organization, including nonprofits.

Elite Enterprise Model

Greatness is not primarily a matter of circumstance; greatness is first and foremost a matter of conscious choice and discipline.[1]

—JIM COLLINS

ELITE ENTERPRISE MODEL

The elite enterprise model that I developed for achieving enduring greatness is based on proven principles that I have applied over many decades. My innovative model was developed to answer that elusive Holy Grail question in business: What specifically makes a company elite, and importantly, how do you build and sustain such an exceptional enterprise?

So, what exactly makes a company elite? Great companies can be built and sustained for generations by brilliantly implementing my elite enterprise model. My model includes the three foundational pillars of *leadership*, *strategy*, and *execution*, all driven by seventeen core principles. There are six principles under leadership, six under strategy, and five under execution. See exhibit 1 for a summary of each foundational pillar and its respective core principles.

For a company to climb to the summit and become elite, it must first get the right leadership team in place. Once an elite team is built, the company must develop a brilliant strategy. The strategy must then be superbly executed. Getting all three elements right—at an elite level and on a disciplined basis—is no easy task. If you closely examine all the elite companies that have endured, you will find—without exception—that they are exceptional at all three foundational pillars of enduring greatness. On the other hand, if you study companies that have either fallen or have never reached the summit of elite, you will likely find that they have not performed well on either one or two of the elements. Under catastrophic situations, failure has occurred in all three areas.

ELITE SIMPLY MEANS THE BEST

The term *elite* as used in *Ascend to Greatness* simply means "the best"! In more quantifiable terms, following are enterprise results I believe qualify a company as elite: proven superior shareholder value over at least a ten-year period as measured by total return as compared with a reliable benchmark, usually the S&P 500 or the comparable results found in a peer group's proxy statement.

Clearly, the best companies achieve elite status because they consistently outperform merely good or mediocre ones. Superior value creation, in the broadest of terms, is what ultimately climbing to the summit of elite is all about. I believe that enterprises that implement and strictly adhere to the elite enterprise model outlined in *Ascend to Greatness* and that do so with fanatical discipline should increase their chances of reaching the highest possible summit. Furthermore, I believe that such an organizational achievement is possible for just about any enterprise that chooses to pursue it. As Jim Collins states, "Greatness is not primarily a matter of circumstance; greatness is first and foremost a matter of conscious choice and discipline." This is so true. The leadership team must first make the conscious choice that they want to achieve greatness, and then they must implement the elite enterprise model with discipline.

IMPORTANT CAVEAT

An important caveat to remember, however, is that you can't make a silk purse out of a sow's ear. Every good cook knows that a master chef must start with exceptional ingredients to create a delightful dish. The same applies to a company and its leadership. If the company is based on a flawed concept, or if the goods or services are not something that the end user must or should have, then even the greatest leadership team cannot make a mediocre product or concept great.

Too many leaders have failed because they started with an idea that nobody cared about or a product that doesn't fill a need. Conversely, think of winners like Apple, Netflix, Uber, or any of the other new innovations that ascended to billion-dollar unicorn enterprises. Thus, before attempting to make a company great, think sow's ears and silk purses.

ABOUT THIS BOOK

Ascend to Greatness is organized into four sections. The first three sections cover the respective core principles under leadership, strategy, and execution. In section four, key metrics and mechanisms are covered that can help drive and accelerate the implementation of the seventeen principles.

EXHIBIT 1

Elite Enterprise Model

I. Foundational Pillar: Leadership

Principle #1: Leadership core characteristics
Principle #2: The right people in the right positions
Principle #3: Talent acquisition
Principle #4: Talent management and leadership development
Principle #5: Distinctive culture
Principle #6: Learning entity
Metrics and mechanisms tool kit

II. Foundational Pillar: Strategy

Principle #7: Purpose, values, and vision
Principle #8: Unique practices
Principle #9: Organizational structure
Principle #10: Building lifelines
Principle #11: Innovation and technology
Principle #12: High-performance plan
Metrics and mechanisms tool kit

III. Foundational Pillar: Execution

Principle #13: Disciplined execution
Principle #14: Growth engine
Principle #15: Commercial excellence
Principle #16: Operational excellence
Principle #17: Administrative excellence
Metrics and mechanisms tool kit

SECTION ONE

Leadership

Introduction

Veni, vidi, vici.[1]

———

—JULIUS CAESAR

JULIUS CAESAR

A marvelous example of elite leadership can be found in studying one of the greatest—and arguably *the* greatest—military commanders of all time, Julius Caesar. Julius Caesar was an exceptional leader. I believe that he manifested his greatness through five prodigious core personal characteristics: *creativity, fearlessness, instinct, proactiveness, and discipline.* He consistently achieved superior results, and his troops trusted him absolutely and would go to the extreme to support him. He was a brilliant strategist. His ability to consistently execute at an elite level was extraordinary.

All one has to do is examine some of his greatest battles, such as the Gallic victory, where he prevailed because of strategy, leadership, and the ability of his troops to execute superbly. From an execution viewpoint, the Roman legions had no peer. They were elite, well trained, and disciplined. After winning the battle of Asia Minor, Julius Caesar coined the phrase *veni, vidi, vici,* which is Latin and means "I came, I saw, I conquered." This is the mindset that is required by the leadership team to build an enduring elite company.

Once the leadership team commits to relentlessly pursuing enduring greatness, there's no turning back. Metaphorically speaking, it's like crossing the Rubicon. This phrase is attributed to Julius Caesar's crossing the Rubicon River in 49 BC. The river is between Italy and what was then Gaul. Once Caesar crossed the river into Italy with his army, that action was irrevocable. It started a civil war against the Roman senate and Pompey. The same principle applies when an enterprise makes a commitment to pursuing greatness. That decision is irrevocable—there's no turning back—because it will put the enterprise on a path that will likely require some painful decisions about people, culture, strategy, and execution.

BUILD A TEAM FOR THE FUTURE

Exceptional leaders almost universally possess the five key core personal characteristics that Julius Caesar possessed. Remarkable leaders use these strong characteristics effectively. As a consequence, they make an outsized positive impact on the performance of their organizations. These five characteristics—more than any other—will be the main drivers to building an elite leadership team and ultimately a great company. We will review these characteristics in more detail in chapter 1.

When it comes to business enterprises, Steve Jobs is, of course, the obvious example of a leader who possessed the five core indispensable characteristics in abundance. Not only was he an elite leader who had an outsized effect on the performance of Apple, but he also brought exceptional talent to the company. The team that he brought to Apple had a disproportional positive effect on building the most elite company the world has ever seen. That performance continues today unabated.

What Steve Jobs did at Apple is exemplary. When he built his team, he had the future in mind. Steve Jobs intuitively knew that for Apple to ascend to greatness, he needed a team that was able to execute at the most elite level possible. This required putting the right people in the right positions who had lots of runway in front of them. That is, his team had outsized talent and the abilities to take the company to the summit of elite. Thus, he built a team for the future state and not for the present. He made no compromises and insisted on the most elite talented people.

DISCIPLINED LEADERSHIP

As stated throughout *Ascend to Greatness*, the three foundational pillars are inextricably linked. The foundational pillars must all be implemented at an elite level to achieve enduring greatness. What links and drives the three pillars is discipline. This is the common denominator. Without discipline, it's impossible to ascend to the summit.

Although the principle of disciplined execution is listed specifically under the foundational pillar of execution, it equally applies to the other two pillars. That's because these other two pillars also need to be executed in a disciplined manner. As explained in section three of *Ascend to Greatness*, I advocate for using an integrated management system to impel elite-level disciplined execution. The same goes for executing the other core principles under the foundational pillars of both leadership and strategy.

LEADERSHIP OVERVIEW

In section one, we will review the foundational pillar of *leadership*. There is a total of six core principles, and they are covered in chapters 1 through 6. Leadership success is all about having the right people. I call this simply *people excellence*. Without enough of the right people occupying the right positions, an organization is destined to fail.

Since people excellence is so important to achieving enduring greatness, I have segmented this vital element into four distinct principles. These four core principles are all interrelated and necessary to building an elite leadership team. The remaining two principles under leadership include the need for a distinctive culture and the importance of developing a learning enterprise.

The following chapters deal with the most important core principles—mentioned in the chapter titles—necessary for building an extraordinary leadership team and an enduring elite company:

Chapter 1. Leadership Core Characteristics
Chapter 2. The Right People in the Right Positions
Chapter 3. Talent Acquisition
Chapter 4. Talent Management and Leadership Development
Chapter 5. Distinctive Culture
Chapter 6. Learning Entity

CHAPTER ONE

Leadership Core Characteristics

The task of the leader is to get his people from where
they are to where they have not been.[1]

—HENRY KISSINGER

ELITE LEADERS BUILD GREAT TEAMS

Elite companies are built and sustained by remarkable leaders. The first step in any journey to the summit is to build an elite leadership team. Without extraordinary leaders, the other two foundational pillars of enduring greatness—strategy and execution—will fail. So, what is an elite leadership team, and how do you create one and sustain it over a long horizon? It all starts with the five core personal characteristics of an elite leader.

In this chapter, we will define the five most vital core personal characteristics that each member of the leadership team must possess at an elite level to build an enduring great company. Then, in chapters 2, 3, and 4 we will review just how you go about building and sustaining an outstanding leadership team that possesses these elite characteristics.

A NEW BREED OF ELITE LEADERS

Because of increasing turbulence from shocks and disruptions, leaders today are confronted with tremendous challenges. In addition to turbulence, leaders face an increasingly competitive landscape and ever more vocal activist investors. With growing volatility and uncertainty, particularly as the pace of technology is accelerating, a new breed of leader is required to navigate what's on the horizon. That's why the leadership team of the enterprise must possess the five core personal characteristics. These core characteristics are the glue that holds the leadership team together across the globe. These traits should always be self-evident whenever a team member interacts with anyone inside or outside the enterprise.

Without the five core personal characteristics, it will be difficult, if not impossible, for leaders of an organization to achieve and sustain greatness. All leaders are ultimately defined by the strength, depth, and quality of these core personal characteristics. When building all the key positions with the right people in the organization, it is imperative to assess these characteristics as much as possible. This is especially important when it comes to the chief executive officer (CEO) and all of his or her direct reports. The most effective way to assess and develop these personal characteristics is through an elite talent management and leadership development program that includes providing people in key positions with indispensable experiences. This is vital because most leaders are developed over some time; they grow into their positions.

WHY ARE THE FIVE CORE PERSONAL CHARACTERISTICS SO IMPORTANT?

The reason the five core personal characteristics are so important is that daily, leaders have to make crucial decisions that will cumulatively determine the success or failure of their organizations. Obviously, some of these decisions are going to be more impactful than others. As part of this decision-making process, leaders are constantly confronted with the all-important dilemma of what to do and what not to do.

The importance of cumulatively making the right decisions cannot be overstated. Leaders must think critically about each decision. This sentiment was captured perfectly by Miriam Gottfried in a *Wall Street Journal* article titled "Apollo's $433 Billion Makeover Man." The author states, "Josh Harris, the co-founder of Apollo Global Management Inc., obsessively weighs the risks and implications of decisions he makes: whom to hire for a role … whether to move forward with an investment."[2] As the article points out, leaders must obsess over decisions because they are so consequential. This is where the five core personal characteristics come in and why they are so fundamental to decision-making. Extraordinary leaders draw on the strength of their core characteristics to consistently make good decisions. Cumulatively, these decisions are the building blocks to achieving enduring greatness.

THE FIVE CORE PERSONAL CHARACTERISTICS OF ELITE LEADERS

Selecting the right people can make the difference between excellence and mediocrity. It can also make the difference between success and failure. The old adage that people are our most important asset is only half true. In reality, the *right* people are an enterprise's most important asset. In his insightful monograph *Turning the Flywheel*, Jim Collins notes, "Those who lead organizations from good to great first get the right people on the bus (and the wrong people off the bus) and then figure out where to drive the bus. They always think *first* about 'who' and then about 'what.'"[3] So, who are the right people? This question will be explored and answered in chapters 1 through 4.

Over the decades, I have closely studied elite leaders. I have also had the opportunity to interview some remarkable leaders, and importantly, I've had the privilege of working with some through both my board work and advisory practice. What I have discovered is that there are, broadly speaking, five special core characteristics that all elite leaders (i.e., right people) have in common. The main difference between the most outstanding leaders of all time and everyone else is that the former manifest these characteristics at the highest possible level of excellence. In other words, these leaders are defined by the exceptional strength, depth, and quality of the core personal characteristics. Although few CEOs have abilities that are consistently at the highest possible level of excellence, what's important is that leaders possess such abilities in a high enough degree to guide their organizations to greatness.

The five personal core characteristics of elite leaders include *creativity, fearlessness, instinct, proactiveness,* and *discipline.* My view is that the first three personal characteristics are primarily innate and are not quickly learned, but they can certainly be further developed and sharpened. The fourth and fifth characteristics can be learned and developed, but not everyone has the ability to take them to an elite level.

Let's now explore how these essential core personal characteristics are defined and applied in the business world. *Please note that for each personal core characteristic of an elite leader, I use an expansive definition that is comprised of a multitude of vital personal traits.*

CORE CHARACTERISTIC #1: CREATIVITY

What exactly is a creative leader? A creative leader is first and foremost very smart and possesses high emotional intelligence. A creative leader can think critically and is exceptional at problem-solving. A creative leader is a visionary, is imaginative, and perhaps can see things that others are unable to. Moreover, a creative leader usually manifests these vital personal traits: passion, inquisitiveness, and natural innovativeness. A creative leader brings a unique perspective and insight to matters of importance, has a distinctive ability to connect the dots, has the skill to think differently, and consistently examines issues with wisdom, sound judgment, and common sense.

A creative leader possesses an innate ability to connect effectively at all levels of the organization and is an exemplary storyteller and teacher. A creative leader develops and communicates an exceptional long-term vision for the company and has a relentless drive for ascending the summit of elite. A creative leader is also someone who inspires the organization to passionately embrace the strategy of the company, especially its purpose, core values, and vision.

CORE CHARACTERISTIC #2: FEARLESSNESS

A fearless leader is, first and foremost, courageous and bold. Moreover, a fearless leader usually manifests these fundamental traits: is a confident warrior; is not afraid to be audacious, but at the same time is cautious and calculating; has unwavering faith that he or she will ultimately prevail no matter the circumstance; perseveres and knows how to deal with adversity productively; is not fearful of going where others may not go; is a survivalist; possesses a mental toughness and has a healthy paranoia; is methodical; is demanding; has the moral courage to do the right thing; and has a quiet, calming confidence under the most extreme conditions.

A fearless leader is an intrepid explorer of greatness. A fearless elite leader is utterly intolerant of mediocrity. In addition, a fearless leader is self-confident but not arrogant, and is a role model who knows how to win and inspire others through excellence, discipline, and a strong sense of purpose. A fearless leader demonstrates continuous self-improvement with the sole objective of personal growth.

CORE CHARACTERISTIC #3: INSTINCT

An elite leader instinctively thinks about the future. An instinctive leader understands that seeing and creating a better future is essential to sustained success. An instinctive leader usually manifests these fundamental tendencies: always follows his or her so-called sixth sense when deciding what to do and what not to do; is inclined to be proactive as opposed to reactive; consistently gets in front of issues before they turn into significant problems; and instinctively has a knack for identifying good opportunities that win in the marketplace. And an instinctive leader has a unique ability to make the right decisions about people, which benefits the enterprise for generations.

An instinctive leader augments and reinforces his or her innate ability to make better strategic decisions with insight, perspective, discipline, and critical thinking abilities. Just as important, an instinctive elite leader does not believe in attribution; instead, he or she is a strong advocate of relying on an intuition that is underpinned by as much data and unimpeachable facts as possible.

CORE CHARACTERISTIC #4: DISCIPLINE

A disciplined elite leader manifests consistency of action and is well controlled and committed. A disciplined leader consistently demonstrates an ability to concentrate on the task at hand and does not allow emotion or attribution to cloud his or her objectivity. In addition, a disciplined leader usually manifests the following traits: is authentic in all respects; is relentlessly focused on accomplishing clearly stated objectives; regularly achieves exceptional results; is not easily distracted; does not deviate from articulated communication; thinks before speaking; and exemplifies at the highest level the twin moral fibers of integrity and ethical behavior.

A disciplined leader has a passionate commitment to the purpose, values, and vision of the company and is focused on the journey to achieving enduring greatness. A disciplined elite leader grasps the importance of taking full responsibility for results and truly understands the meaning of accountability. A disciplined leader is mature and pragmatic enough to share credit when there's success. And a disciplined leader accepts total responsibility for failures, not pointing the finger at others. When failure does occur, an elite disciplined leader has the courage to apologize and learn from mistakes, and then establishes mechanisms to ensure that they are not repeated.

A disciplined leader is decisive, even when there's insufficient information available. A disciplined leader has an unshakable faith in his or her ability to deliver on promises made consistently; his or her word is sacrosanct. And a disciplined leader is the main driving force behind a distinct high-performing culture.

CORE CHARACTERISTIC #5: PROACTIVENESS

A proactive elite leader has a strong bias for action. A proactive leader builds a culture in the organization that easily and flawlessly adapts and acclimates to disruptive change. Also, a proactive leader has an obsessive focus on survival and preparing for unexpected events before they unfold. A proactive leader understands that preparation for severe turbulence and unforeseen events needs to occur during good times. Proactive leaders invest appropriate resources into building prodigious lifelines to better prepare the organization for any event—expected or unexpected— in order to provide a certain margin of safety for the enterprise. Thus, when disruptions and shocks do occur, the enterprise is well prepared and virtually immunized from the illness that strikes the unprepared.

Proactive leaders continuously scan the environment to better predict the future with appropriate analytical tools. They utilize all their core personal characteristics to identify developing storms and opportunities. With the ability to detect early on both opportunities and threats, proactive leaders adapt quickly to any circumstance. They are flexible and agile to seize opportunities, while at the same time can survive and possibly thrive under any disruption or shock.

DISCIPLINED HABITS

The five core personal leadership characteristics outlined in this chapter must be consistently driven and underpinned by disciplined habits. Ultimately, it is the daily practices that help build consistency of action. Extraordinary leaders use their superior habits to make an outsized performance impact on their organizations. As the great Greek philosopher Aristotle pointed out, "We are what we repeatedly do. Excellence, then, is not an act, but a habit."[4] Exceptional habits are essential to building elite leadership teams and ultimately a great company.

CHAPTER TWO

The Right People in the Right Positions

The greatest people are self-managing—they don't need to be managed. Once they know what to do, they'll go figure out how to do it. What they need is a common vision.[1]

—STEVE JOBS

THE RIGHT PEOPLE IN THE RIGHT POSITIONS

So, who are the right people? Who are the wrong people? What are the most critical positions in the organization? All these fundamental questions and more will be explored in this chapter.

To be successful and ultimately ascend to greatness, the leadership team must commit significant resources to people selection, retention, development, and succession. As explained earlier, I call this "people excellence." People excellence must be driven by an uncompromising process that achieves elite-level results. For a rigorous process of people excellence to work well, leaders must have ongoing robust dialogue. That dialogue must be underpinned with facts, metrics, and mechanisms to ensure that the right people are selected, retained, developed, and promoted. There must be a total commitment to ensuring that the right people are in the right positions and the wrong people are removed from the organization or moved to another seat. Without this disciplined and robust process, the company will ultimately fail in its quest to ascend the summit of elite.

WHO ARE THE RIGHT PEOPLE?

As we learned in the previous chapter, it all starts with the five core personal characteristics. These are the foundational building blocks to put together an elite team. The right people are the ones who possess an abundance of the five core personal characteristics; they consistently manifest them at an elite level. Amplifying this, the right people are passionate about and fit well with the culture of the company. I believe that culture fit is essential in selecting individuals to fill all positions, especially the key seats. Right behind culture fit, the right people need to embrace fully and be most passionate about the core values, purpose, and vision of the company. Moreover, the right people work well in a team environment. They are responsible, are accountable, and consistently deliver on their commitments.

Conversely, the wrong people are usually the ones who don't consistently exemplify the five core characteristics at an elite level. The wrong people don't fit well with the culture and don't fully embrace the strategy of the enterprise. The wrong people are not accountable, and they consistently miss on their commitments. Also, the wrong people need constant supervision and guidance. They are not well suited to a team environment.

WHAT ARE THE MOST IMPORTANT POSITIONS?

The most critical positions in the organization are usually the ones that are directly responsible for executing the strategy of the company and realizing its vision. These positions will vary from company to company depending on size, complexity, type of industry, and other variables. The two most important elite enterprise model core principles for getting the right people into the right positions and the wrong people out of the organization are talent acquisition and talent management and leadership development.

WHAT ARE THE MOST IMPORTANT TEAMS AND KEY POSITIONS?

Without an extraordinary leadership team, it's impossible to build an enduring great company. Select companies understand that the journey to greatness must begin with superior people who make an outsized impact on the performance of the organization. So, how do leading companies go about identifying the most crucial positions necessary to build elite teams?

When building exceptional teams, it is fundamental to identify all key positions. In this section, we will review what I believe to be the most influential teams and also reveal what the critical positions are, starting with the CEO. In addition to the appointment of the CEO, an executive leadership team also needs to be selected and built at an elite level.

After the CEO and the executive leadership team, it becomes a little less clear what the most critical positions in the organization are. What you will find in most companies is that the next group is called either the global leadership team or the Top 100, or some derivative of these terms. The framework for building and developing an elite global leadership team usually includes the elements outlined as follows. Finally, another group that has an outsized effect on the organization is the board of directors. These are all also key positions. Let's now review all these teams, along with the position of CEO, in more detail.

THE CEO

An elite company cannot be built or sustained without the supremely vital position of CEO. The CEO is the leader of the company. CEOs make an outsized impact on the success or failure of an enterprise. Thus, to build and ultimately sustain an elite company, the journey to greatness must begin with an exceptional CEO. The board of directors must ensure that the company is led by an elite CEO. This is the board's most important role. It is somewhat surprising how many news stories have appeared over the past decade about boards falling short on their most crucial responsibility. The record is replete with examples of boards making either wrong hiring decisions or bad firing decisions and promoting the wrong person to the CEO seat.

When selecting and appointing a CEO, the board must ensure that the individual has what it takes to elevate the company to greatness. CEOs must exemplify the five key core leadership characteristics at an elite level. These core characteristics must be extraordinarily strong, deep, and of remarkable quality. Boards need to ensure that the leader of the company has these exceptional characteristics; otherwise the journey to the summit will be arduous, if not impossible. These characteristics must be underpinned by the character of the CEO. CEOs must first and foremost possess the twin moral fibers of integrity and ethical behavior. Integrity means doing the right things for the right reasons and in the right way. Integrity and ethical behavior are ultimately the cornerstone of a leader's reputation and legacy and, importantly, the foundation on which great companies are built. As the author M. H. McKee wrote, "Integrity is one of several paths—it distinguishes itself from others because it is the right path ... and the only one upon which you will never get lost."[2]

THE EXECUTIVE LEADERSHIP TEAM

The executive leadership team, or ELT, is usually comprised of all the key direct reports to the CEO. These are all critical positions. The more common direct reports to the CEO include chief financial officer, chief information officer, chief people officer, segment/group presidents, chief operating officer (if the company has one), and chief legal officer. In addition, some enterprises have a chief risk officer, chief revenue officer, chief marketing officer, chief strategy officer, chief commercial officer, chief technology officer, chief digital officer, and/or chief sustainability officer, among executives with numerous other titles. What's important is that the ELT needs to include the leaders of the organization who are directly responsible for executing the strategy and vision of the company under the leadership of the CEO.

For an organization to climb to the summit of greatness, all critical positions need to be filled with the right people. This means that each individual who makes up the ELT needs to be the right person who is in the right position—no exceptions! This means 100 percent that there mustn't be anyone in this group who is not the right person in the right position; otherwise it will impair and certainly slow the company's ascent to the summit of elite. As you will see when we discuss the global leadership team, the benchmark percentage number is usually lower.

Just as it is imperative for the CEO to possess at an elite level the five core leadership characteristics, the ELT group must also possess a healthy supply of these characteristics. The best way to ensure that the ELT is filled 100 percent with the right people in the right positions is to promote from within through a world-class process of talent management and leadership development. The CEO is responsible for ensuring that this group performs at the highest level. The board of directors provides counsel to the CEO about each group member's performance.

GLOBAL LEADERSHIP TEAM

The global leadership team, or GLT, is usually comprised of all the other most important positions in the enterprise as defined by the ELT, with input from the CEO. The size of this group will vary depending on how large the enterprise is and how deep down in the organizational structure the ELT wants to go. Usually, the GLT is made up of all the direct reports of each ELT member. Some organizations go even deeper by including the next level below this. For some companies, this can be a rather sizable group.

Just as it is paramount for the CEO and ELT to possess at an elite level the five core leadership characteristics, the GLT group must have these characteristics too. That's because the GLT group is usually responsible for driving the strategy of the company across the globe on a daily basis. Not everyone in the GLT necessarily needs to be deemed to be in a key position. This is where the CEO and ELT need to make crucial decisions. Obviously, it is easier simply to keep the GLT a smaller group and designate all the positions as essential seats. This is what I recommend. I would then recommend using the Top 100 as a bigger group that includes both key positions (CEO, ELT, and GLT) and rising stars who will fill these seats in the future. To make the GLT more focused, some companies further segment this group into separate teams, such as the operational leadership team and the finance leadership team. I recommend this approach with a particular focus on the operational leadership team. These are the individuals that are responsible for managing the various business units and they can have an outsized effect on the performance of the company.

The GLT group needs to have at least 90 percent of the key positions filled by the right people. That's the minimum benchmark metric. Obviously, to achieve greatness, this metric needs to be constantly above the 90 percent mark. Because of retirements, job changes, and other unforeseen events, it is challenging to sustain this number close to 100 percent.

TOP 100

For large companies, the Top 100 could be the Top 200 or some other, more significant number that properly reflects the scale of the enterprise. For ease of discussion, we will simply use "Top 100" throughout. The Top 100 at some companies is usually the same as the GLT. There are, however, exceptions to this, which I recommend. Some larger companies include certain high-potential individuals who are not part of the GLT. These individuals tend to be younger rising stars who need development and exposure to the top talent in the organization. Thus, these individuals are invited to attend the Top 100 meeting, which includes GLT members as well. These high-potential individuals are viewed as being able to fill some of the critical seats in the future, including the CEO position, to sustain the enterprise for generations. Elite companies understand that they must invest in future leaders early to build an enduring great enterprise.

As part of the Top 100, I recommend implementing a mechanism that can be utilized for identifying and developing the future senior leaders of the organization. I call this the "future leaders watch list." It's a mechanism for early identification of outsized talent. This watch list should be an integral component of the leadership development program. Once these individuals have been identified, a robust development plan needs to be put in place for them as part of the succession planning process. These potential future senior leaders need to be closely monitored and mentored.

BOARD OF DIRECTORS

Every member of the board of directors is in a critical position. This seems obvious to say, but it's not unusual to find boards that may include members who are not the right people to take the enterprise to enduring greatness. Boards make an outsized impact on the future of a company. They have the sole power to hire and dismiss a CEO. When they get this wrong, the future of the company may be adversely affected. This is why every single position on the board is a key seat and why it should be treated as such with a robust process for assessment, evaluation, and accountability. Boards that do this well can truly differentiate themselves and help create value for the enterprise and its shareholders.

With more than two decades of board of directors' experience and having served as chairman of the board as well as chairman of various committees, I have observed what works and what doesn't work when it comes to building an elite board. Elite boards need to be built through a disciplined and robust succession planning process. Finding the right board member is essential to building and sustaining a value-creating elite board. This means that identifying the right prospective team members requires a strong process, a hands-on approach, and patience. An effective succession planning process for board members should rely mostly on internally developed candidates, augmented by board search firms. I believe that you need a perfect blend of the two, but with a bias toward candidates who are well-known and have a history of performance and teamwork. Just as it is a high-risk proposition to hire unknown executive level talent from the outside, it is high-risk to completely outsource the board search process to a recruiting firm.

The governance and nominating committee, which is responsible for overseeing board recruitment, needs to develop a process that is exemplary. This is fundamental because a strong board succession planning process can be a paragon for the entire organization. And it can be infectious. This means the process must be disciplined, organized, and well managed. The process should also include directors who are skilled at interviewing. A strong process should include a healthy dialogue between the committee, the CEO/chairman, and the entire board. Appropriate metrics should be utilized to ensure that the process consistently produces elite board members who fit well with the culture of the board.

FRAMEWORK FOR THE RIGHT PEOPLE IN THE RIGHT POSITIONS

A question I'm often asked is, "How do you specifically determine what the critical positions are and, importantly, who the right people are to fill them?" There are many paths that one may follow in deciding how to construct the critical positions for an organization and who should fill them. Based on my experience, I recommend a simple two-step framework that has worked well for me in practice.

Step #1: It is vital first to define what a crucial position is. In making this determination, one must answer the question "Does the position have a material effect on the organization's performance and its ability to achieve its stated vision?" Stated another way, can the position be materially impactful to any or all the foundational pillars? I would argue that any position that ultimately has the potential to have an outsized effect on the company's ability to realize its vision is a key position. With that in mind, I believe that the CEO, ELT, and GLT positions all meet the criteria. As a result, here is the recommended summary of the key positions of an organization:

- Start with the CEO, the most critical position in the organization.
- The next group is the ELT, which includes all vital positions. This group will make an outsized impact on the company's ability to realize its vision. This group includes all the direct reports to the CEO. The size of this group will obviously vary among companies, but it's not unusual to see a number that ranges somewhere between eight to twelve people. The key metric with this group is that you need to have 100 percent of these positions filled with the right people.
- The next group is GLT, which includes all essential positions. Just like the ELT, this group will make an outsized impact on the performance of the company. This group includes all the direct reports to the ELT. The size of this group will obviously vary among companies, but it's not unusual to see a number that ranges somewhere between seventy-five and one hundred people. The key metric with this group is that you need to have at least 90 percent of the key positions filled with the right people.

Step #2: The next step is to determine who the right people are who should fill these critical positions. It all starts with the candidates' need to possess the five core personal characteristics at the highest level possible. And the right people are the ones who have demonstrated an impeccable record of performance and leadership during their rise to the top of the organization. Consider the following questions when determining the right people for the right positions. These questions should be assessed for each person who is being considered for a critical position:

- What is the strength, depth, and quality of the five core leadership characteristics? Has the individual consistently manifested these characteristics at the highest level possible?
- What profile has emerged as the candidate has passed through the talent management and leadership development program? Does that profile fit the requirements of the key position?
- Is the individual deeply passionate about the company's core values, purpose, and vision?
- Does the individual fit with the culture of the company?
- Is the individual responsible, showing no need to be tightly managed?
- Does the individual work well in a team environment?
- Does the individual consistently deliver on commitments made?
- Does the individual instinctively think about the future?
- Is the individual accountable for failure, never blaming others or outside factors?

All these questions need to be properly assessed before a person is put into one of the critical positions in the company. Each position decision will cumulatively affect the journey to greatness.

UTILIZE A POWERFUL TOOL TO MANAGE THE KEY POSITIONS

With some exceptional software platforms on the market, it is now easier to manage the most vital positions in the enterprise. When selecting a software product to manage the critical positions, it is important to ensure that it includes robust tools for managing and developing talent. For example, the following information should be provided for each critical position: online profiles, individual succession plans, development plans, performance reviews, and key metrics—especially the percent of key seats filled with the right people.

Once the right tool is selected, it is essential to visually display electronically all the critical positions in the company in the format of an organizational chart. I usually recommend using a simple coloring scheme for all the key positions, that is, each box on the organizational chart is color coded as follows:

Green seats: This means that the right person is in the right position. There's no action required.

Yellow seats: This means one of two things, either that the person needs development or the person is due to retire within the next twelve months. Both scenarios require action. Development plans will need to be closely monitored. If an individual does not respond appropriately to his or her development plan, the position should then be coded red.

Red seats: This means one of three things: (1) It is not the right person, and he or she needs to be removed from the company; (2) the person is not in the right position and needs to be moved to another seat; or (3) the position is vacant and needs to be filled. With red seats, immediate action is required. When a person is not in the right position and needs to be moved to another, it is imperative that the individual is first given the benefit of the doubt.

CHAPTER THREE

Talent Acquisition

You're only as good as the people you hire.[1]

———

—RAY KROC

ELITE LEADERS FOCUS ON PEOPLE EXCELLENCE

Enduring great companies are built by elite leaders who focus on people excellence. No matter how gifted a CEO may be, the enterprise is unlikely to thrive and might just fail without an exceptional team at the top and throughout. The late CEO of Apple, Steve Jobs, was reportedly fanatical about fielding an elite team. His focus was truly on people excellence. He refused to accept even one nonelite player because he knew of the direct correlation between outsized talent and results. The logic of having a team of elite players is undeniable. Having such a team is the best antidote to mediocrity and irrelevance.

Much has been written on the subject of selecting and hiring elite players, so in this chapter we will examine the topic from a slightly different perspective. Our focus will be on reviewing specific best practices that should be adopted by organizations interested in building an exceptional elite-level talent acquisition process. Many of these best practices are employed by leading companies and have been proven over the years to be effective.

BEST PRACTICES FOR TALENT ACQUISITION

People excellence requires skill, focus, and discipline. Exceptional hiring teams clearly understand that the hiring process needs to be rigorous and it must utilize all the modern tools, mechanisms, and metrics that are available to support making quality hiring decisions. Here are essential best practices that elite leaders focus on when acquiring talent to build elite teams. The following practices are part of my elite enterprise model for people excellence:

BUILD A ROBUST TALENT ACQUISITION PROCESS

Selecting elite team members, developing them, and retaining them is the most important responsibility of a leader. This responsibility begins with building an exceptional talent acquisition process that is driven by a mindset that views hiring as strategic and not superficial. This starts with the leadership team's understanding that there's nothing more critical for the future than establishing an elite-level hiring process and getting the right people in the right positions.

UNDERSTAND THAT TALENT IS NOT ALL CREATED EQUAL

Competition for talent continues to intensify. Elite leaders understand that when it comes to talent, not everyone is created equal. Exceptional people will usually make an outsized positive impact on the performance of the company. The objective is to find as many of these talented people as possible, get them in the right positions, and unshackle them and let them perform.

KNOW THAT TALENT COMPETITION IS INTENSIFYING

Talent competition continues to intensify; everyone is chasing the best and the brightest. Elite companies are successful at recruiting talent because they have a strong culture as well as core values, a purpose, and a vision that all genuinely resonate with prospective candidates. Of course, performance, brand ranking, and market position of the enterprise are also major factors in a candidate's decision, but what's usually a deciding factor when choosing between comparable firms are culture fit and the how the individual feels about the core philosophy (purpose, values, and vision) of the company.

WHEN IN DOUBT, DON'T HIRE

When in doubt about a prospective candidate, don't hire. Hire only when the right candidate is found. Do not hire someone just to fill a position.

TREAT EVERY HIRE AS CRITICAL

The enterprise must have the right mindset to view every hire as crucial to its long-term health. There needs to be the same level of intensity around all hiring decisions no matter what position is being filled. This means that the same level of focus that is employed when hiring an officer of the company is used for an entry-level position. This is what separates the elites from everyone else. Every hiring decision in business is important. Cumulatively, all hiring decisions will have an impact on the performance of the company and its ability to climb to the summit.

LIMIT GROWTH BASED ON THE ABILITY
TO PROPERLY FILL POSITIONS

Limit growth of the enterprise based on its ability to attract enough of the right people. That's because when growth of the company exceeds the ability to fill the key positions with the right people, the enterprise will undoubtedly encounter difficulties. A shortage of enough elite players will derail a company from achieving its ultimate objective of greatness. Thus, to avoid this pitfall, decisions about people excellence must always be disciplined, aligned, and balanced with the growth of the company.

KNOW THAT RECRUITING FROM THE OUTSIDE FOR SENIOR-LEVEL POSITIONS IS HIGH-RISK

Recruiting from the outside for talent—particularly for senior-management-level positions—is fraught with high risk. If possible, promote from within the organization. The failure rate for hiring leadership positions from outside is unacceptably too high. It has been generally reported by reliable sources that the failure rate of hiring leadership positions from the outside is in the area of about 60 percent. Thus, almost two out of three outside hires are going to result in failure. With such a high failure rate, it is impossible to build an enduring great company.

If a company is reliant mainly on hiring from the outside for management and senior-level positions, this typically points to ineffective and possibly failed processes of talent acquisition and talent management and leadership development, including succession planning. Thus, it is absolutely necessary for companies to learn how to hire smartly at the lower level. These lower-level hires then need to be developed into exceptional managers and senior leaders through an elite talent management and leadership development process.

HIRE AROUND THE FIVE CORE LEADERSHIP CHARACTERISTICS

Achieving people excellence begins by hiring talented people who possess the five core leadership characteristics. How does the candidate's profile and experience compare with the five core personal characteristics? What is the strength, depth, and quality of each core characteristic? These are essential questions that must be answered.

HIRE AROUND THE CULTURE FIT AND CORE VALUES

Use culture fit and core values as a baseline for interviews. Future employees must be passionate and aligned with both the culture and the core values of the enterprise. How does the candidate fit with the culture of the company?

How does the candidate fit with the core values of the company? These are essential questions that must be answered.

HIRE PEOPLE WITH GROWTH POTENTIAL

Individual growth is fundamental to building a pipeline of future leaders. Leading companies understand this and they are focused on hiring people that have lots of runway. It's also imperative that people with growth potential are properly nurtured and developed.

POSSESS EXCEPTIONAL INTERVIEWING SKILLS

A successful elite talent acquisition process must consistently deliver quality hires. The talent acquisition process must be managed by an elite leader who appoints people who are skilled at hiring. This means that the enterprise must first identify individuals who are utterly exceptional at selecting talent. As part of this skill base, the hiring team needs to excel at interviewing. This is a skill that is not easily found.

VALIDATE REFERENCES

Another important part of quality hiring is the reference check. Checking references should never be delegated, they must be verified exhaustively by skilled interviewers. References can't be superficial; they need to be broad and deep because there's a lot that can be learned from speaking with the right people who have worked with the candidate for many years. In addition to references, obviously background checks, as well as cognitive testing, need to augment hiring decisions.

DEVELOP A DEEP PIPELINE OF TALENT

An important aspect of quality hiring is having dependable sources to draw upon. This can be accomplished by establishing a productive pipeline, for example, reliable independent hiring firms that have historically delivered high-quality candidates, top universities that have delivered exceptional graduates, and other third-party groups. In addition, current employees can sometimes be an abundant source for finding outstanding new employees. Another source that should be considered are family members of elite employees. Some companies have policies against the practice of hiring family members, but my experience is that when managed properly, this can be an excellent source for talent.

ENSURE THAT PEOPLE DECISIONS ARE DISCIPLINED

People decisions must be consistently disciplined. Leaders need to be intolerant of mediocrity. When a people change needs to be made because of a hiring mistake, it should be completed quickly, but not before the person is given the opportunity to demonstrate his or her value. This can be accomplished by providing the individual with a personal improvement plan or by moving him or her to another position, provided the circumstances require this type of action. Otherwise, if it's clear that the individual needs to be removed from the company, then do not delay or hesitate to deal with the matter. However, involuntary separations should always be conducted with dignity and fairness.

DEVELOP AN INTENSIVE ONBOARDING PROGRAM

A strong onboarding program is indispensable. Immerse all new hires in an intensive onboarding program that reinforces the culture, core values, and strategy of the company. However, onboarding is just the beginning of the training journey. There needs to be continuous improvement and training throughout an employee's career.

TREAT AFTER-ACTION REVIEWS AS INDISPENSABLE

After-action reviews need to be conducted for selection failures and successes with the objective of learning. It is vitally important to learn from both hiring mistakes and hiring successes and that appropriate actions are identified. Critical lessons learned need to be incorporated into the key people excellence processes to ensure that what works continues and what doesn't is stopped.

CONDUCT EFFECTIVE EXIT INTERVIEWS

Robust exit interviews need to be conducted when a team member voluntarily departs from the company. Appropriate mechanisms need to implemented to ensure proactive action is taken to remedy any emerging issues that are discovered as part of the exit process.

DEVELOP FUTURE LEADERS

A powerful internal talent management and leadership development process must continuously provide the enterprise with people who possess the right skills. A robust succession planning process needs be an integral part of the equation. This is covered extensively in chapter 4.

IMPLEMENT MECHANISMS AND METRICS

Mechanisms and metrics must be established and utilized to drive improved selection and hiring performance.

Many of the foregoing practices are referenced and further discussed throughout section one. We will conclude this chapter by exploring the elite hiring practices at Google and Amazon with the objective of learning from some of the best.

ELITE COMPANY EXAMPLE—GOOGLE HIRING PRACTICES

The hiring process of Google (Alphabet) has, over the years, proven to be world class. It is one to emulate given the outstanding performance of the company. In their excellent book *How Google Works*, authors Eric Schmidt and Jonathan Rosenberg provide insight on how the company approaches hiring. Following are some select quotations that capture the importance of hiring the right people and the type of focus that is necessary to achieve elite-level results.

The first quotation from *How Google Works* refers to the need to use the same level of intensity no matter what position you're hiring for. As stated earlier, this level of focus is what usually separates the elites from everyone else. Every position in business is critical because cumulative hiring decisions will make an enormous impact on the long-term performance of the company. Here is what the authors say about this essential habit: "The company's leaders pursued interviewing with the same level of intensity for every candidate. It didn't matter if the person would be an entry-level software engineer or a senior executive. Googlers made it a priority to invest the time and energy to ensure they got the best possible people."

The second quotation relates to the concept of the "herd effect." Leaders must understand the impact of this approach when building an elite company. Here is the quotation: "The best workers are like a herd: They tend to follow each other. Get a few of them, and you're guaranteed that a bunch more will follow. This 'herd effect' can cut both ways: While A's tend to hire A's, B's hire not just B's, but C's and D's too. So if you compromise standards or make a mistake and hire a B, pretty soon you'll have B's, C's, and even D's in your company."

The third quotation refers to hiring passionate people, which is something I strongly believe in. Passionate people are infectious and will help drive elite performance. Here is what the authors have to say about this: "Passionate people don't wear their passion on their sleeves; they have it in their hearts. They *live* it. ... If someone is truly passionate about something, they'll do it for a long time even if they aren't at first successful. Failure is often part of the deal."

The fourth quotation relates to the importance of hiring people who have a deep affection for learning. This is a vital personal characteristic that underpins the lifeline principle of being a learning entity. The authors capture the importance of learning well with this statement: "Our ideal candidates are the ones who prefer roller coasters, the ones who keep learning. These 'learning animals' have the smarts to handle massive change and the character to love it. ... Once you hire those learning animals, keep learning them! Create opportunities for every employee to be constantly learning new things."

The fifth quotation relates to need to be exceptional at interviewing. The interviewing skills of the organization need to be elite if the company aspires to greatness. As stated earlier, hiring is strategic and requires people with elite skills. The authors capture this idea well: "The loftier your hiring aspirations, the more challenging and important the interview process becomes. ... The most important skill any business person can develop is interviewing."

The final quotation is truly relevant because it deals with hiring biases. Biases come from not having a deep understanding of human psychology or of what drives performance. It also comes from not possessing elite hiring skills. The authors capture this idea perfectly: "Great talent often doesn't look and act like you. When you go into that interview, check your biases at the door and focus on whether or not the person has the passion, intellect, and character to succeed and excel."[2]

ELITE COMPANY EXAMPLE—AMAZON HIRING PRACTICES

Just like Google, Amazon's hiring practices are also elite. Amazon has attracted the best and the brightest, and their results prove it. In the November 21, 2019, *Wall Street Journal* article "Amazon Takes Over from GE as CEO Incubator," Dana Mattioli writes extensively about Amazon's world-renowned leadership principles and how Amazon has displaced

GE as a CEO incubator. Let's review some salient points from the article, with a focus on employee selection and talent management and leadership development.

The first quotation from the article relates to Amazon's legendary management principles and how these are used in hiring and employee reviews. Here is how the article captures this important point: "At Amazon, candidates who pass a phone interview then meet in person for up to six back-to-back meetings with different employees one-on-one. Each employee is digging for examples for how the candidate's experience relates to a specific leadership principle or competency of the job. One of the interviewers is specifically trying to glean whether the person embodies the leadership principles." This is a strong process for selecting employees. I have used a similar one over the years. It works. However, it's imperative that the people conducting the interviews are skilled and have the ability to assess the core values properly.

The second quotation relates to other practices that are used in the company for developing and promoting its culture: "In addition to its ... leadership principles, there are more general practices that are aimed at keeping teams nimble and that let data guide business decisions. Cross-functional teams should be small enough that two pizzas would suffice for dinner. Many meetings start with thirty minutes of silence as everyone reads the same six-page document. Employees pitching new products create fictional press releases to focus on the benefits to customers." These are interesting mechanisms that warrant consideration. I like the six-page document idea instead of using PowerPoint presentations (they are banned at Amazon). I also like the idea of the fictional press release and of not using presentations.

The final quotation from the article shows the power of Amazon in not only developing elite CEOs but also retaining the start-up mentality of its leaders: "In the Big Tech era, Amazon has become the incubator for CEOs and entrepreneurs. Amazon's ethos is a scrappy startup mentality that encourages employees to constantly innovate and challenge the way things are typically done." Developing talent and unleashing elite team members to innovate and be entrepreneurial can be a powerful force to drive an organization's ascent to greatness.

CHAPTER FOUR

Talent Management and Leadership Development

My number one job here at Apple is to make sure that the top 100 people are *A+ players*. Everything else will take care of itself.[1]

—STEVE JOBS

ELITE TALENT MANAGEMENT AND LEADERSHIP DEVELOPMENT

Great teams are built, developed, and sustained through a robust, results-oriented talent management and leadership development process. The indispensable component of succession planning must also be an integral part of this process.

The future performance of the company relies on what the company does today to manage and develop talent for tomorrow. Therefore, it is imperative that the CEO and the board invest a considerable amount of quality time on getting this core principle of talent management and leadership development right. As part of this critical process, there must be an ongoing robust dialogue about managing and developing talent, all underpinned by unassailable facts.

The first part of this chapter will be on reviewing specific best practices that should be adopted by organizations interested in building an exceptional talent management and leadership development process. The second part of this chapter will be devoted to succession planning. Many of the best practices outlined in this chapter are employed by exceptional companies and have been proven over the years to be compelling at managing and developing elite talent.

BEST PRACTICES FOR TALENT MANAGEMENT AND LEADERSHIP DEVELOPMENT

Exceptional leaders clearly understand that it's impossible to achieve enduring greatness without first having remarkable talent. Here are some essential best practices that elite leaders focus on when developing and managing talent to build elite teams. The following practices are part of my elite enterprise model for people excellence:

BUILD A STRONG TALENT MANAGEMENT AND LEADERSHIP DEVELOPMENT PROCESS

Retaining and developing talent is one of the most fundamental responsibilities of the leadership team. This responsibility begins with creating an exceptional talent management and leadership development process that includes succession planning. It is essential that the leadership team properly manage and inspire talent to perform at an elite level. Talent needs to be developed so that the organization always has a healthy pipeline of individuals to take on new challenges. The development of talent needs to be connected to a robust succession planning process that gets results.

BUILD A ROBUST SUCCESSION PLANNING PROCESS

Succession planning is about creating the future. For a company to better control its own destiny, the succession planning process must be aligned with the strategy of the company. The succession planning process must also be robust and should periodically be reviewed by the board of directors. The CEO needs to take ownership of succession planning, and the board needs to own the CEO succession. As part of succession planning, potential candidates need to be identified for all critical positions.

PROVIDE FUTURE LEADERS INDISPENSABLE EXPERIENCES

Leadership development programs need to be impactful and achieve superior results. It's crucial that future leaders are developed so that the enterprise is sustained for generations. A critical aspect of the leadership development program is to continuously provide key positions with what I call indispensable experiences. Some critical indispensable experiences that future leaders should be provided include international stretch assignments, being responsible for an income statement by running a business, and managing an important strategic project. As part of this training, a company should utilize staff leadership rides. This inspiring development program teaches leadership lessons on crucial battlefield decisions that were made under extreme conditions and how those decisions correlate to today's business environment.

PROMOTE FROM WITHIN FOR SENIOR MANAGEMENT POSITIONS

As explained in the previous chapter, there is ample evidence in the writings that promoting from within over the long term clearly yields better results. Some of reasons for this include less disruption to the organization, enhanced promotion and maintenance of the culture of the company, and generally lower costs. However, the most important reason is that hiring executives from the outside is like gambling and rolling the dice: sometimes you are a lucky and win, but most times you lose. And sometimes losing can be catastrophic by entrusting someone who is essentially unproven with the keys to part or all the enterprise.

So, why take outsized risks when it comes to the future of the company? If you think about this issue pragmatically, then you must ask yourself how an enterprise can truly assess a person just by a résumé, a couple of interviews, and references that are for the most part perfunctory in nature. I would argue the enterprise can't! People can only be adequately assessed by many years of working with them and seeing how they perform as they pass through the company's talent management and leadership development program. Thus, I believe that a company should not go outside for senior executive positions unless the individual has previously worked for the company and departed for various career advancement reasons. Bringing someone back with elite skills who had previously worked for the enterprise is a much lower risk proposition than bringing in someone who is essentially an unknown.

A GLOBAL LEADERSHIP TEAM MEETING MUST BE AN INTEGRAL PART OF TALENT DEVELOPMENT

The global leadership team meeting and/or the Top 100 meeting should be an integral part of the development plan for current and future leaders. This is a vital mechanism for learning and sharing best practices, for dialoguing and charting the future course of the company, and for creating a platform for the leadership team to connect and dialogue about areas of collaboration. Importantly, it's also a powerful mechanism for reinforcing the culture and strategy of the company.

TALENT DEVELOPMENT AND SUCCESSION PLANNING MUST BEGIN WITH AN EFFECTIVE PERFORMANCE APPRAISAL

Talent development and succession planning must begin with a robust performance appraisal process. Performance appraisals must be viewed as strategic. Each manager must conduct a performance appraisal of all direct reports, and the senior leader of each group must critically review and approve all these appraisals. A strong performance review provides the necessary input into an individual's development plan.

Talent development and succession planning will not achieve elite status without a disciplined performance appraisal process. The essential objectives of a performance appraisal are not to only assess the strengths and weaknesses of each individual but also to highlight any potential derailers. The reviewer must sit down and have an honest and candid dialogue with the individual being assessed. A key area of dialogue needs to be about any identified leadership derailers, which are defined as "a behavior that gets in the way of our progress. A derailer is not just a weakness. We all have many weaknesses that we may never choose to improve or need to master. A derailer is a weakness that requires improvement if we are to realize our potential."[2] A few common leadership derailers include hubris, lack of composure, lack of focus, and indifference. As part of the robust dialogue, the manager needs to agree with the individual on a specific development plan to address the identified derailers.

AN INTERNAL UNIVERSITY IS VITAL FOR TALENT DEVELOPMENT

An internal university augmented with tailored outside training should be an integral part of employee management and development. As part of this talent development, there needs to be a focus on sharpening and further enhancing as many of the core personal characteristics as possible. In addition, team members need to be properly trained in critical thinking and problem-solving skills.

ASSIGN YOUR MOST TALENTED PEOPLE TO YOUR GREATEST OPPORTUNITIES

As stated throughout section one, talent is not all created equal. That is why it's important to assign your most talented people to develop the best opportunities for the enterprise. A common mistake that some organizations make is to assign their best people to their most severe problem areas. By doing this, an organization may miss out on achieving a breakthrough objective that is instrumental in realizing the vision of the company.

ENGAGE EFFECTIVELY WITH TEAM MEMBERS

A robust employee engagement program is a must for all organizations. It is essential that enterprises seek continuous feedback from employees. Employee engagement is indispensable for taking the temperature of the organization and for implementing meaningful change. Engaging effectively with team members is critical because employee satisfaction is fundamental to retaining talent and maintaining a distinctive culture.

There are many software products and other tools that are effective at capturing timely and constructive comments from employees. Some common mechanisms include the use of employee surveys that are conducted by both third parties and internal human resources personnel. Also, many companies are augmenting these mechanisms with pulse surveys. In general, surveys should be done as frequently as possible, as long as they are effective. Every company needs to determine the appropriate frequency that works best in its environment, which is often driven by the culture of the organization. Interim feedback from team members ensures that continuous and valuable real-time information is received by the leadership team so that appropriate corrective action can be implemented.

There are numerous mechanisms that are utilized by companies to obtain feedback from employees—far too many to mention here. What is essential to remember, however, is that companies are now utilizing more innovative approaches to employee engagement and retention. Of particular importance are mechanisms that enable proactive action in response to useful feedback. Employees need to see that the process is working. One example is the company town hall meeting. Today, many town hall meetings are conducted quarterly, and they can be effective at engaging with employees and receiving feedback. Another example is from the great grocery chain Wegmans. They have what is called the Ask Bob initiative. Here is how a *Fortune* article from March 2020 about the hundred best companies to work for captured this mechanism: "One big theme on our list? Employees want leaders who will listen. No one knows that better than Wegmans, a fixture on our list for 23 years. Wegmans is renowned for its Ask Bob initiative—an open line of communication between the company's 50,000 employees and its senior vice president of operations, Bob Farr. Farr takes pride in reviewing and personalizing every response to employees. Since 2002, the program has given responses to a stunning 16,000 messages."

EMPOWER TEAM MEMBERS

As part of their development, team members should be empowered to do great things. Remarkable leaders focus intensely on embedding empowerment in the DNA of the organization through effective mechanisms that free people from bureaucratic policies and suffocating practices. This is an important way to identify and observe future leaders of the company. Leaders need to ensure that decision-making is pushed down to individuals and to small teams. However, with empowerment comes accountability and responsibility. Empowerment does not mean allowing individuals total freedom to do as they please. They must be accountable to management, and their work should be properly reviewed. For empowerment to work well in an organization, the CEO must support it and live it every day. The CEO also needs to ensure that implemented empowerment mechanisms are functioning as designed.

EMBRACE DIVERSITY

Talent management and leadership development needs to passionately embrace diversity and inclusion. Leading companies understand the power of building an enterprise that promotes diversity and inclusion. I believe that building a diverse and inclusive group of future leaders will strengthen the organization. Studies have shown that companies that embrace diversity and inclusion usually perform at a higher level. Sheryl Sandberg, in an article in the *Wall Street Journal* on September 30, 2015, really captured the power and competitive advantage of this important practice when writing,

"There is a wealth of evidence that diversity helps teams and organizations perform better in terms of innovation, creativity, revenue and profits."

ACT FAST

When a company knows that a change needs to be made in a critical position because of unsatisfactory performance, it is crucial to act fast. However, the enterprise must first ensure that the person is not simply in the wrong position. It's important to give that person the benefit of the doubt and let him or her prove himself or herself. I've seen people flourish when moved to another seat because they were just simply in the wrong position. When a person is moved to another seat, it is essential to establish key objectives and properly define success.

DEVELOP LEADERSHIP PRINCIPLES

Amazon's leadership principles are used daily in all aspects of their business. These leadership principles instill discipline and are part of Amazon's high-performance culture. See exhibit 2 at the end of the chapter for a list of all the principles, along with a definition for each one.

SUCCESSION PLANNING NEEDS TO BE STRATEGIC

Few people are natural-born leaders. The majority of leaders are instead nurtured and developed through a powerful talent management and leadership development program. As these talented individuals mature through indispensable experiences, they eventually grow into the type of leaders that are necessary to take the company to the summit. The objective of succession planning is to continuously identify, assess, and develop talent through a disciplined process. Leading companies understand that a robust leadership development and talent management process for succession planning is an exceptional capability that separates the elite from everyone else. To ensure that they have a sufficient pipeline of strong executive talent, exceptional enterprises actively engage in succession planning that gets results.

A prolific succession planning process requires considerable resources. Elite companies don't view this commitment as a cost but as an opportunity to build a world-class organization. Studies have shown that there's a direct correlation between enterprise performance and an exceptional succession planning process. Succession planning has never been more relevant than it is today. Although most companies have some form of succession planning in place, the evidence shows that plans sometimes fall short because they are either outdated or just simply ineffective at building a deep pipeline of talent for the future.

SUCCESSION PLANNING GUIDELINES

Elite CEOs and boards ensure that there is a total focus on building an organization that is prepared to endure for generations. Extraordinary leaders understand that superior results are derived from a world-class succession planning process that impels the long-term health and viability of the enterprise. Here are some key guidelines to follow in creating an elite succession planning process:

- Succession planning must be viewed as a strategic process. This is the process where future leaders are identified, assessed, and developed. The process must be driven and owned by the CEO because the future of the company depends on its strength and effectiveness. The board is directly responsible for CEO succession and should also oversee the entire succession planning process.
- A world-class succession planning process should ensure that the company is never forced to recruit the CEO from the outside. When this happens, it usually means that the board has fallen short of its most important responsibility. This mistake can be avoided by implementing a superior succession planning process that ensures there is a consistent large pool of qualified candidates.

A viable succession plan should also ensure that all identified high-potential candidates are developed over a period of decades, with the best emerging over time based on their performance.

- Succession planning must be thoughtful and comprehensive in nature. It should cover the entire C suite and at least one level below, but it is not unusual to see planning mapped out for two levels below the executive leadership team.

- Succession planning must be clearly aligned with and descend from the strategy of the company. And it should also ensure that the culture of the company is embedded in the DNA of each potential future leader.

- On a quarterly basis, the CEO and senior managers should review the pipeline of talent. They should also discuss progress and position assignments.

- At least annually, the board should conduct an in-depth review of the company's succession plan. The review should be done with the CEO and, at times, might include key senior officers. It is the CEO's job to provide insight into each key seat in the form of a written summary, augmented with a verbal report.

- The independent directors should periodically meet in executive session to discuss the CEO succession plan. The board and the CEO should have a robust dialogue about the most desirable competencies and characteristics of a future CEO and should use this profile for measuring all potential candidates against. The dialogue should be centered on the five core personal characteristics.

- The succession plan must be well organized with essential information, such as which executives are ready immediately to step into a new position; which executives will be ready in the near term (one to three years); which high potential key employees will be ready in the future (three to five years); and perhaps which potential candidates will be ready beyond five years.

- The succession plan should include detailed development plans for each potential successor and should include such elements as stretch assignments, overseas experience, mentoring, and specific internal and external training. Star candidates should be provided with indispensable experiences, including running a business.
- A succession plan should include key metrics and tools, such as 360° assessments.

CEO SUCCESSION SHOULD ENSURE THE SUCCESSOR IS A SUCCESS

I am a passionate believer in the idea that it is the moral obligation of a departing CEO and the direct responsibility of the board of directors to take substantive action to ensure that the incoming CEO is a success. There are five basic minimal lifelines that a company needs to provide a newly appointed CEO to ensure future success:

- A newly appointed leader must be assigned an experienced and talented mentor, but that assignment needs to be natural and authentic; it can't be a forced relationship.
- A newly appointed leader must have an unwavering board of directors and executive team support.
- A newly appointed leader must be provided with appropriate outside training on leadership, such as Harvard's programs.
- A newly appointed leader should be assisted in establishing an outside relationship with a trusted confidant, someone who can provide counsel and support.
- A newly appointed leader must be assisted in obtaining a board of director's seat at another company.

Boards that fall short of providing these five essential lifelines to a newly appointed CEO should reassess their internal succession planning process. Elite CEOs, however, go way beyond the five basic lifelines provided by a strong board. First and foremost, these remarkable leaders devote their entire careers to building an enduring organization. They do this by first building a distinctive culture, one that is deeply ingrained in the organization. A strong culture is built on the foundation of a clear purpose and vision, guided by embedded core values. Nothing is more important for a leader than ensuring that a healthy culture permeates the enterprise. In addition, elite CEOs build an abundance of lifelines over their tenure. As a consequence, newly elected CEOs who inherit a healthy culture and plentiful lifelines will no doubt start their tenure on much stronger footing, which significantly increases the probability of future success. With these elements in place, successors have a clear advantage over other newly appointed CEOs who don't inherit these strengths.

A good example of an elite leader providing his successor with exceptional elements for success is Steve Jobs. Mr. Jobs's successor, Tim Cook, inherited a company that was extraordinarily strong and inimitable. It is not surprising that Tim Cook has been a tremendous success and that Apple continues its remarkable and unmatched climb. Today, Apple is viewed by many knowledgeable people as the best-managed company in the world. This did not happen naturally or by accident. The foundational seeds were planted by Steve Jobs, and they have been harvested by Tim Cook. Apple is clearly in an elite class that operates in the thin air of the summit.

IDENTIFY OR APPOINT A STRONG NUMBER TWO

Whether or not to create a chief operating officer position is a question that periodically comes up in business articles and board meetings. The question, however, should not be centered on the position title but on whether a strong number two exists in the organization. For elite companies, the answer to this question of an already existing strong number two is usually yes. In many enterprises, there's usually more than one person identified. Organizations will often identify individuals who are high-potential candidates from a small, select pool of extraordinary leaders. In cases where there is a clear number two in the organization, it is not unusual for a company to designate this individual and elevate him or her as the heir apparent. When that happens, the title of president and/or chief operating officer will often be given to the successful candidate who will succeed the CEO.

An exceptional number two candidate often comes from such positions as chief operating officer, president of a large business segment or group, and even the CFO role. With the chief operating officer title, you will often see the additional title of president. However, titles are not important. What is most important is that the CEO has someone whom he or she can trust to execute superbly and be a true partner in climbing to the summit of greatness.

In today's hypercompetitive and chaotic environment, an exceptional number two is indispensable. I would argue that if you look closely at high-performing elite companies, you will usually find an exceptional number two who helps the CEO to build ample lifelines as the company ascends to the summit. At times, the number two person may not be officially announced as such, but the responsibilities and track record of performance put that individual on a clear path to possibly ascending to the top position. For companies and boards that want to build an elite company, succession planning should not be solely focused on the CEO. It needs to go deeper to identify and appoint an extraordinary number of individuals who have the potential to be elevated to number two and ultimately to the CEO position.

EXHIBIT 2

Amazon's Leadership Principles

Amazon has sixteen leadership principles. Here is what the company states on its website about these fundamental beliefs: "We use our Leadership Principles every day, whether we're discussing ideas for new projects or deciding on the best approach to solving a problem. It is just one of the things that makes Amazon peculiar."

Amazon has these management principles deeply ingrained in its culture. This was highlighted in a November 21, 2019, *Wall Street Journal* article, "Amazon Takes Over from GE as CEO Incubator." The author, Dana Mattioli, writes extensively about Amazon's world-renowned leadership principles. Some salient points from the article regarding the principles are as follows: "Amazon's management culture is especially well-defined and hammered endlessly into its executives, say those who have worked there. ... Today it is used in hiring, employee reviews and business decisions." Clearly, Amazon's culture has a fanatical focus on the company's management principles, and these principles have worked well given the extraordinary value of the company.

The following are Amazon's leadership principles on the company's website, as of August 2021:

- **Customer Obsession.** Leaders start with the customer and work backward. They work vigorously to earn and keep customer trust. Although leaders pay attention to competitors, they obsess over customers.
- **Ownership.** Leaders are owners. They think long term and don't sacrifice long-term value for short-term results. They act on behalf of the entire company, beyond just their own team. They never say "that's not my job."
- **Invent and Simplify.** Leaders expect and require innovation and invention from their teams and always find ways to simplify. They are externally aware, they look for new ideas from everywhere, and they are not limited by "not invented here." As we do new things, we accept that we may be misunderstood for long periods of time.
- **Are Right, A Lot.** Leaders are right a lot. They have strong business judgment and good instincts. They seek diverse perspectives and work to disconfirm their beliefs.
- **Learn and Be Curious.** Leaders are never done learning and always seek to improve themselves. They are curious about new possibilities and act to explore them.

- **Hire and Develop the Best.** Leaders raise the performance bar with every hire and promotion. They recognize exceptional talent, and willingly move them throughout the organization. Leaders develop leaders and take seriously their role of coaching others. We work on behalf of our people to invent mechanisms for development like Career Choice.

- **Insist on the Highest Standards.** Leaders have relentlessly high standards—many people may think these standards are unreasonably high. Leaders are continually raising the bar and driving their teams to deliver high-quality products, services, and processes. Leaders ensure that defects do not get sent down the line and that problems are fixed so they stay fixed.

- **Think Big.** Thinking small is a self-fulfilling prophecy. Leaders create and communicate a bold direction that inspires results. They think differently and look around corners for ways to serve customers.

- **Bias for Action.** Speed matters in business. Many decisions and actions are reversible and do not need extensive study. We value calculated risk taking.

- **Frugality.** Accomplish more with less. Constraints breed resourcefulness, self-sufficiency and invention. There are no extra points for growing head count, budget size, or fixed expense.

- **Earn Trust.** Leaders listen attentively, speak candidly, and treat others respectfully. They are vocally self-critical, even when doing so is awkward or embarrassing. Leaders do not believe that their or their team's body odor smells of perfume. They benchmark themselves and their teams against the best.

- **Dive Deep.** Leaders operate at all levels, stay connected to the details, audit frequently, and are skeptical when metrics and anecdote differ. No task is beneath them.

- **Have Backbone; Disagree and Commit.** Leaders are obligated to respectfully challenge decisions when they disagree, even when doing so is uncomfortable or exhausting. Leaders have conviction and are tenacious. They do not compromise for the sake of social cohesion. Once a decision is determined, they commit wholly.

- **Deliver Results.** Leaders focus on the key inputs for their business and deliver them with the right quality and in a timely fashion. Despite setbacks, they rise to the occasion and never settle.

- **Strive to be Earth's Best Employer.** Leaders work every day to create a safer, more productive, higher performing, more diverse, and more just work environment. They lead with empathy, have fun at work, make it easy for others to have fun. Leaders ask themselves: Are my fellow employees growing? Are they empowered? Are they ready for what's next? Leaders have a vision for and commitment to their employees' personal success, whether that be at Amazon or elsewhere.

- **Success and Scale Bring Broad Responsibility.** We started in a garage, but we're not there anymore. We are big, we impact the world, and we are far from perfect. We must be humble and thoughtful about even the secondary effects of our actions. Our local communities, planet, future generations need us to be better every day. We must begin each day with a determination to make better, do better, and be better for our customers, our employees, our partners, and the world at large. And we must end every day knowing we can do even more tomorrow. Leaders create more than they consume and always leave things better than how they found them.

CHAPTER FIVE

Distinctive Culture

With the right people, culture, and values,
you can accomplish great things.[1]

—TRICIA GRIFFITH

CULTURE IS THE CORNERSTONE OF ENDURING GREATNESS

Because culture is the cornerstone of enduring greatness, it should be at the top of the list for all leaders. An elite company cannot be built and sustained without a distinctive culture. A distinctive culture is one that is harmonious and high performing, where everyone is passionate about the strategy of the company. A distinctive culture is in essence an underpinning lifeline of a company. Conversely, a company that has a dysfunctional, disharmonious, or even toxic culture will most likely not perform well over a long horizon. Extraordinary leaders understand the importance of having a distinctive culture where everyone is aligned, disciplined, and focused on implementing the elite enterprise model. There can be no deviation. An organization must first win the culture war before it can thrive as an enduring enterprise.

It is fundamental to remember that once a company's culture is embedded, it's difficult to change it, particularly if it's toxic. In most companies, an unhealthy culture usually just happens; no one plans it. No company intentionally tries to create a dysfunctional culture; such a culture just happens naturally over time (sometimes over decades) and for a multitude of reasons, including not having the right people or having no clear purpose, no core values, or no vision.

Ultimately, a distinctive culture is driven by the leadership team, particularly the CEO. I believe that culture is the one principle where the CEO can make a dramatic and outsized impact on the company. A distinctive culture can also attract top talent to a company. This is an area that CEOs need to pay close attention to because it's a prerequisite not only to building an elite company but also to sustaining it. Culture is so important that some CEOs have appointed a chief culture officer.

The way the leadership team acts, thinks, and behaves is instrumental to determining the type of culture an enterprise will ultimately have. The strength and caliber of peer connections within the organization will also determine whether there's a strong or weak culture. And most important is a healthy culture, one driven heavily by the core values, purpose, and vision of the company. In a distinctive culture, the unique practices and organizational structure lend themselves to a connect-and-collaborate type of environment that allows employees to flourish and interact in a positive and constructive manner. Thus, in a remarkable culture, you will usually find that everyone is aligned with the values, beliefs, and behaviors that are fundamental to building an enduring great company.

In a distinctive culture, you will also find that a number of essential mechanisms have been implemented to ensure that the strong culture is embedded and sustained. It is my belief, based on a number of companies that I have studied and worked with, that organizations that have established a distinctive culture usually outperform those within their peer group. My experience is also backed up by studies that have shown enterprises with a superior culture outperform others that have an unremarkable culture.

BUILD AN ENDURING CULTURE THAT WINS

No matter how well a company performs, there's always a risk that an enterprise can lose its way and fall from the summit. Sometimes, the wounds are self-inflicted by complacency and/or arrogance, which are usually driven by the loss of discipline. Some examples of this include making a disastrous large acquisition or the board of directors ousting an elite leader (think Apple and Steve Jobs).

On the other hand, wounds can be inflicted by outside forces such as innovation disruptions and economic shocks. Elite companies find a way to immunize the enterprise against these negative and adverse forces of change by creating a winning culture that endures and by building ample lifelines. So, how does an organization build a distinctive culture that wins and endures for generations? I've developed a recipe for building a winning culture, which includes the following critical elements:

- the way the CEO and leadership team behave and communicate,
- the way people embrace the strategy of the company,
- the way people in the organization connect, interact, and collaborate,
- the way the company promotes an entrepreneurial environment,
- the way learning and continuous improvement are embedded in the organization,
- the way the governance system functions,
- the way the company implements mechanisms, and
- the way the board of directors behaves, thinks, and acts.

CRITICAL ELEMENTS FOR CREATING A WINNING CULTURE

All the meaningful elements that we will discuss in this section are normally found in most distinctive cultures. Let's examine each element in detail. Please note that all elements of building a distinctive culture are crucial, but none are more so than the tone at the top set by the CEO.

#1. THE WAY THE CEO AND LEADERSHIP TEAM BEHAVE AND COMMUNICATE

Leadership excellence must underpin a distinctive culture. The way the CEO and the leadership team behave and communicate—along with the core values, purpose, and vision—is the most profound driver of culture. Do leaders walk the talk? Do they manifest integrity in every action, every word, and every deed? Do their actions embrace and passionately demonstrate a commitment to teamwork and connectivity? Do leaders communicate effectively with clarity and consistency? Is there unity of purpose within the global leadership team? Does the team regularly reinforce the core values of the company? Do they stay true to the vision and business model in a disciplined manner? Do they instill a culture of innovation and technology? Do they strongly embrace learning? In a distinctive culture, the answer to all these questions is a resounding yes.

Another aspect of leadership behavior is how the enterprise treats its employees. This can have a notable effect on the performance culture of the company. This behavior becomes especially vital during difficult and turbulent times. Employees will remember how they were treated during periods of chaos and distress. Elite leaders need to consistently, under all conditions, demonstrate empathy, respect, and flexibility when dealing with team members. Another important element of treating people well is establishing a safe, diverse, and inclusive environment where team members can flourish and perform to the best of their abilities.

A distinctive culture can also be shaped by the way the leadership team proudly communicates and promotes the rich history of the company. Effectively telling the story of the company and reinforcing its importance can help shape a strong culture. This can be accomplished through various means, including the company's internal university, a global leadership team meeting, on the company's website, or through various digital channels.

#2. THE WAY PEOPLE EMBRACE THE STRATEGY OF THE COMPANY

How an organization's strategy is embraced is a key driver of a healthy culture. At the top of the list are the purpose, values, and vision of the company, which I collectively refer to as a *core philosophy*. When people embrace it enthusiastically, a powerful core philosophy has an outsized effect on the culture of the company. When the core philosophy is deeply embedded in the culture of the company, it provides a strong foundation— it's the engine that propels the company forward. Enterprises that profoundly live their core philosophy daily with passion and discipline usually outperform the competition.

The unique practices, organizational structure, the building of lifelines, innovation and technology, and the high-performance plan are all also integral parts of the company's strategy—and they all impact culture. Therefore, they need to be enthusiastically embraced by everyone in the organization because they are also powerful drivers of a distinctive culture.

#3. THE WAY PEOPLE IN THE ORGANIZATION CONNECT, INTERACT, AND COLLABORATE

The way people in the organization connect, interact, and collaborate with each other on a daily basis is essential to a distinctive culture. This is one of the best indicators of the type of culture that exists in an organization. It all begins with hiring the right people who are most passionate about the purpose, values, and vision of the company. Hiring and developing the right people who have the highest integrity and who consistently behave in a way aligned with the spirit of the company's core values is paramount. The right people are passionate about doing things the right way and for the right reasons. They are also disciplined in thought, word, and deed, which is vital to a remarkable culture.

Companies with a superior culture understand the importance of having physical locations organized in such a manner that they promote the core philosophy and unique practices of the company. Physical locations can make a sizable impact on how people connect, interact, and collaborate and thus should not be ignored. The importance of having physical locations that are well designed and organized applies across the enterprise.

In addition to attending to its physical environment, a company needs to be thoughtful about how it organizes itself virtually. As the world discovered during the COVID-19 pandemic, the work-from-home (WFH) environment suddenly changed everything, with the most adverse effect being on culture and innovation. I believe that the WFH virtual world will remain with us in some form. Many are predicting a hybrid system, which will vary greatly depending on the organization and the industry it operates in. Thus, companies need to be attentive to how they build their virtual environments with the primary focus on how sustained WFH will especially influence culture, innovation, and employee development. Companies that ignore this will do so at their own peril.

#4. THE WAY THE COMPANY PROMOTES AN ENTREPRENEURIAL ENVIRONMENT

An entrepreneurial spirit provides elite organizations with a competitive advantage and is often a critical recipe element of a distinctive culture. Creating an entrepreneurial spirit throughout the enterprise is not easy. It usually begins by establishing a home where entrepreneurial managers feel empowered to make decisions and drive change throughout the organization. This is an excellent way to cultivate an environment where people want to come to work and take the initiative to succeed.

When team members are enthusiastic about an organization's entrepreneurial culture, their enthusiasm can be infectious and motivational. It can attract talent and help promote an entrepreneurial environment throughout the company. However, to properly sustain such a dynamic culture, such enthusiasm must be carefully managed. This includes ensuring that the governance system does not demotivate people and discourage them from doing the right thing that can ultimately benefit the company.

#5. THE WAY LEARNING AND CONTINUOUS IMPROVEMENT ARE EMBEDDED IN THE ORGANIZATION

Learning and continuous improvement are fundamental to the long-term success of the company. These two facets complement each other and are essential drivers of a distinctive culture. They both help to strengthen and improve the company while simultaneously sustaining a healthy culture. As part of learning and continuous improvement, people need to feel free to question and challenge the status quo without the fear of retribution.

There are some fundamental areas where learning is especially important, including the development of talent and the sharing of lessons learned. Learning also needs to be deeply embedded in the company through potent mechanisms. In addition to learning, an enterprise needs to have a continuous improvement mindset. A continuous improvement mindset can be achieved by implementing an effective integrated management system across the entire enterprise. This is discussed in detail in chapter 13.

#6. THE WAY THE GOVERNANCE SYSTEM WORKS

Does the governance framework eliminate unnecessary rules and bureaucracy? Does it promote trust and accountability? Does it enforce, without exception, the core values of the company? Does the governance framework allow the enterprise to be nimble? Does it promote sustainable practices? Are teams properly empowered? Is there a high level of trust between the leadership and the teams that execute the strategy? In a healthy and distinctive culture, the answer to all these questions is an emphatic yes!

Empowering teams to execute the strategy of the company without lots of suffocating rules and regulations can be a strong driver in building a distinctive culture that is high performing. Also, pushing decision-making down to teams who are accountable and responsible can generate the right momentum that is necessary for turning an organization's flywheel. The importance of empowerment is perfectly captured in General Stanley McChrystal's book about teams. Here is what he said:

Teams whose members know one another deeply perform *better*. … A team fused by trust and purpose is much more potent. Such a group can improvise a coordinated response to dynamic, real-time developments. … Team members cannot simply depend on orders; teamwork is a process of reevaluation, negotiation, and adjustment; players are constantly sending messages to, and taking cues from, their teammates, and those players *must* be able to read one another's every move and intent. … Purpose affirms trust, trust affirms purpose, and together they forge individuals into a working team.[2]

As General McChrystal discovered, empowering teams helps to build a high-performing, sustainable culture. The same principle of empowerment applies in the business world as well. However, as stated earlier in *Ascend to Greatness*, with empowerment there must be accountability and responsibility. No one in the organization, including the CEO, has total empowerment. This is where the genius of the "and" that Jim Collins discusses in many of his books comes into play. You can have empowerment *and* accountability at the same time; they need to coexist.

#7. THE WAY THE COMPANY IMPLEMENTS MECHANISMS

Dynamic mechanisms are utterly indispensable to building an enduring company that is powered by a distinctive culture. For a distinctive culture to be built and sustained, it is imperative to implement mechanisms that have teeth. Sometimes these mechanisms, if implemented correctly, can cause pain. This is a good thing.

An example of a mechanism with teeth is one that embeds the ethical values of a company's code of conduct into the culture of the company. When this is done properly, companies will most likely apply their code of conduct forcefully throughout the organization, which means no exceptions to violations of the policy. This also means that even if the

CEO violates the policy and dismissal is warranted, the code is enforced. This sends a powerful message to the entire organization that the code of ethical conduct is sacrosanct.

#8. THE WAY THE BOARD BEHAVES, THINKS, AND ACTS

The behavior and decision-making of the board of directors can play a role—sometimes significantly—in both the culture and long-term health of the company. A board of directors who are not collaborative or do not work well as a team can adversely affect the performance of a company. As part of this ineffectiveness, boards sometimes make wrong decisions—such as the ouster of a good CEO—that can have a long-term negative effect.

CHAPTER SIX

Learning Entity

An organization's ability to learn, and translate that learning
into action rapidly, is the ultimate competitive advantage.[1]

——

—JACK WELCH

LEARNING ENTITY

Learning needs to be a focal point in developing talent. This is especially
critical when it comes to developing future leaders. As part of this
development process, enterprises need to ensure that constructive lessons
are learned from mistakes, and they must take appropriate measures to
ensure that they are not repeated. Moreover, organizations need to utilize
learning to teach success stories. Learning must also be instrumental in
better predicting future threats and identifying potential opportunities.

The focus of this chapter is on understanding the value of a learning
entity and the key elements that are fundamental to implementing this
core principle. However, before examining the essential aspects of a
learning entity, let's briefly connect with a principal climbing metaphor
that underpins the concepts in all my books. Mountaineering authors
Mark F. Twight and James Martin provide easily transferable advice about
learning that seems tailor-made for organizations and their leaders. In

their insightful book *Extreme Alpinism: Climbing Light, Fast, and High*, they state as follows:

> Experience acts as a shield against disaster. An experienced climber spots potential problems and takes the right steps to avoid them. Experience provides the raw material for imagining hard routes in the mountains. ... Learn how to learn. Write everything down ... Read the stories of grand masters of alpinism. ... And learn from your mistakes. The intelligent climber makes each mistake only once, and he is cured.[2]

This sage advice is something that enterprises can surely benefit from in today's turbulent and chaotic world. The importance of the ability to continuously learn from both success and failure cannot be overstated. When companies repeat mistakes, the cumulative effect on the performance of the company can be severe.

An organization must implement an appropriate number of mechanisms to ensure that the company learns valuable and actionable lessons. As the legendary Jack Welch once said, "An organization's ability to learn, and translate that learning into action rapidly, is the ultimate competitive advantage." How true this is. The ability to learn must be translated into action by mechanisms.

FUNDAMENTAL ELEMENTS TO BUILDING AN EXCEPTIONAL LEARNING ENTITY

There are seven fundamental components that I have identified to building a successful and high-impact learning organization. They include the following:

- a real-time scan of the environment,
- the global leadership team meeting,
- an internal university,

- a learning excellence team,
- joint ventures and strategic alliances,
- after-action reviews, and
- lessons learned from indispensable experiences.

For these elements to be successful, it's crucial to understand that they must be underpinned and driven by vigorous processes and discipline. Let's examine each one a little closer.

#1. A REAL-TIME SCAN OF THE ENVIRONMENT

Scanning the environment in real time is a fundamental element of learning. In fact, it's so critical that it's covered extensively under two separate principles in my elite enterprise model: building lifelines and high-performance plan. I'm repeating it here because what is learned from scanning the environment needs to be communicated within the organization and needs to be integrated into training programs.

The relevant information that is gleaned from scanning the environment needs to be incorporated into the strategic planning process. Enterprises need to use learning in such a way that it gives them the ability to better predict future outcomes, both positive and negative. Without the ability to learn and to better predict outcomes, the high-performance plan will fall short of what is required to drive excellence and ultimately achieve a company's vision.

#2. THE GLOBAL LEADERSHIP TEAM MEETING

Three valuable outcomes of the global leadership team meeting should be learning, critical thinking about the future, and improved connections between team members. Moreover, for a global leadership team meeting to be effective, elite leaders need to establish mechanisms and metrics that both instill discipline and measure results.

The first outcome of the global leadership meeting is learning. This is the forum where lessons learned can be shared and spoken about with all the leaders of the enterprise. This is the group that will implement the necessary changes for failures and will likewise be responsible for adopting winning strategies. Moreover, this forum is perfect for reinforcing the culture of the company. It's also the right forum for unifying everyone around the strategy of the enterprise, particularly its vision.

Another main function of the global leadership meeting is to introduce fresh critical thinking into the organization. This is usually done by bringing in from the outside thought leaders who speak on various subjects such as innovation and technology trends. Also, this is the forum for a robust dialogue on future trends that are either probable or likely to impact the enterprise. A way to achieve this is to bring in outside facilitators who are experts in specific areas of interest. This exercise is valuable because it will ultimately be a key input into developing a high-performance plan.

The other essential outcome of the leadership meeting should be to strengthen connections between team members. This can be accomplished by allowing time for people to connect by sponsoring events that strengthen peer connections and holding team-based workshops. Facilitating connections between team members creates an environment for collaboration and sharing ideas.

#3. AN INTERNAL UNIVERSITY

The importance of learning was captured perfectly by George Bernard Shaw when he said, "Success does not consist in never making mistakes but in never making the same one a second time."[3] An effective way to ensure that learning is instilled in the organization is to create an internal university. An internal university usually takes many forms depending on the size of the company and the level of allocated resources. Most organizations supplement the internal university with outside professional training.

For an internal university to be successful, it should have a clearly defined core purpose. The curriculum of the university should always be guided by its core purpose. Otherwise, the university will ultimately fail.

The primary objectives of the university should be to train future leaders and key employees, to communicate the strategy of the company, and to sustain a strong culture. In addition, the internal university must be results oriented with appropriate metrics established to measure success. These fundamental points, as well as other salient items, are explored in more detail in the next several paragraphs.

Many elite companies have internal universities. These universities usually have dedicated physical facilities that are augmented with virtual online classes. An online platform can be very practical for companies spread across the globe. As was learned during the COVID-19 pandemic, online classes can be an indispensable tool. I believe that the virtual online platform for internal universities will continue to grow, particularly for companies that have limited resources to invest in physical facilities.

Corporate universities can be useful for developing top management, for training entire organizations, and for either changing or sustaining the culture. Successful internal universities build an enterprise-specific curriculum that conforms to the company's strategy and all the related principles outlined in *Ascend to Greatness*. Some organizations have good intentions with their internal universities, but unfortunately, these universities sometimes lose their way and become ineffective. The best way to avoid this trap is to never lose focus on the reason for its existence.

One of the risks often pointed out about internal universities is that managers are not exposed to fresh outside ideas. This can be countered by simply using a mix of internal and external professors. Also, hiring someone from a prestigious university to organize and even oversee the university can mitigate this risk.

Internal universities also need to be closely linked to the global leadership team meeting. The leadership of the company needs to ensure that there is coordination in areas of emphasis, including but not limited to culture, future trends, lessons learned, and innovation and technology. An online platform should be developed for continuous learning and for reinforcing the culture and values of the company.

An example of a company with a remarkable internal university is

Apple. Learning was so important to the great Steve Jobs that he created Apple University to ensure lessons learned were properly documented. This idea is captured perfectly by Walter Isaacson in the inspirational book *Steve Jobs*. Here is what Isaacson wrote: "In order to institutionalize the lessons that he and his team were learning, Jobs started an in-house center called Apple University. He hired Joel Podolny, who was dean of the Yale School of Management, to compile a series of case studies analyzing important decisions the company had made. ... Top executives spent time teaching the cases to new employees, so that the Apple style of decision making would be embedded in the cultures."[4]

#4. A LEARNING EXCELLENCE TEAM

I'm usually not too enthralled with committee-type structures because they ultimately tend to become bureaucratic, political, and ineffective. However, there are exceptions—and a learning excellence team is one of those. A learning excellence team should be formed in the company, and it should function as a focal point for developing future leaders and supporting employee learning in accordance with the purpose, core values, and vision of the enterprise. What's essential is for the team to be small and be led by a talented person who never deviates from the purpose.

The learning leadership team should be responsible for developing a results-oriented curriculum for the internal university in concert with outside experts. More specifically, the team should focus on establishing and evaluating leadership development programs. The learning team should also monitor trends and best practices and incorporate these into the leadership development programs. Finally, the learning excellence team needs to establish appropriate metrics for measuring success. Two key metrics should be leadership retention rates and promotion rates after completing a specific curriculum.

A learning leadership team can be a potent force if it focuses on creating a learning culture that places a heavy emphasis on lessons learned across the enterprise and on future trends. I believe that a well-focused learning team can be a catalyst for improving the overall learning and critical thinking experience of team members. This, in turn, should also enhance the performance culture of the company.

#5. JOINT VENTURES AND STRATEGIC ALLIANCES

Well-established joint ventures and strategic alliances can be a powerful force in supporting a learning entity. There is so much that can be learned from outside business partners and alliances. Enterprises need to implement appropriate mechanisms to ensure that lessons learned from these potentially valuable sources are shared and communicated within the company. Any best practices that are superior to what is currently being utilized within the organization should be adopted. As you will see in section three of *Ascend to Greatness*, the Roman Legion was very adept at embracing best practices learned from others.

During my career, I have experienced notable successes with joint ventures. What I have learned over many decades of being involved with these types of ventures was indispensable to me as a leader. The areas that were particularly of value were innovation and technology, people excellence, and execution excellence.

#6. AFTER-ACTION REVIEWS

An after-action review, also known as a post-event debrief, is a formal process established by the enterprise to thoroughly and completely review important initiatives with the sole objective of learning and improving. The debrief needs to occur after both negative and positive outcomes. The biggest user of this mechanism is the US military, particularly special operations. The military refers to these debriefings as after-action reviews. There's a lot that business leaders can learn from the military. Some of the more salient lessons learned from the military are covered next, under lesson 7. For a post-event debrief assessment to be successful, it must be driven by honesty and transparency. It's also necessary that the proposed recommended actions emanating from the event are implemented immediately.

After-action reviews are vital because human memory tends to be, at times, selectively poor. We sometimes tend to attribute results to a different cause from what the facts suggest. This cognitive bias can attribute success and failure either disproportionally or completely inaccurately. Worst of all, this can result in flawed decision-making by leaders and boards. This is why after-action reviews are important as they are powerful mechanisms that prevent history from being rewritten. Companies that are exceptional at learning through post-event debriefs will most likely not suffer from attribution errors.

#7. LESSONS LEARNED FROM INDISPENSABLE EXPERIENCES

The lessons learned from indispensable experiences are effective in helping one to transfer those valuable experiences to the enterprise. These experiences can come from elite leaders and exceptional organizations. These shared experiences are something that an enterprise and its team can surely benefit from. For example, it is common for CEOs and some members of the executive leadership team to belong to the board of directors of other companies. Often, the experiences of other companies are wonderful resources for learning valuable lessons. It's also common for executives to belong to various professional groups and councils. These likewise can be great sources for learning.

Something that I personally benefited from during my career was visiting and engaging with elite companies that were not competitors. What I discovered over the years is that many leaders are very welcoming and are eager to share the story of some of their successes. Through all these identified sources, there is an opportunity to possibly connect with elite leaders who have valuable experience and insight that can benefit your company. This is a resource that should be captured as vital lessons learned and then appropriately applied within the organization.

In addition to learning from and engaging with elite leaders and enterprises, one can learn much by studying premiere organizations such as the US military. What's important is to find valuable and actionable lessons learned that can improve the performance of the company, while avoiding as much as possible mistakes others have made.

In terms of valuable lessons learned from the military, I will say that the US military is elite and is unmatched in the world, so it offers business leaders many lessons to be learned. A wonderful mechanism to capture some of these lessons is to implement an executive leadership development program called Staff Ride. The objective of the staff ride is to learn leadership lessons from historic battles as imparted by generals and other high-level military personnel and then to apply those lessons to the business environment. Here is how the program is conducted:

An organization partners with the US Army War College in Carlisle, Pennsylvania, to design a compelling leadership program for its company. Usually, a group of about fifteen to twenty executives, along with military personnel, travel to a famous battle site such as Normandy or Gettysburg to learn what happened on the battlefield. The critical decisions—both right and wrong—that were made during those battles are then connected to the business world. These battlefield decisions are viewed through the lens of experts who comment on important factors that influenced the outcome of each battle. Participants complete assigned reading before attending so that they fully understand the historical context.

I was fortunate to have attended a staff ride in both Normandy and Gettysburg. Here are the salient lessons I learned from these outstanding life-changing experiences and how they apply and translate to the business world:

Don't fight a fair battle. Overwhelming power puts the enemy at a significant competitive disadvantage. Companies need to build strength and position themselves to dominate their market and the competition. Facebook, Amazon, Apple, Google, Microsoft, and Disney are exceptional at this.

Know the importance of a learning entity and after-action reviews. The military operates in a learning culture that values lessons learned. After-action reviews are performed for important actions that succeed and fail. The military clearly understands human behavior, so the purpose of the post-event debrief is to eliminate attribution and hindsight biases.

Communicate the commander's intent. One of the main reasons that the military is elite is that team members have total clarity on the commander's intent. Everyone on the team knows the mission, and there's no ambiguity or confusion about what must be done. In business, companies clearly understand the importance of having a clearly stated purpose and vision statement. They provide total clarity on what the company is striving to achieve.

Develop distinct lines of command. No confusion exists in the military as to who the decision makers are. Regardless if it's an army division or a small special operations team, such clarity is vital to the success of the mission. In organizations, clearly understood lines of command and decision-making responsibility are essential to realizing the vision of the company.

Operate at the speed of trust. Everyone in the military knows what trust is when they find themselves in a life-or-death situation. It needs no explanation. Military units operate superbly because of the speed of trust. What this means is that there is a high level of trust within each unit, which results in fast decision-making. In battle, high trust and speed of decision-making—along with resolve and execution—is vital to success. Elite companies understand this well and are exceptional at empowering and trusting their teams to act with a high sense of urgency in making smart decisions.

Have a shared consciousness. Having a shared consciousness is simply having a holistic understanding of the environment and high levels of connectivity. In other words, everyone on the team is on the same page. In business, everyone gets on the same page by having a distinctive culture and a clearly understood purpose, core values, and vision.

Perform succession planning and leadership development. Before going into battle, every team member is keenly aware of the chain of command at least two levels down. The military understands well the importance of succession planning and developing team members who can assume a leadership position whenever it's necessary. Elite enterprises also devote significant resources to ensure that both succession planning and leadership development are executed at an elite level.

Offer training. The military spends considerable resources on training. They understand the correlation between extensive training and success on the battlefield. This mindset is captured in an ancient aphorism that says, "Cry in the dojo, laugh on the battlefield."[5] This disciplined focus on training and learning is an effective habit that leading enterprises vigorously embrace and implement.

Prioritize planning and strategy. The military's success can be traced in part to detailed planning and strategic thinking. Consider also the military adage about planning: once the first bullet is fired, all plans go out the window. This is where the military's other strengths, including adaptability, discipline, and leadership training, come into play. Detailed planning and strategic thinking, along with disciplined execution, is also an area in which leading companies excel.

Understanding innovation and technology. The military understands the connection between innovation and the impact of emerging disruptive technologies. Cybersecurity, stealth technology, drones, autonomous vehicles, and cutting-edge weapons systems all underpin the US military's elite status. As demonstrated throughout *Ascend to Greatness*, extraordinary enterprises likewise understand how vital innovation and technology are to achieving sustained success.

SECTION TWO

Strategy

Introduction

All men can see these tactics whereby I conquer, but what none can see is the strategy out of which victory is evolved.[1]

—SUN TZU

A NEW PARADIGM FOR STRATEGY

In this section, we will review the foundational pillar of strategy and its six core principles that are necessary for building and sustaining an elite enterprise. These six principles are covered in chapters 7 through 12. The definition I provide for the foundational pillar of strategy is broader perhaps than definitions that you will find in some textbooks. I believe that a new paradigm is necessary. Strategy needs to be viewed more broadly. I believe that all six principles identified in this section need be an integral part of a brilliant strategy as they are all linked.

STRATEGY OVERVIEW

Strategy must begin with developing a clear statement of purpose, core values, and vision. Strategy is then simply how an organization is going to successfully realize its vision, guided by its purpose, while strictly adhering to its core values. The remaining five principles under strategy must then all be perfectly aligned with the purpose, values, and vision of the company.

For a company to achieve its vision, it needs to have an innovative business model. For ease of explanation, consider that the business model is segmented into two separate principles. One principle relates to the unique practices of the company, and the other is focused on the organizational structure. With respect to the unique practices, these are the recipe elements for how the company will differentiate itself in the marketplace. The unique practices provide unambiguous guidance to everyone in the organization on what to do and what not to do. The organizational structure is then designed to execute those elements in the most effective and efficient way possible.

Visionary leaders consistently focus on building a company that will endure for generations. A crucial core principle that is needed for accomplishing this objective is the building of lifelines. Lifelines are utterly indispensable. They not only protect a company against adverse turbulent events but also help build exceptional capabilities, both of which are necessary for ascending to the summit of elite. I believe that there are seven fundamental lifelines that must be built for a company to withstand any turbulence and possibly even prosper under the right conditions.

The other two remaining principles of innovation and technology and a high-performance plan are driving forces that enable and accelerate the execution of the vision statement. Innovation and technology need to permeate the organization in all areas so that the company does not lose its way and become complacent or possibly irrelevant. Most importantly, innovation and technology are major disruptors in the marketplace. Innovation is a strong incubator of ideas for new products and services. And technology can provide the enterprise with a competitive advantage in the marketplace by digitally improving the customer experience.

The high-performance plan, which is more commonly known as the strategic plan or strategic planning, consolidates and summarizes all the key breakthrough objectives of the enterprise in both quantitative and qualitative terms over a stated time span of either three or five years.

Each time frame is then used as a building block to ultimately reach the summit, that is, to realize the vision of the company. I like the term high-performance plan because it elevates planning to the same level as the other principles under the foundational pillar of strategy.

A high-performance plan needs to be closely linked to the vital mechanism of scanning the environment in real time. A high-performance plan also focuses an enterprise on consistently achieving superior results. Superior performance over a long horizon is what separates the elite from all the others and ultimately leads a company to greatness.

DISCIPLINED STRATEGY

As stated throughout *Ascend to Greatness*, the three foundational pillars are inextricably linked. The foundational pillars must all be implemented at an elite level to achieve enduring greatness. What links and drives the three pillars is *discipline*. This is the common denominator. Without discipline, it is impossible to ascend to the summit. Although the principle of disciplined execution is listed specifically under the foundational pillar of execution, it equally applies to the other two pillars. That's because the other two pillars also need to be executed in a disciplined manner.

As explained in section three of *Ascend to Greatness*, I advocate for using an integrated management system to impel elite-level execution excellence. The same goes for executing people excellence and other principles under the foundational pillar of leadership that were covered in section one, as well as for developing a brilliant strategy, which is covered in this section.

STRATEGY PRINCIPLES

There are six principles under the foundational pillar of strategy that are covered in section two. The following chapter titles indicate the principles that are essential to building an enduring elite company:

CHAPTER SEVEN

Purpose, Values, and Vision

The future belongs to those who believe in the beauty of their dreams.[1]

——

—ELEANOR ROOSEVELT

CREATE THE FUTURE

When creating the future, a company must first decide on a purpose statement and the company's core values. The organization then needs to create a vision for the future. I collectively call these three elements the *core philosophy* of the company. So, how do you create a powerful core philosophy? I strongly believe that a modern core philosophy should include three fundamental parts, as follows:

- purpose—the reason for being
- values—guiding principles
- vision—aspirational objective.

In this chapter, we will focus on how to create that crucial purpose statement and the underpinning core values that should drive all actions of the enterprise. We will also review why it's essential to create a vision for the enterprise, one with a bold objective. When an enterprise strives to reach elite status, it is necessary to develop a clear and powerful core philosophy. The absence or the existence of a confused one will most likely result in the company's ultimately falling short of its goal of ascending the summit.

GROUNDBREAKING WORK

Before we review some exceptional core philosophies, it's important to understand who was responsible for the groundbreaking work that was done in this area. The thought leadership on a vision framework emanated from the extraordinary work of Jim Collins and Jerry Porras at Stanford University back in the early 1990s. This resulted in several publications, starting with "Organizational Vision and Visionary Organizations" (*California Management Review*, Fall 1991), which was followed by "Building Your Company's Vision" (*Harvard Business Review*, September–October 1994). Collins and Porras also outline the vision framework in their venerable book *Built to Last* (October 1994). Finally, the vision framework is again detailed in a book by Jim Collins and Bill Lazier, *BE 2.0* (2020), which is an updated version of their insightful book *Beyond Entrepreneurship* (1992).

In their various publications, the authors use the term *vision framework* to capture the elements necessary to build a great company. Their vision framework consists of core values, purpose, and BHAG—big hairy audacious goal. Prior to using the initialism BHAG, Collins and Lazier used *mission*. The authors provide excellent examples and guidelines in their work. I particularly recommend reading *BE 2.0* because it's the most recent publication that clearly spells out how to construct a proper vision framework. We will review some of the guidelines and insights provided by the authors in this chapter.

As detailed earlier, I use the term *core philosophy* as opposed to *vision framework*. Also, I use the term *vision* instead of the initialism BHAG. The other two elements of purpose and core values are identical. The reason I use *vision* instead of *BHAG* is because of my work with companies in implementing this fundamental element; the term *vision* worked well for them. I also had to develop the term *core philosophy* because the use of *vision framework* could possibly confuse matters. However, it doesn't matter which approach is taken; they both work well. What's important is that these essential elements be properly developed as they are the foundation.

Throughout all their published materials, the authors perfectly capture the critical parts of a company's vision framework. Here is what the authors say about core values: "[These] are the handful of guiding principles by which a company navigates. They require no external justification." Collins and Porras state that the core purpose "is an organization's most fundamental reason for being. It should not be confused with the company's current product lines or customer segments. Rather, it reflects people's idealistic motivations for doing the company's work." And they state that BHAGs "are ambitious plans that rev up the entire organization. They typically require 10 to 30 years' work to complete."

The business world would not be the same today had it not been for the extraordinary thought leadership of all the authors. Their groundbreaking research and writings have been contributors in helping to build some of the greatest companies in the world. We should all be deeply grateful for their work.

CORE PHILOSOPHY: PURPOSE, VALUES, AND VISION

In the remainder of this chapter, we will review the elements of purpose, values, and vision collectively as a separate principle under my elite enterprise model. After several decades of working with purpose, values, and vision, I have made several observations that can benefit companies when developing their core philosophy. These common mistakes are outlined below.

PURPOSE—THE REASON A COMPANY EXISTS

Through my advisory practice, I have discovered some common mistakes that organizations make in preparing their core purpose. I often see organizations creating a purpose statement that either is too long or combines other elements. By doing this, the purpose loses some or all of its effectiveness. It's not uncommon to find people within an organization who believe the purpose, the mission, and even the vision to be the same thing. A key test for a robust purpose statement is to ask, can every employee repeat it verbatim without thinking about it? Another is, do employees demonstrate passion for the purpose of the organization? Also, do they know the difference between purpose and vision? I would argue that it's difficult to get passionate about a purpose statement that is long and lacks clarity.

It's fundamental to remember that a purpose statement defines an organization. It's the reason for its existence; it's the why. The purpose statement should be relatively short and should be known, embraced, and applied with passion by everyone in the organization. Purpose is something that should be perpetually pursued. Collins and Porras advocate that a purpose statement should guide the company for at least one hundred years. On the other hand, a vision is something that needs to be attained within a shorter time frame. Everything a company does must be guided by its purpose while striving to achieve its vision. All things that are pursued in an organization that deviate from the purpose and vision are a waste of time and resources.

In his insightful book *Start with Why*, author Simon Sinek captures the criticality of a clear purpose statement. Here is what he says: "It all starts with clarity. You have to know *why* you do *what* you do. If people don't buy *what* you do, they buy *why* you do it, so it follows that if you don't know *why* you do *what* you do, how will anyone else? If the leader of the organization can't clearly articulate *why* the organization exists in terms beyond its products or services, then how does he expect the employees to know *why* to come to work?"[2]

When developing an exceptional purpose statement, you should follow these helpful guidelines:

- Ensure the purpose statement is authentic.
- Ensure it is succinct.

- Ensure it reflects the actions and culture of the company and its employees.
- Ensure it is constantly communicated and reinforced.
- Ensure it is constantly pursued.
- Get everyone in the organization passionate about it.
- Ensure everyone in the company can repeat it verbatim without hesitation.
- Do not change it for a long time frame.

So, what are the enterprises that know how to put a powerful purpose statement together? It's not a coincidence that these are some of the best-performing companies in the world. See my list below.

EXEMPLARY PURPOSE STATEMENTS

Here is a list of some of the more exceptional purpose statements. Please note that the majority of the statements begin with "To."

- **Microsoft:** "To empower every person and organization on the planet to achieve more."
- **Google:** "To organize the world's information and make it universally accessible and useful."
- **Southwest Airlines:** "To connect people to what's important in their lives through friendly, reliable, and low-cost air travel."
- **Instagram:** "To capture and share the world's moments."
- **Facebook:** "To give people the power to build community and bring the world closer together."
- **Amazon:** "To be Earth's most customer-centric company, where customers can find and discover anything they might want to buy online."
- **Mastercard:** "Every day, everywhere, we use our technology and expertise to make payments safe, simple and smart."

- **Tesla:** "To accelerate the world's transition to sustainable energy."
- **Nordstrom:** "To provide outstanding service every day, one customer at a time."

Clearly, these companies have worked hard to create strong purpose statements. I especially like Google's and how they promote it. When you go to their website, the first thing you see in vivid colors is their statement. There's no confusion as to what their purpose is; they prominently display it. If your organization is in the process of developing a purpose statement or reworking one, the examples outlined above not only should be inspirational but also can function as a practical guide.

VALUES—GUIDING PRINCIPLES

Core values are the key principles by which a company navigates. For core values to be effective, they need to support the purpose, vision, culture, and unique practices of the company.

Collins and Porras beautifully capture the essence of core values: "A small set of timeless guiding principles, core values require no external justification; they have *intrinsic* value and importance to those inside the organization." Although Collins and Porras advocate for a small set of guiding principles, it's not uncommon to see organizations with a large number of values, well in excess of the three to five the authors recommend. All you have to do is scan corporate websites to find a large variance in values from firm to firm.

I have scanned dozens of websites and have noted that many of the core values usually range in number between four and ten. As was mentioned earlier, Collins and Porras recommend using between three and five, no more. The authors state, "We found that none of the visionary companies we studied in our book had more than five: most had only three or four." The authors go on to say, "Only a few values can be truly *core*—that is, so fundamental and deeply held that they will change seldom, if ever."

I'm aligned with the authors on this because too many core values often can be unworkable. This is because it can be difficult for people to be passionate about so many core values. More importantly, it can be problematic trying to embed all the core values in the culture of the company with robust mechanisms. In light of my extensive experience with helping companies develop their core values, I believe that the perfect number is between four and five. However, I believe that every company is different and more core values can actually work in the right environment.

In his book *Start with Why*, author Simon Sinek captures how valuable core values are to making the purpose of the company a reality. Here is what he says: "Once you know *why* you do what you do, the question is *how* to bring your cause to life. *How* we do things manifests in the systems and processes within an organization and the culture." He goes on to say, "Understanding *how* you do things and, more importantly, having the discipline to hold the organization and all its employees accountable to those guiding principles enhances an organization's ability to work to its natural strengths."[3]

The most common mistake that I have discovered when working with companies on their core values is the lack of strong mechanisms to reinforce and embed these values in the culture of the company. When there is such a lack, core values often become superficial and are simply given lip service, with no real intrinsic value to the company. Another common error is that core values are not always clearly defined. The lack of a clear definition can lessen their effectiveness.

CORE VALUES NEED TO BE EMBRACED AND DEEPLY EMBEDDED

Employees need to passionately embrace and live the guiding principles of the company every moment of their careers. Without this strong commitment, the core values will not be as effective. Thus, it's vital for the company to get buy-in right from the beginning. This can be achieved by hiring around the core values and ensuring that the talent brought into the enterprise is aligned with them. Moreover, the company has to implement mechanisms to ensure that the core values have teeth in order for them to be both meaningful and impactful.

CORE VALUES GUIDELINES

There are guidelines that should be considered by organizations whenever they develop powerful core values. The following are the most critical:

- Core values must be deeply ingrained principles that guide the actions of everyone in the company.
- Core values must be authentic, fundamental, and timeless.
- Everyone in the organization must be passionate about the core values.
- Core values must be vigorously maintained and promoted throughout the organization.
- Appropriate mechanisms must be implemented so that the core values are embedded into the culture of the company.
- Core values should be clearly defined.
- Core values should rarely be changed.
- Properly implemented core values should, at times, cause pain, the pain coming from strict adherence.

In the next section, I provide some extraordinary examples of core values that can be used by companies as a point of reference and as inspiration for establishing strong guiding principles.

EXEMPLARY CORE VALUES

When developing core values, it's helpful to include a brief definition for each one in order to put them all in perspective and to avoid any possible confusion. The best place to start is with a review of the websites of accomplished enterprises to see how they define their core values. For illustrative purpose, I have included examples of core values with definitions. These elite enterprises include Danaher, Facebook, and Mastercard.

Robust core values are fundamental for climbing to the summit of elite. Below are some exceptional core values that can assist enterprises in developing their own. I especially like Danaher's core values because they focus on innovation, continuous improvement, the customer, winning teams, and the owners. Danaher lives its core values, and their performance proves it. For companies thinking of developing their own core values, I would recommend that at least three of them be focused on the customer, innovation, and continuous improvement.

DANAHER—FIVE CORE VALUES

The best team wins. Exceptional people thrive in Danaher's fast-paced, results-oriented culture. And our values start with our people.

- We value our associates and their unique contributions, and we invest in their growth.
- We're passionate about recruiting, developing, and retaining the most talented and diverse team possible.
- We put the most skilled, collaborative, engaged team on the field of play every day.

Customers talk, we listen. One of our team's most important responsibilities is to listen to our customers.

- We continually seek deep insight into the needs of our customers, both explicit and implicit.
- Our strong customer focus helps us create innovative solutions that directly address those needs.
- Through our processes and our products, we seek to deliver greater value every day and to improve our customers' experience beyond their expectations.

Kaizen is our way of life. Through Kaizen, or continuous improvement, we address customer needs with actions that benefit the greater good.

- Customers challenge us, and we challenge ourselves, to continuously improve. We set the bar high for ourselves and each other.
- With our strong culture rooted in the Danaher Business System, we constantly strive to make things better in a meaningful way— for our company, our customers, and the world.
- Our drive for continuous improvement keeps us ahead of our competitors, creating enduring value and lasting impact on a global scale.

Innovation defines our future. One of the most important ways we drive continuous improvement is through innovation that makes a difference.

- Customers look to us to find opportunities and define the future— to deliver innovative products, services, and solutions that address their most pressing needs.
- Innovation is our ultimate competitive differentiator. We pursue out-of-the-box ideas, both large and small, to add value and advance innovation.
- We improve people's lives by delivering technologies that matter. By helping our customers achieve amazing things, we enhance quality of life around the world.

We compete for shareholders. By living our core values, we deliver the highest possible value to our shareholders.

- Our strong track record enables us to continually invest back into our businesses and our people to help them realize their full potential.
- We earn our shareholders' investment by maintaining the highest standards of integrity, outstanding service for our customers, and a deep commitment to building a better business every day.

FACEBOOK—FIVE CORE VALUES

- **Be bold.** Building great things means taking risks. We have a saying: "The riskiest thing is to take no risks." In a world that's changing so quickly, you're guaranteed to fail if you don't take any risks. We encourage everyone to make bold decisions, even if that means being wrong some of the time.

- **Focus on impact.** To have the biggest impact, we need to focus on solving the most important problems. It sounds simple, but most companies do this poorly and waste a lot of time. We expect everyone at Facebook to be good at finding the biggest problems to work on.

- **Move fast.** Moving fast enables us to build more things and learn faster. We're less afraid of making mistakes than we are of losing opportunities by moving too slowly. We are a culture of builders; the power is in your hands.

- **Be open.** We believe that a more open world is a better world. The same goes for our company. Informed people make better decisions and have a greater impact, which is why we work hard to make sure everyone at Facebook has access to as much information about the company as possible.

- **Build social value.** Facebook was created to make the world more open and connected, not just to build a company. We expect everyone at Facebook to focus every day on how to build real value for the world in everything they do.

MASTERCARD—FOUR CORE VALUES

- **Trust.** We act with integrity and respect; we encourage openness.
- **Partnership.** We work as one team to the benefit of all—consumers, retailers, business partners, governments, and the communities we serve.
- **Agility.** We act with a sense of urgency and deliver value through our innovation and execution.

- **Initiative.** We are empowered to take bold and thoughtful action, and we hold ourselves accountable for delivering results.

VISION—WHAT DOES THE FUTURE LOOK LIKE?

In this last part of the chapter, we will review the third element of a modern core philosophy: the vision. The vision should typically look at a future horizon of ten to thirty years.

In the Jim Collins and Bill Lazier book *BE 2.0*, mentioned above, the authors provide the best guidelines on how to develop a powerful BHAG (which I call vision). Before we examine the guidelines they recommend, it's relevant to quote them on how they view this vital third element. Here is what they write: "It doesn't really matter whether you call it 'mission' or 'BHAG' or anything else that works for you. What matters is that you commit to something that meets the tests of a BHAG." They go on to provide the key tests of a powerful BHAG (or vision). Here are the questions— verbatim—that the authors believe need to be answered affirmatively:

- Do you and your people find the BHAG exciting?
- Is the BHAG clear, compelling, and easy to grasp?
- Does BHAG connect to the purpose of the enterprise?
- Is the BHAG undeniably a goal, not a verbose, hard-to-understand, convoluted, impossible-to-remember mission or vision "statement"?
- Do you have substantially less than a 100 percent chance of achieving the BHAG yet at the same time believe your company can achieve the BHAG if fully committed?
- Would you be able to clearly tell if you've achieved the BHAG?

In addition to posing the questions, the authors go on to say, "The best BHAGs make you think big. They force you to engage in both long-term *and* short-term intensity. The only way to achieve a BHAG is with relentless sense of urgency, day after day, week after week, month after month, for years. … For BHAG-driven people, the extended discomfort, the enduring quest, can itself be a form of bliss. When you commit to a BHAG, it lives with you."

As both a CEO and as an adviser to companies, I have developed BHAGs or vision statements. Based on those indispensable experiences, I've created helpful guidelines. However, please keep in mind that these are simply high-level ground rules. They may work better for private companies than they do for public companies. Given the competitive landscape and the regulatory environment, it's more difficult for public companies to adhere to all these guidelines. As you will see in the following examples, public companies do not always provide specific numbers and/or dates.

- The vision objective should be for a period in the future, usually around ten to thirty years. However, what is more important is to define a time frame that works best for the enterprise because everyone is different. I've seen some effective visions that cover a time frame of less than ten years. Ideally, I recommend somewhere around ten to fifteen years. I believe that a period greater than fifteen years is simply too long and unrealistic in today's fast-moving world.

- As explained later under the principle of a high-performance plan, the selected vision time frame needs to be broken down into distinct building blocks. For example, if a company sets forth a time frame of fifteen years to realize its vision, that period needs to be broken down into five separate three-year plans.

- A specific breakthrough objective or several objectives should be stated in the vision statement, ones that can be clearly measured and understood by everyone in the company. Breakthrough objectives need to be bold. Think big! For example, "We will be at $10 billion in revenues by the year 2035." Revenues are easily measured. Or, "We will be the most admired and respected brand in the United States by 2035." Brands can also be measured; these rankings are common in the United States. Or, "We will operate profitably in one hundred countries by the year 2035." Or, "New products will account for 40 percent of our revenues by the year 2035." Again, these targets are easily measured.

- A succinct description of the long-term vision should be included. The written description should be pithy and no more than a couple of sentences. I've seen visions that range from one sentence to a couple of paragraphs. There's a lot of flexibility with the written description, but I recommend brevity—preferably one sentence—because then it's easier for everyone to remember and to understand.
- Most important, a vision statement needs to be meaningful, powerful, and impactful. It needs to excite the organization. Everyone needs to be passionate about the long-term direction of the company and what it's trying to achieve.
- Once you realize your objective, you move on and establish your next vision for the enterprise. This is how elite companies are built and sustained.

POWERFUL VISION STATEMENTS

Let's examine some powerful vision statements from elite companies, including Tesla, Southwest Airlines, and Mastercard.

TESLA

"To create the most compelling car company of the twenty-first century by driving the world's transition to electric vehicles."

This is an excellent example to use in establishing an organization's vision. It's one of the best I've seen. It clearly points to the future and is audacious, impactful, and inspirational. It's a goal that employees of Tesla can get very passionate about. This vision can be measured by determining the percentage of cars produced annually that are electric. The trend can be plotted to determine progress. Like the other examples, this vision offers no specific time frame for achieving the goal. Given Tesla's amazing progress as of 2021, they appear to be well on their way toward realizing their vision. Also, the vision statement aligns perfectly with the purpose of the company: "To accelerate the world's transition to sustainable energy."

SOUTHWEST AIRLINES

"To become the world's most loved, most flown, and most profitable airline."

This is a wonderful vision statement. I believe that it answers all the questions posed in the above stated guidelines. The company has established clear and bold objectives. The goal of being the world's most-loved airline, along with the most flown and the most profitable, is audacious. The statement is also succinct and easy for all team members to remember and easily recite. All three elements can be measured and are generally publicly available. The only missing element is a time frame for each one of the measurable objectives. Given that the airline is a public company, it's likely that they have kept that information internally. Nonetheless, this is a good vision statement.

MASTERCARD

"A world beyond cash."

This vision is succinct and extremely bold, probably the most audacious I've seen. I believe that it generally answers all the questions posed in the above guidelines. This statement requires envisioning a world where cash is no longer used. Given the acceleration of technology, it's conceivable that we could be in world beyond cash in twenty-five years or so. This is also a measurable vision to a certain extent because spending transacted on credit cards can be determined and trends can be plotted. Just as with the Southwest Airlines example, there's no time frame on this vision statement.

CORE PHILOSOPHY STATEMENT

Once a company has defined its purpose, values, and vision, I advocate that these elements be included in a simple one-page core philosophy statement. The statement should start with the purpose of the company, be followed by its core values that are clearly defined, and end with the vision. The core philosophy statement should be posted on the website of the company. The statement should also be continuously communicated and embedded in the culture of the company.

CHAPTER EIGHT

Unique Practices

There are no shortcuts to true excellence.[1]

———

—ANGELA DUCKWORTH

INNOVATIVE BUSINESS MODEL

The business model includes two interconnected parts: the *unique practices* of the enterprise and the *organizational structure*. Companies that solve the value-creation equation by getting both the unique practices and the organizational structure right will generate superior returns over a long horizon. The reason for this is simple: an innovative business model will usually provide a unique competitive advantage in the marketplace.

The unique practices of the company need to be clearly defined and articulated in such a manner that everyone in the company knows what to do and what not to do. The organizational structure is then built to execute each crucial element of the clearly and succinctly identified unique practices of the company. Because the business model is so important to the success of the company, I believe that the unique practices and the organizational structure should be treated as two separate core principles. Thus, we will review the principle of unique practices that are necessary for creating a sustainable competitive position in this chapter. We will then review the principle of organizational structure in chapter 9.

CREATE A UNIQUE AND SUSTAINABLE COMPETITIVE POSITION

Let's now examine in detail the first principle under an innovative business model, the unique practices of an elite company. The unique practices need to be a formula for success. Please note that throughout this chapter, I will use the terms, *unique practices*, *activities*, and *recipe* interchangeably.

In my *CEO Lifelines* series of books, I highlight an exceptional company called Roper. In the books, I identify what I believe to be Roper's unique practices that have driven the company's extraordinary performance over the past fifteen years. In addition, I highlight Nucor's unique activities that have propelled the company to greatness. Both Roper's and Nucor's recipe elements should be used as best-of-class examples of how to create the unique practices for your organization. We will reexamine both of these again in this chapter because I have updated these companies' unique activities. Furthermore, I've added what I believe to be Apple's unique practices; these are covered later. For additional examples, I recommend the works of both Michael Porter and Jim Collins where they highlight companies with innovative recipes.

To obtain further insight into how a certain elite company has chosen to position itself to win in the marketplace, I recommend reviewing 10-K SEC filings, annual reports (particularly the CEO letter), and investor presentations. From this information, it is relatively easy to identify the unique practices of a company. Although it may not be possible to clearly spot every single element of the recipe, the majority should readily stand out.

CREATING UNIQUE PRACTICES

Creating the unique practices of a company is all about making deliberate choices. An enterprise must develop a specific formula for success in relation to how it plans to compete in the marketplace. For more insight into this, I recommend Michael Porter's groundbreaking book from 1980, *Competitive Strategy.*

When you are developing and documenting the unique activities of an organization, I recommend keeping them to around five. Previously, I've written that an enterprise can have as many as eight recipe elements. However, the more I work with companies on this vital part of the business strategy, the more convinced I become that the right number is in the area of five. As you will see in three world-class examples below, they all have five recipe elements.

Let's now review exceptional examples of unique practices of three elite US companies, Roper Technologies, Nucor, and Apple. I have closely followed these enterprises; they consistently perform at an elite level. Their ability to excel at leadership, strategy, and execution is evident in everything they do.

ROPER TECHNOLOGIES

Roper's unique practices are extraordinary and are a paragon for any company wishing to develop its own elements that can differentiate it from competitors. Here is an excerpt from Roper's CEO letter to shareholders included in the 2019 annual report that provides wonderful insight into Roper's business performance: "In 2019, our shareholders enjoyed an above-market return of +34%. … Over the past 15 years, our shareholders have earned a compound annual return of +18% and a total shareholder return of +1,174%, more than four times the total return of the S&P 500. … During this time, gross margin expanded 1,390 basis points, EBITDA margin expanded 1,370 basis points, and net working capital improved from +17.3% of revenue to (5.3)% of revenue."

Roper has a relentless and disciplined focus. An examination of Roper's annual reports and investor presentations reveals five key elements that make up the company's unique practices. Roper's five innovative recipe elements are as follows:

1. Win in niche markets by having a diverse set of businesses with leading market positions.
2. Focus on proprietary and differentiated customer solutions that generate high margins, recurring revenue streams, and exceptional cash flows.
3. Maintain an asset-light business model that delivers exceptional cash performance with minimal needs for working capital and capital expenditures.
4. Implement a decentralized operating structure where business leaders are accountable for results and operate within a nimble governance system.
5. Implement centralized capital deployment that effectively redeploys free cash flow in acquisitions that deliver growth and high cash returns.

Let's examine these elements a little closer. At a high level, the five practices clearly spell out to everyone in the organization what to do and what not to do. As you examine each element, you see that the leadership team has specific guidelines on what it needs to focus on. For example, Roper is not going to acquire a company that requires significant investment in capital expenditures and working capital. This is because they are clearly focused on asset-light businesses. Also, Roper is not going to burden its operating companies with needless rules and bureaucratic policies because the company passionately believes in a nimble governance framework. And they are not going to acquire a company that has low operating margins and a mediocre free cash flow profile because the Roper leadership team has the opposite mandate. Roper has its flywheel working, which has been the economic driver of its extraordinary performance.

NUCOR

Nucor's success is anchored in its decades-long history of extraordinary leadership, strategy, and execution. But before we get into that, let's examine the company's 2018 annual CEO letter to shareholders: Here is what CEO John Ferriola wrote:

Our five drivers to generate long-term sustainable growth are:

1. being a low-cost producer;
2. being a leader in the markets in which we compete;
3. moving up the value chain to expand our capabilities for our value-appreciative customers;
4. expanding our channels to market; and
5. achieving commercial excellence to complement our operational strength.

These five unique practices that make up Nucor's business model are underpinned by metrics, mechanisms, and core beliefs. Here are some of the most important that I was able to glean from Nucor's public filings:

- Teammates are both the company's greatest asset and a competitive advantage.
- Nucor maintains a laser focus on profit per ton of finished steel—the economic driver of steel producers.
- Nucor has a culture of high productivity and exceptional performance.
- They have a flexible nonunion workforce that is empowered to make decisions.
- They have an unofficial no-layoff policy.
- They have made a commitment to pay well for high performance, and they have a policy of no guaranteed incentives or retiree benefits.
- They use electric arc furnaces and a scrap-based process (mini-mill), as opposed to large, fixed-cost integrated mills.

- They have a relentless focus on costs, safety, process improvement, and maintaining a strong balance sheet.
- They maintain a focus on innovation and technology advancements.

One reason I can speak with such confidence about Nucor is because I spent more than three decades working in the steel industry as a key partner and provider of environmental and other knowledge-based solutions to the global steel industry, including Nucor.

The global steel industry is one of the most highly competitive industries in the world. It is also prone to major swings in production, pricing, and certain input costs, such as scrap metal prices. The global steel industry is dominated by China. The World Steel Association notes that in 2019 steel production in the world was 1,870 million tons, with China accounting for approximately 996 million tons or more than 53 percent of the world's production. But production is only part of the story.

The global steel industry has a glut of steel production with most excess capacity residing in China. China, along with several other countries, has historically exported a significant amount of steel to the United States, which has put constant pressure on the price of steel. Although Nucor and all other US steel producers have historically benefited from tariffs, the market continues to be challenged by cyclicality and other key factors. So, how is it that Nucor is an elite company in an industry characterized by overcapacity and highly volatile pricing while its many steel competitors across the world continue to struggle?

I believe that the reasons for Nucor's success can be categorized into three distinct areas: people excellence, financial discipline, and competitive structure. First, the people. Nucor is truly focused on and passionate about its people and has built a strong culture that drives the company. Amazing mechanisms have been built that really work. Some of the mechanisms include Nucor's innovative no-layoff policy; its pay for performance that offers no guarantee payments or benefits; its strong safety culture; and its practice of listing every employee or teammate on the cover of the annual report. Nucor is a company that works in every way.

Second, let's look at Nucor's financial discipline. Nucor has a relentless focus on costs and process improvements and a discipline of maintaining a strong balance sheet to ensure it can weather all storms. The company's key financial metric of profit per ton of steel produced is also vital to the company's success story.

Third, competitive structure. What I mean by competitive structure is Nucor's focus on mini-mills as opposed to less flexible and more expensive integrated steel mills. Nucor's focus on locating plants mainly in the South with a favorable nonunion labor environment is another vital element of the competitive structure. And finally comes the company's relentless focus on innovation and technology.

Nucor's unique practices are the reason that the company was identified as a Good to Great firm in Jim Collins's seminal book by the same name. This is clearly another extraordinary business model that can be used as a guide in developing one for your business.

APPLE

As mentioned earlier in *Ascend to Greatness*, I believe that Apple is the best-managed company. It was the first company to reach that utterly amazing market valuation of one trillion dollars (and two trillion dollars). Apple excels at all three foundational pillars, and there is no company that has performed consistently better. Apple has been so innovative that they demand premium prices for their products and services. They have created enormous brand value. Their profitability and cash flow metrics are simply extraordinary. There's ample evidence to demonstrate Apple's innovation and technological development prowess. A few examples: They disrupted the PC industry first with the Apple computer and then again with the iPad. They totally changed the music industry and revolutionized the smartphone business. There's overwhelming demonstrable evidence that Apple has its flywheel working tremendously well, which means the company should be able to sustain its greatness for many years to come.

Apple's practices are innovative. Let's examine what I believe to be the unique activities that fundamentally define Apple's business model:

1. an ecosystem where hardware, services, and software are all seamlessly integrated between devices, driven by a proprietary and closed operating system,
2. innovative development of new disruptive products and services that set the industry standard,
3. simplicity, functionality, and aesthetics all creatively designed and supremely engineered into products,
4. luxury brand differentiation, superior customer engagement, extraordinary customer loyalty, all enhanced by beautifully designed retail stores, and
5. operation as a highly integrated enterprise, as a cohesive and flexible company with one income statement.

Apple made it clear from that beginning that all its products would be fully integrated and driven by a closed operating system. This decision was prescient because it provided Apple with a competitive advantage. The company's decision to engineer innovative products that have strong functionality, are easy to use, and are aesthetically pleasing was brilliant. Also, its decision and commitment to making the customer experience extraordinary was rewarded with pricing leverage and loyalty. And finally, Apple's decision to organize itself as one highly integrated and collaborative company was likewise a smart move.

SHOULD THE UNIQUE PRACTICES BE CHANGED?

The most relevant question that often comes up with respect to the unique practices of an enterprise is, should these activities be changed and, if so, how often? The simple answer to the first half of the question is yes, they should be changed. However, they should only be changed when the competitive environment has adapted and copied some or all the unique practices of the company or, more importantly, when an organization recognizes a trend early on and spots an opportunity to be disruptive. This is where scanning the environment in real time provides an early warning system. One of my favorite examples of this is Netflix. Netflix had already disrupted the market with the DVD model, using the mail system as opposed to the large, fixed-cost-structure model employed by Blockbuster with all its stores scattered throughout the country. Although Netflix was the market leader, the company disrupted itself by pivoting to streaming. Netflix recognized very early that streaming technology was the future.

Here are some helpful guidelines that can assist with the decision regarding changing recipe elements:

- Changes to the recipe elements should be infrequent, but the frequency is dictated more by future trends and the ability to spot them early.
- Keep what is working. Change only recipe elements that are not working.
- When changes need to be made to the recipe, it should normally involve only one or two elements.
- Refrain from changing all the recipe elements at the same time, as this implies that a company may have lost its way.

CHAPTER NINE

Organizational Structure

I discovered that the best innovation is sometimes the
company, the way you organize a company.[1]

———

—STEVE JOBS

ORGANIZATIONAL STRUCTURE OF THE ENTERPRISE

Now let's move on to the second principle of an innovative business
model: the organizational structure. At a very high level, I believe, there
are essentially three types of organizational structures that are commonly
used by enterprises. These three organizational structures include the
decentralized, hybrid, and integrated models. It's important to stress,
however, that there are no two organizational structures that are alike,
and there are numerous variations of each model. Said another way, every
company is organized differently!

The organizational structure of a company should be designed around
the company's unique practices. Leaders need to focus intensely on the
organizational structure because it's essential to effective execution of the
unique practices of the company. Moreover, the structure should align well
with the culture of the company and the management style of its leadership.
To revisit what the great Steve Jobs once said, "I discovered that the best

innovation is sometimes the company, the way you organize a company." It's utterly amazing that one of the best CEOs of all time identified the organizational structure as a vital innovation that provided Apple with a distinct competitive advantage. This piercing insight is something that every leadership team should take to heart.

Enterprises using a decentralized business model are usually organized so that business units operate independently as essentially stand-alone businesses. Organizations using a hybrid model are built around a system that takes parts from both the decentralized and integrated models. Then there is the integrated model, where the entire enterprise is usually set up as a cohesive unit that operates as a whole. Irrespective of which model is utilized, the model must be underpinned by well-designed, efficient, and standardized processes. These processes must be accompanied by a framework that allows the enterprise to execute its vision flawlessly, without the bureaucratic policies that normally slow or cripple an organization.

ORGANIZATIONAL STRUCTURE KEY OBSERVATIONS

During my business career, I've been blessed to see the inner workings of numerous companies. As a result, I have formed some thoughts on how a company should be optimized through an innovative business model structure. Also, I have studied the organizational structure of several elite companies. Thus, my own analysis and study of the different organizational structures has revealed some not too surprising truths. Here are my key findings and thoughts:

- There is no perfect or magical organizational operating structure.
- No two organizational operating structures are identical; there's an endless number of structures that can be adopted.
- Much can be learned by studying how other enterprises are structured and adopting some of their best ideas.
- The organizational model must fit the operating style of the leadership team.

- The organizational model must allow for a connect-and-collaborate environment that promotes innovation.
- The organizational model must fit and be aligned with the enterprise's specific unique practices.
- The organizational model must fit with and reinforce the culture of the company; it shouldn't damage it.
- When designing the optimal organizational structure, one must make critical decisions about business segments, groups, platforms, brands, product lines, and how results are reported.
- An organizational structure change does not have to be transformative to be effective; it can simply entail such actions as the realigning of segments.

With these findings and thoughts in mind, let's now examine all three business models more in depth.

TYPE I: DECENTRALIZED MODEL

A question I often get from various sources is this: Is a highly decentralized business model—including conglomerates—relevant in today's competitive and turbulent environment? Or is there still room for some diversified and decentralized enterprise to continue in existence and perform well?

As you would expect, the answer is complex.

Decentralized business structures, particularly those with a portfolio of diversified businesses, have been around for a long time, having come into prominence in the 1960s. In recent years, activist investors have changed the landscape. They are demanding more focus, more commonality, and better performance. In addition, adaptive companies have taken unilateral and proactive action to totally transform themselves. The list of enterprises that have announced some form of breakup or transformation over the last several of years is impressive. There are, however, some companies that have resisted and bucked this trend, with the most notable being Honeywell and Roper. Both these enterprises believe in their business model and continue along as successful diversified companies.

For the decentralized model to be optimal, an enterprise must ideally have a powerful entrepreneurial culture, strong enterprise controls, and business units that are consistently high performers, posting exceptional operating results. Another essential condition for a decentralized business model to be consistently successful is to have businesses that operate mainly in noncyclical end markets.

Stability is important for this model to be effective since the cost is usually higher than for either the hybrid or centralized model. For example, the structure of a decentralized company may include a global headquarters, segment headquarters, regional headquarters, and sometimes even multiple headquarters within a country since each business platform operates independently. Often with a decentralized model, the enterprise tends to have a portfolio of diversified businesses.

Thus, the answer to the question I started with is as follows: it depends on the forces of change, all shaped by the type of business platforms the enterprise has and what end markets it participates in. Given today's competitive marketplace and the rise of activist investors, the need to operate with the lowest cost structure possible is now paramount. Consequently, the truly decentralized business model has somewhat fallen out of favor and has evolved to become more of a hybrid model. I believe that the decentralized model will continue to be less utilized in the future and that some form of the other two models will be more the norm. However, I also believe that in special cases such as Roper, the decentralized model will continue to work well for a select group of companies.

TYPE II: HYBRID MODEL

The hybrid model can take many forms, including a matrix organization and the one-company initiative. Based on all the various forms that I have personally experienced, I prefer the one-company structure, which is explained below. For a hybrid model to be exceptional, it must have a team of strong and talented functional leaders, including elite-level financial officers, information technology officers, supply chain specialists, and human resources officers, to name a few. Trust and teamwork are important in a hybrid enterprise structure.

Under the hybrid model, an organization must possess operational excellence capabilities. These capabilities, necessary to capture benefits from scaling the company, include an integrated management system, shared services, and global supply chain management. Since this structure reduces the need for regional business headquarters, these facilities are usually either eliminated or significantly reduced in size and/or number. This model is appropriate for both nonhomogeneous and homogeneous businesses (multiple or single business platform). Also, this model ideally requires a company to operate in an entrepreneurial manner.

As explained above, a popular derivative of the hybrid structure is the one-company initiative. This structure has been around for a long time. The concept has been utilized in various forms by a multitude of companies to optimize their respective organizations and also to unify their cultures. I used a similar structure in several businesses with good results. This structure works well when an enterprise has business platforms that are nonhomogeneous and when there are multiple ERP (enterprise resource planning) systems.

For the one-company structure to function effectively, it is critical to spell out key responsibilities of each business segment and the corporate center. To achieve maximum optimization, it is also essential for each segment to have installed a one-instance ERP system. The one-company model I championed was structured to capture scale benefits and promote a strong culture while allowing each business unit to operate independently, as follows:

- **Business segment responsibilities.** Each business segment operated separately and was led by a group president. The business segment was responsible for all its daily activities, including operations, engineering, products and services, innovation and technology, marketing/sales/distribution channels, customer relationships, brand management, site management, and digital strategy.

- **Corporate center responsibilities.** The corporate center had three primary roles, each distinctively different. Here are the specific elements within each role:

  o *Business strategic services.* Role number one includes strategy development and coordination. The most important elements of strategy development include core philosophy, high-performance plan, capital allocation, governance, and board of directors.

  o *Business segment functional support services.* Role number two includes such services as human resources, legal, information technology infrastructure, compliance and governance, risk management, internal audit, financial reporting, treasury, and taxes.

  o *Business segment operational support services.* Role number three includes critical support elements such as acquisitions, global supply chain, manufacturing excellence, integrated management system, and environmental, health, and safety management.

In essence, the one-company initiative allows for optimization of services—such as global supply chain—while allowing the business segment to operate independently so it may focus on its fundamental objective of supremely serving the customer.

TYPE III: INTEGRATED MODEL

The integrated model is often referred to as the centralized model. On the surface, the integrated model is compelling from a cost savings and efficiency standpoint. Many companies have moved to some form of this structure because of activist investors and the need to continuously perform at a high level under the lowest cost structure possible.

Over the years, I've had the privilege of visiting several Fortune 100 companies that operated under the integrated business model. What I observed is that the model worked beautifully for them and the demonstrated cost savings were impressive. Still, enterprises considering this model must ensure they have a modern and fully integrated information technology (IT) infrastructure using one ERP system. However, for some companies, the cost of implementing a one-instance global ERP system can be prohibitive and simply unrealistic. Secondly, for the centralized model to work at a high level, a homogeneous business enterprise is preferable to different and distinct business platforms, which is what is typically found with the hybrid and decentralized models.

During my research of various organizational structures, I discovered that Apple offers the best example of a successful integrated enterprise model. In the book *Steve Jobs*, the author Walter Isaacson talks about the significance of the business model to Apple. Here is what he said: "[Steve Jobs] did not organize Apple into semiautonomous divisions; he closely controlled all his teams and he pushed them to work as one cohesive and flexible company, with one profit-and-loss bottom line."

Steve Jobs offered some additional interesting perspective on how a company should be organized when he said, "One of the keys to Apple is [that] Apple's an incredibly collaborative company. You know how many committees we have at Apple? Zero. We have no committees. We are organized like a start-up. One person's in charge of iPhone OS software, one person's in charge of Mac hardware, one person's in charge of iPhone hardware engineering, another person's in charge of worldwide marketing, another person's in charge of operations. We are organized like a startup. We are the biggest startup on the planet."[2]

A lot can be learned by studying Apple and especially understanding the perspective of Steve Jobs. He went to great lengths to explain that the way he organized the company was an important innovation. This is something that should be appreciated by all leaders. It should also provide the inspiration for leadership teams to reexamine how they are organized.

FIVE EFFECTIVE PRACTICES TO OPTIMIZE THE ORGANIZATIONAL STRUCTURE

In the remainder of this chapter, we will review five practices that leaders should consider when designing their organizational structure. Many of these activities, such as building a flat organization and simplifying the business, are universal and apply to all enterprises. The five practices include the following:

- Build a flat and responsive organization.
- Build a value-creating corporate center.
- Simplify the business.
- Optimize the legal, tax, and reporting structures.
- Reimagine the business model.

PRACTICE #1: BUILD A FLAT AND RESPONSIVE ORGANIZATION

For a company to achieve greatness, it must be nimble, resilient, and driven by exceptional people. A key component to building a nimble and resilient company is the way in which the company is structured. When designing how the enterprise will operate through its organizational structure, it is important for the leadership team to design a flat organization. This simply means that leaders have as many direct reports as possible.

If the best and brightest people are hired and they operate within a nimble governance framework of accountability and responsibility, there's no need to micromanage them. To the contrary, they should be unshackled and allowed to perform at a high level. It's also crucial that each team be led by an exceptional leader who may make a disproportionate impact on the company and its long-term performance. Exceptional people, when not micromanaged and not stifled by bureaucratic procedures and processes, will most likely outperform. Elite companies know this well, so they structure a flat organization that unleashes talented teams.

PRACTICE #2: BUILD A VALUE-CREATING CORPORATE CENTER

No matter what organizational structure is adopted by an enterprise, one element that must always be at the forefront is a corporate center. This is to add value. Unfortunately, corporate centers sometimes fall short of this measure. Most CEOs grapple at some point in their tenures with the age-old question of how the corporate center can add value. In a white paper, the Boston Consulting Group captured the essence of this dilemma as follows: "CEOs of multinational corporations are under constant internal and external pressure to add value to the portfolio of businesses so that the whole is worth more than the sum of its parts. Many CEOs, however, struggle to devise a strategy for the corporate center and to translate that strategy into an organizational design that actually adds value."[3] The good news is that the corporate center can be designed to add value. Following is how to create a value-enhancing corporate center irrespective of the organizational structure the enterprise adopts as part of the business model:

The value-creation process must begin with understanding what the corporate center should not be. An arrogant view that the corporate center is the global headquarters is completely the wrong mindset to have. In addition to engendering hubris, the global headquarters mindset usually manifests itself in many other value-destroying characteristics, including centralized decision-making, bureaucracy, high overhead costs, and office design that offers little or no opportunity for interaction. On the other hand, a value-creating center is completely different and is characterized by such positive attributes as entrepreneurialism, decentralized decision-making, lean staffing, minimal bureaucracy, and an office designed for maximum interaction that stimulates innovation and creativity.

There are some specific key areas where the corporate center can add value. The following elements can be used as an assessment tool by the leaders to determine the effectiveness of their corporate center structure:

- establishing a strong core philosophy,
- developing an innovative business model,
- instilling a culture of innovation and technology,
- establishing a robust high-performance planning process,
- building an abundance of lifelines in a disciplined manner,
- setting the tone for the enterprise on integrity and business conduct,
- working with the business unit leadership team to develop a long-term strategy,
- establishing an enterprise-wide integrated management system,
- providing the business units with exceptional capabilities, such as the ability to successfully execute acquisitions,
- establishing disciplined capital allocation policies,
- ensuring that the enterprise capital structure is optimized,
- appointing a value-creating board,
- keeping the governance framework nimble and effective,
- maintaining an optimized cost structure, and
- establishing an entrepreneurial environment.

PRACTICE #3: SIMPLIFY THE BUSINESS

It is not uncommon to pick up a business article and read about a leader who is trying to simplify his or her organization because it has grown too complex with too much bureaucracy. Elite leaders maintain a relentless focus on simplifying that which is complex because they understand the connection to a more adaptive, efficient, and flexible organization.

The concept of simplicity was captured perfectly by the outstanding author Walter Isaacson in the book *The Innovators* when he wrote, "Most true geniuses ... have an instinct to simplicity."[4] True geniuses such as Steve Jobs recognize and harness the power of simplicity. This is evident from the way Jobs organized Apple to the way he focused on the product design. Steve Jobs of Apple actually captured the concept of simplicity better than anyone. Here is what he said: "Simple can be harder than complex. You have to work hard to get your thinking clean and make it simple. But it's worth it in the end because once you get there, you can move mountains."[5]

Simplicity always wins over complexity. Simplicity applies to just about everything from the core purpose, to core values, to vision, to product design, to critical processes, and especially to the organizational structure. Simplicity is a mechanism that keeps an organization from falling prey to stifling bureaucracy. Suffocating bureaucracy is something that I have experienced over the decades and have observed as being one of the most common elements that prevents a company from achieving greatness. Bureaucracy usually starts with good intentions. Unfortunately, these good intentions normally result in added layers of people. These multiple layers of people will often implement complex rules along with numerous policies and procedures. This environment usually builds slowly and over a long period of time; the enterprise does not become bureaucratic overnight. Sadly, the net result of bureaucracy is a higher cost structure and inefficient processes.

PRACTICE #4: OPTIMIZE THE LEGAL, TAX, AND REPORTING STRUCTURES

An exceptional capability that elite companies possess is an ability to optimize the company's legal, tax, and reporting structures. These structures can make a material impact on the company in terms of both economic success and risk management.

With respect to the legal structure, it is vital that a company protect itself as much as possible from existential risk. The devastation caused by asbestos litigation is just one of many examples. In the simplest form, a company should consider structuring its business units as separate, wholly owned subsidiaries.

From a tax standpoint, there are some weapons that a company may utilize with smart tax planning strategies. Strategic tax planning is a must because tax rates change and nothing is static. That's why it's essential to scan the environment, to be proactive, and to have an exceptional team of tax experts available to help navigate complex legislation.

With respect to reporting structures, these represent the way the company organizes segments, groups, divisions, branches, product lines, and administrative centers. All these will ultimately affect, to a certain degree, the performance of the company. In some instances, the effect on the company could be material. Leaders should not underestimate the importance of properly organizing the process by which critical information is reported and managed.

PRACTICE #5: REIMAGINE THE BUSINESS MODEL

Reimaging the business model applies to both the unique practices and the organizational structure. Elite companies excel at creating an innovative business model and at successfully reinventing their organization. Let's examine some companies that have flawlessly executed their own reinventions. Many of these elite companies have already been mentioned in *Ascend to Greatness*, including Roper, Disney, Alphabet, Amazon, Microsoft, and Danaher.

Roper transitioned from an industrial enterprise to a diversified technology company. They now design and develop software and engineered products and solutions for a variety of niche end markets. Disney reinvented itself by building a collection of inimitable brands through brilliant acquisitions such as Lucasfilm, Marvel Studios, and 20th Century Fox (now 20th Century Studios). Google transformed itself into Alphabet because of the growth outside its core search engine business, represented by holdings such as YouTube, YouTube TV, and Nest. Amazon transformed itself from just an e-commerce site to a force in cloud computing. Microsoft likewise transformed itself around several other platforms with the most important being its Azure cloud computing platform and its Office 365. Danaher transformed itself from a diversified industrial company into principally a life sciences and diagnostic company.

All enterprises need to have the same mindset as the leading companies cited above to reach the summit of greatness. Visionary leaders and boards need to reimagine what the company can become in order to successfully transform an organization. When business models are reimagined, it's important also to revisit how the company is structured because an organizational structure that may have worked in the past may not work in the future.

CHAPTER TEN

Building Lifelines

Bad companies are destroyed by crisis. Good companies
survive them. Great companies are improved by them.[1]

——

—ANDY GROVE

LIFELINES AND MOUNTAINEERING METAPHORS

I use mountaineering metaphors throughout all my books to capture the
essence of the challenge leaders face in today's tumultuous, unpredictable,
and hypercompetitive global marketplace. Just as mountaineers rely on
lifelines to ensure safety, elite leaders metaphorically rely on lifelines to
survive any unexpected turbulence as they embark on their journey to
ascend the summit of greatness. The enterprise lifeline serves as a useful
narrative device that further illustrates the threats all leaders are confronted
with today because of ever-increasing disruptions and shocks.

One of the most effective mountaineering metaphors that I have used
in my books that applies specifically to this principle is the "death zone." In
the book *The Climb: Tragic Ambitions on Everest*, authors Anatoli Boukreev
and G. Weston DeWalt define the death zone as "any elevation above 8,000
meters where extended exposure to sub-zero temperatures and oxygen
deprivation combine and kill, quickly."[2]

In the world, only fourteen mountains rise above eight thousand meters in height, with the highest peak being Mount Everest at 8,848.86 meters (29,031.69 feet) above sea level. The second highest—and considered the most dangerous and difficult to climb—is K2, which rises 8,611 meters (28,251 feet). In business, ascending to the summit of greatness is more like trying to climb K2 because it is this peak that is the most difficult and most dangerous. Companies, like mountaineers, don't exist with guarantees that they will succeed; both mountaineers and CEOs are always in danger of perishing (or failing) on their respective climbs to the summit. The best-prepared and most skilled climbers (and companies) have the best chance to safely reach the summit. This process is where the lifelines come in.

COMPANY DEATH ZONE

The death zone in business can be a sudden change in the marketplace due to a disruptive new innovation. Take for example the impact of Apple's iPod on the music industry. The disruptive innovation may also be an external global shock such as the COVID-19 pandemic. There are numerous others as well, including economic and geopolitical shocks. The shock can also really be a series of shocks that cumulatively have a material adverse impact on the company. In all these cases, enterprises that are unprepared for a sudden change may find themselves with little oxygen and little hope of making it safely down the mountain. To survive, companies must build a prodigious number of lifelines so that they can survive any unexpected storm.

The need to prepare for the death zone is more important today than at any other time in history. This was on full display in 2020 with the pandemic that devastated companies across the globe. In my previous book, published in 2017, I was prescient in stating that we have now entered a new period of immense turbulence and instability. I called it the Global Chaos Crisis. I also stated that before it's too late, companies immediately need to start building an abundance of lifelines. The events that unfolded in 2020–21 as a result of COVID-19 unfortunately proved my 2017 prediction to be true.

LIFELINES ARE CRITICAL TO BUILDING
AN ENDURING ELITE COMPANY

The ultimate goal of every leader should be to create and sustain an elite enterprise, one that transcends generations. A fundamental step in creating and sustaining such an enterprise is implementing my elite enterprise model. One of the seventeen principles outlined in my model is the need to build ample lifelines. Lifelines are necessary to withstand any turbulence the enterprise will encounter in its long and arduous journey to the summit. The ultimate objective of building a prodigious number of lifelines is to come out of any major storm quickly, unscathed, and possibly even stronger.

One sure way to ensure that an enterprise is derailed from its journey is to fail to build the necessary lifelines that can be drawn upon when events quickly spiral out of control. An organization must be well prepared to survive any known or unknown threats. That's because under extreme conditions, preparedness in the form of lifelines can mean the difference between surviving or dying on the mountain. It's the oxygen. Leaders must recognize that beginning any climb to the summit of elite without an appropriate number of lifelines will make the journey, at best, extremely challenging and perilous.

POSSESSING A HEALTHY PARANOIA

Mountaineering rule number one states, "Hope for the best, but plan for the worst." Elite leaders who build lifelines analyze all possible scenarios, so they can hope for the best but prudently plan for the worst. Elite leaders clearly understand that they must manage in good times just as they do in bad times. This means having the right mindset and a healthy paranoia to operate the company in a disciplined manner under all economic environments. Under this mindset, costs are controlled even during the best of times, and a certain level of investment is consistently made to strengthen the enterprise.

Throughout his timeless book *Only the Paranoid Survive*, Andy Grove from Intel emphasizes why leaders need to possess a healthy paranoia. That is so true because no one is immune from the forces of change. In addition, Jim Collins, in his insightful monograph *Turning the Flywheel*, provides his perspective on the importance of possessing a healthy paranoia about survival and the need to adequately prepare. No one has said it better than Jim Collins; his words are very powerful: "The only mistakes you can learn from are the ones you survive. Leaders who navigate turbulence and stave off decline assume that conditions can unexpectedly change, violently and fast. They obsessively ask, 'What if? What if? What if?' By preparing ahead of time, building reserves, preserving a margin of safety, bounding risk, and honing their discipline in good times and bad, they handle disruptions from a position of strength and flexibility. Productive paranoia helps inoculate organizations from falling into the five stages of decline that can derail the flywheel and destroy an organization."[3] Leaders need to take to heart the insightful advice provided by both Mr. Grove and Mr. Collins. It should always be kept in the forefront of their minds.

As we will review later in this chapter, fundamental disruption and shocks appear to be happening with ever-increasing regularity and severity. It's not a matter of if, it's a matter of when. We just don't know when the next shock will occur and how severe it will be. That is why leaders must possess a healthy paranoia about preparedness and survival. Metaphorically speaking, the more oxygen canisters, the greater the chance of survival. The only realistic antidote to disruptions and shocks is being fanatical about building an immense number of lifelines.

SURVIVING AND FLOURISHING IN TURBULENT TIMES

The more lifelines that are built over a long horizon, the stronger the enterprise will be. These lifelines often make the difference between success and failure. In some cases, failure can mean the death of the enterprise.

I've personally experienced as a CEO three major consecutive shocks that had a devastating effect on our company. First, in 2008, my first full year as CEO, our company was crushed by the financial crisis. The following year (2009), we faced the H1N1 swine flu just as we were significantly expanding our business footprint in Asia. The year after that (2010), we faced the European sovereign debt crisis. For our company, the European sovereign debt crisis was as equally as devastating as, and possibly more devastating than, the 2008 Great Recession. The reason for this is simple: more than 50 percent of our business was concentrated in the European Union. I would say that these three consecutive years marked by major forces of change qualify as severe. As bad as these events were, nothing equaled the devastation faced by some companies because of the COVID-19 pandemic. Although I was not a CEO during this dark period, I served on boards and advised companies on how to deal with the destructive impact of the pandemic on their businesses. Thus, I can attest to how critical it is to have in reserve plentiful lifelines of the sort needed to survive amid the most extreme conditions.

Before we examine the importance of lifelines, let's first review where the most notable external turbulent events come from. Adversity in business can come in many different forms. I have segmented the most severe external forces of change into two major categories. The first category is disruptive innovation and technology. The second category is severe shocks. In addition to these two powerful forces of change, there are numerous others that emanate from both external and internal sources. An example of an external source is litigation—such as asbestos—that can pose an existential threat to the enterprise. An example of an internal source is a series of significant management missteps that put the enterprise on a pernicious path of decline. One could write an entire book on the number of external and internal sources of turbulence; we will not cover the myriad of possible forces of change in this chapter. Instead, we will focus more narrowly on the two most severe external forces of change, which include the following:

DISRUPTIVE INNOVATION AND TECHNOLOGY

Disruptive innovation and technology can pose a direct threat to the survival of an enterprise. The threat from disruptive innovation and technology continues to rise, and companies that ignore this fact do so at their own peril. Disruptive innovation and technology has upended numerous industries. This has resulted in some companies either disappearing completely or simply being relegated to mediocrity or irrelevance.

SEVERE SHOCKS

A major global economic, geopolitical, or health shock or, even worse, a series of severe events may dramatically weaken or even possibly destroy an enterprise. History is replete with examples of shocks, including the Great Depression, the 9/11 terrorist attacks, the Great Recession, the European sovereign debt crisis, and economic crisis resulting from the COVID-19 pandemic. If you examine all the events in just the last twenty years, you see that the frequency is striking. This should cause all CEOs some disquiet. Some of these shocks, such as COVID-19, should spur all boards and CEOs to immediate action. Enterprises must adequately prepare for unforeseen events. The data is just too compelling to ignore!

A CALL TO ACTION

As stated earlier, disruptive events and devastating shocks occur with some regularity. Thus, there must be a call to action by CEOs and boards to ensure that their enterprises are fully prepared for any eventuality. Companies that fail to prepare adequately for future disruptions and shocks and that fail to adapt to the ever-changing business landscape do so at their own peril. The evidence is just too compelling to ignore. Let's examine just one key data point, the Fortune 500 list.

If you examine the entire history of the Fortune 500 list (1955 to 2019), you will probably be surprised to learn that an astonishing 448, nearly 90 percent, of the company names on the 1955 list don't appear in the 2019 list. Mark J. Perry of the American Enterprise Institute wrote the following in a blog post about this surprising piece of information:

The fact that nearly nine of every 10 Fortune 500 companies in 1955 are gone, merged, reorganized, or contracted demonstrates that there's been a lot of market disruption, churning, and Schumpeterian creative destruction over the last six decades. It's reasonable to assume that when the Fortune 500 list is released 60 years from now in 2079, almost all of today's Fortune 500 companies will no longer exist as currently configured, having been replaced by new companies in new, emerging industries, and for that we should be extremely thankful. The constant turnover in the Fortune 500 is a positive sign of the dynamism and innovation that characterizes a vibrant consumer-oriented market economy, and that dynamic turnover is speeding up in today's hyper-competitive global economy.[4]

Such statistics are shocking. They support my argument that there is a need for companies to implement my elite enterprise model as an antidote. Moreover, I don't completely agree with the statement that a constant turnover is a positive sign. It is obviously true to a certain degree, but I would argue that a nearly 90 percent disappearance rate is excessive and perhaps points to other reasons the failure of an unknown number of entities that are no longer in existence. I suspect that some leadership teams missed the message about what was to come in the future. This idea was captured perfectly by the cofounder of Google Larry Page when he stated, "The main thing that has caused companies to fail, in my view, is that they missed the future."[5]

Of course, without a proper study being done, it is impossible to draw definitive conclusions from the nearly 90 percent disappearance rate. However, I suspect that an undefined percentage of companies disappeared from the list primarily for the reason stated by Mr. Page. Missing the future can mean many things, but I would argue that the possibilities can be narrowed down to two primary reasons. First, leaders did not build enough of the enterprise lifelines discussed in *Ascend to Greatness* that would have, to a certain degree, insulated them from most, if not all, turbulent events. Second, because circumstances are always changing, these companies were likely too slow to adapt to a change or may not have even recognized the need to change because of internal complacency and/or arrogance, which is usually driven by the loss of discipline.

Here is what Andy Grove has to say about complacency: "Success breeds complacency. Complacency breeds failure. Only the paranoid survive."[6] With respect to hubris, Jim Collins captures it well in his insightful book *How the Mighty Fall*. Mr. Collins points out that the first stage of decline is "hubris born of success." Here is what Collins says about stage one: "Great enterprises can become insulated by success; accumulated momentum can carry an enterprise forward, for a while, even if its leaders make poor decisions or lose discipline. Stage 1 kicks in when people become arrogant, regarding success virtually as an entitlement, and they lose sight of the true underlying factors that created success in the first place. When rhetoric of success … replaces penetrating understanding and insight … decline will very likely follow. Luck and chance play a role in many successful outcomes, and those who fail to acknowledge the role luck may have played in their success … have succumbed to hubris."[7]

CREATE YOUR OWN FUTURE

Mountaineers, like companies, also face many obstacles that can slow or even terminate the ascent to the summit. Avalanches, which tend to be the deadliest, are at the top of the list. Unexpected storms, high winds, equipment malfunction, and team members' bad choices are some of the more common obstacles. Great mountaineers know how to adapt to the situation. It's no different in business. Companies face formidable obstacles that can slow or even derail their ascent to the summit of elite. A great recession, a disruptive innovation, a geopolitical event, a crippling cyberbreach, or even an unpredictable pandemic can dramatically affect the climb. Businesses, just like mountaineers, need to be able to adapt to any circumstance.

Visionary leaders know how to create a brighter future. These leaders know that for a company to endure, it must build ample lifelines to ensure that the enterprise can withstand any form of disruption or shock. As history has proven over and over again, these events are inevitable. Thus, elite leaders know that having an abundance of lifelines not only will position the company to survive turbulent events but also allow the company to prosper by enabling the seizing of opportunities. Elite companies know how to turn disruption and shocks into a competitive advantage.

All one has to do is examine what happened during the 2008 Great Recession and the 2020 coronavirus pandemic, where some firms failed and others were crippled. On the other hand, the well-prepared companies that possessed lifelines demonstrated a superior competitive position over rivals and actually performed well.

WHAT ARE THE MOST ESSENTIAL LIFELINES?

So, what are some of the most essential lifelines that allows a company to continue performing at a relatively high level even during periods of chaos and uncertainty? I believe that there are seven fundamental lifelines that must be built to withstand any turbulence and possibly even allow the organization to prosper under the right conditions. All seven of these lifelines are disciplined proactive actions that will provide the antidote to disruptions and shocks. Let's begin by examining the balance sheet, which I believe is the most important lifeline.

LIFELINE #1. BUILD A STRONG BALANCE SHEET

Maintaining a strong balance sheet with ample cash reserves, manageable debt levels, and lots of liquidity in the form of bank lines is paramount. There's nothing better than a pristine balance sheet to get an organization through any type of turbulence. Just look at Berkshire Hathaway and Apple as extraordinary examples. The amount of cash that they have readily available is utterly amazing, and the decision to keep such cash in reserves is very smart.

As we saw with the COVID-19 pandemic, companies scrambled

to improve their liquidity position and simultaneously reduce costs. Elite companies already had all these elements in place, plus numerous other lifelines that are covered in this chapter. In connection with this preparedness, a helpful calculation may be used to determine just how long an enterprise can operate with its balance sheet before running out of cash. This calculation was explained well by Theo Francis and Thomas Gryta in a *Wall Street Journal* article of March 26, 2020.

Here's how the authors capture the importance of liquidity: "The fast-moving coronavirus has prompted even the biggest US companies to cut their spending and bolster their balance sheets, proving once again how cash is king, especially in times of crisis. After a decade-long US economic expansion, not every company has entered this crisis with the same cushion. Apple Inc. ended the year with $247 billion in cash, securities and account receivables, enough to run its operations for more than a year even if it didn't cut costs or sell a single iPhone." Apple, of course, is the gold standard.

The article goes on to point out that, in general, the technology sector is much better prepared than other sectors for these types of shocks. The article states, "Technology companies generally operate with more cash on hand. … The median amount of cash and other readily available assets on an S&P 500 tech company's books at year-end was enough to let it operate about 270 days in an extreme scenario without revenue or cost cutting, while the median was closer to 60 days for retailers. … As companies prepare to close their books on a tumultuous first quarter, these measures can reveal how ill-prepared they are for the sudden financial stress."

The journal article uses a calculation from *Calcbench* to demonstrate the estimated number of days that a company can operate. Here is the definition that was used by the journal: "Calculated by dividing cash, securities and accounts receivable at the end of 2019 by total operating expenses for the prior 12 months, excluding depreciation and amortization, stock compensation and common write-downs."

LIFELINE #2. INVEST IN AND CREATE THE FUTURE

Consistently investing in the future in a disciplined manner is imperative if one aspires to ascend to greatness. Enterprises must invest in all areas in order to create a better future and drive long-term performance. Elite companies consistently allocate, at least annually, a certain percentage of earnings to build exceptional capabilities, no matter the economic environment. They know how to balance short-term quarterly earnings with the need to invest for the long term to strengthen the enterprise. This balance is achieved by allocating investment dollars within a preestablished range. Under good times, they invest at the higher end of the range; during difficult times they invest at the lower end. What's important is that the organization consistently invests—with discipline—in building strength and capabilities. All these building blocks are so crucial that they are expanded upon in the following points:

INVEST IN PEOPLE EXCELLENCE

Making a long-term commitment to leadership development and talent management, including hiring and retaining the best and the brightest, is essential to building and sustaining an elite company. Without extraordinary people, it is impossible to build an elite company. Investing in people is one of the most fundamental lifelines for a company because these individuals are the ones who will navigate the storms and execute brilliantly the strategy of the company.

COMMIT TO INNOVATION AND TECHNOLOGY

Making a long-term commitment to innovation and technology, including research and development, is vital not only to achieve elite status but also to sustain it. Innovation and technology are the lifeblood of any organization. Companies that don't make a long-term commitment to building these capabilities will eventually pay a heavy price.

DEVELOP EXTRAORDINARY EXECUTION CAPABILITIES

Investing over a long horizon in developing exceptional execution capabilities is crucial to sustained high performance. This includes investing in such elements as supply chain; an integrated management system; project and product management; automated processes; and information technology, just to name a few.

INVEST IN STANDARDIZED PROCESSES

Identifying and continuously investing in standardizing the most critical processes that drive execution excellence is crucial to achieving high performance.

SIMPLIFY AND DELAYER THE ENTERPRISE

There must be a focus on simplifying, delayering, and eliminating as much complexity as possible from the organizational structure and underlying processes. This lifeline, along with building an adaptive and resilient company, should provide the organization with the necessary speed and agility to deal with adversity.

POSSESS A FANATICAL COST CONTROL MINDSET

Instilling a discipline where cost controls are cultural and not structural is paramount. The organization must possess a fanatical mindset when it comes to controlling costs, even during good times. This will better prepare the organization to weather unexpected adverse events. Every dollar that is saved can be invested back into the enterprise.

BUILD A CULTURE OF CONTINUOUS IMPROVEMENT AND LEARNING

Just as it is important to be passionate about cost controls, it is equally necessary to instill a culture of continuous improvement and learning. Continuous improvement and learning should be in the DNA of the organization.

BUILD AN ENTREPRENEURIAL CULTURE

An entrepreneurial culture can be a major driver of elite performance. That's why it's crucial for an organization to invest appropriately in building and sustaining this type of culture. Investment can take many forms and can include such elements as teaching entrepreneurial principles, designing an effective governance framework, and implementing strong mechanisms.

LIFELINE #3. SCAN THE ENVIRONMENT IN REAL TIME

This lifeline is of paramount importance to the long-term success of a company. The objective for scanning the environment is to excel at better predicting the future and doing so earlier and more accurately than others. Being able to see the future can provide an enterprise with a competitive advantage. As Andy Grove famously said, "The ability to recognize that the winds have shifted and to take appropriate action before you wreck your boat is crucial to the future of an enterprise."[8]

An early detection and prediction process is fundamental to preparing an organization for any potential disruption or shock and for detecting opportunities. This allows the company to create a better future. Sentinel systems are indispensable because they provide the ability to take proactive action. This insight is invaluable, especially to getting in front of upcoming major storms. For this early warning mechanism to be effective, it must be connected to a bias for fast action. A proactive mindset must exist, one with a sense of extreme urgency. All critical data gathered by the sentinel process is rendered useless if the culture of the organization is such that the leaders are too slow to react and make decisions.

Scanning the environment is an exceptional capability that all enterprises must develop. It is vital they do so because of the competitive nature of markets, disruptive technologies, and ongoing global shocks. As we have seen with the financial crisis, the coronavirus pandemic, and the ever-increasing rate of disruptive technologies, fierce turbulence is here to stay. The ability to scan the environment is essential so that proactive actions may be taken to either avoid or at least minimize the potential destructive effect from major threats, risks, and uncertainties. Like mountaineers, enterprises must stay ahead of the storm if they are to survive.

What do I mean by scanning the environment in real time? Every company has some form of real time–embedded mechanisms in place to gather data. What separates the elite enterprises from everyone else is that the ability of the former to learn more quickly and effectively from the data gathered. They are able to distinguish between unassailable facts, emerging risks, and attribution (unsubstantiated opinions). Consequently, they are better able to predict trends that are likely to worsen; to detect the disruptive forces of change; and even to identify opportunities.

Elite organizations understand that they must react and adapt quickly based on whatever conclusions they reach by critically analyzing data that is gathered by scanning the environment. That is, they are proactive, they are not bureaucratic, and the responsive actions they take are measured and specifically address identified risks. The exceptional capability to learn and take proactive action is fundamental to understanding at the earliest possible moment what is transpiring in the marketplace. This extraordinary capability can allow a company to get in front of challenges and also seize opportunities more quickly.

So, what are some of the key practices utilized by exceptional companies for scanning the environment? Big data is used by elite companies to better understand customer habits, innovation and technology trends, the competitive landscape, and market changes. It's also used to analyze health-related matters, geopolitical events, demographic information, and regulatory trends. Elite enterprises obsess over data and trends. This is an area where technology, robust processes, and skilled people trained in data analytics and critical thinking can make a difference. Such people delve deep into the multitude of economic, market, competitive, and general industry information that is released daily. They know how to analyze and model the data. They also know how to organize it in a meaningful fashion so that it can be utilized throughout the enterprise.

Some companies have formed internal big data teams staffed by specialized scientists, analysts, and engineers who understand that data and facts must drive critical decision-making. In addition, big data teams build economic models and establish the right indicators necessary for providing early warning signals. They also assemble other subject experts, both internal and external third-party partners, to assist with identifying and interpreting complex data.

LIFELINE #4. FOCUS ON FREE CASH FLOW

Generating free cash flow is the economic engine of an organization. Free cash flow is the ultimate lifeline because it drives the building of a gold-plated balance sheet. Thus, it's essential that an enterprise have a complete focus on free cash flow and that this cash flow is properly utilized as a key metric for measuring long-term success.

Companies that generate prodigious amounts of free cash flow usually dominate their respective markets. Exceptional free cash flow generation allows a company to build cash on the balance sheet, pay down debt, pay dividends, and invest in acquisitions. Just as important, it provides the resources to invest in the future.

LIFELINE #5. ALLOCATE CAPITAL EFFICIENTLY

Capital is, of course, a finite resource that needs to be well managed. When capital is invested efficiently at all times, it ensures a better future for the organization. Just as there must be a fanatical mindset toward controlling costs, there must be a fanatical mindset toward capital allocation. Capital needs to be invested smartly because, cumulatively, all investment decisions will make an impact on the enterprise. It's crucial that precious capital not be squandered.

Efficiently allocating capital requires discipline, robust processes, and extraordinary capabilities. More specifically, the enterprise needs to possess elite talent capable of successfully consummating acquisitions and investing in capital expenditures and other projects that generate a high internal rate of return. Every dollar that is not waste, can be invested in creating a better future.

LIFELINE #6. ACCELERATE THE TRANSFORMATION TO A DIGITAL ENTERPRISE

Innovation and technology are escalating at a rapid pace. The speed at which innovation and technology are disrupting markets is unprecedented. The power of the digital enterprise became crystal clear during the COVID-19 pandemic; those who leveraged digital technology well were the clear winners. Many of these businesses continued to operate at a relatively high level despite having large a number of employees working from home. Digital enterprises ensured that their customers had positive experiences, which strengthened their brand.

No one captures the need to transform into a digital enterprise better than Andy Grove of Intel and Satya Nadella of Microsoft. Here is what Mr. Grove said: "I have been quoted saying that, in the future, all companies will be Internet companies. I still believe that. More than ever, really."[9] Mr. Nadella was just as bold in a *Wall Street Journal* article that appeared in the January 30–31, 2021, edition titled "Businesses Are Being Pushed to Evolve": "What we are witnessing is the dawn of a second wave of digital transformation sweeping every company and every industry. Digital capability is key to both resilience and growth. It's no longer enough to just adopt technology. Businesses need to build their own technology to compete and grow."[10]

As discussed in other parts of *Ascend to Greatness*, I believe that the digital transformation needs to be focused on three critical areas: infrastructure, processes, and the customer. With respect to infrastructure, this includes websites, cloud storage, ability to work remotely and seamlessly, internet speed, and access to data, cybersecurity, and ERP systems. With respect to processes, this is the way the company handles and delivers orders, the way it collects money, the way it pays employees and vendors, and the way it closes its books, just to name a few. With respect to customers, included are all the ways the enterprise interacts through digital channels with the customer utilizing e-commerce, the virtual marketplace, and social media. Also, all three of these areas need to be adequately supported by a wide array of digital tools that can improve their performance.

LIFELINE #7. DEVELOP AN EFFECTIVE RESPONSE PLAN

Developing and frequently testing a crisis response and business continuity plan that can be executed with a high degree of confidence is vital to survival. As we have learned over the decades, crisis and disasters can come in different forms. They can be economically driven as we saw with the 2008 financial meltdown; they can be health driven as we saw with COVID-19; and they can also be natural (hurricanes, earthquakes) or man-made (cyberbreaches, war). What elite companies have learned from such major events is the importance of having a well-developed and well-tested response plan with all the appropriate protocols.

There are two important lessons I have learned from examining exceptional response plans. First, organizations need to prepare in good times for any eventuality. Second, they need to incorporate as many plan elements as possible into their company's daily practices. The need to prepare in good times has already been covered above in the sections on building lifelines. The second lesson is covered next. For an exceptional plan to be implemented, it is vital that key elements be incorporated into the critical processes of the organization. This will make the execution of the plan during the so-called fog of war more seamless. Let's explore a few examples to better explain this point.

An essential practice of any response and business continuity plan is financial modeling. Modeling various scenarios is crucial to surviving any major adverse event. The modeling needs to be as real time as possible so that critical decisions can be made proactively. Elite companies are exceptional at modeling. They utilize financial modeling for long-term planning, for acquisitions, for joint ventures, and for other projects. This exceptional capability can be utilized when the company is confronted with a major disruption or shock.

Another vital element of an exceptional plan is effective communication. Communicating regularly, both internally and externally, is something organizations do all the time. However, great companies have well-developed processes and protocols in place that can be utilized immediately as part of their response plan. Thus, during a major adverse event, there is no need to try to establish appropriate communication channels, because they already exist.

The same goes with the technology infrastructure. As we saw with the coronavirus pandemic, many employees were asked to work from home. Leading companies already had in place exceptional information technology infrastructure and appropriate protocols. So, as they invoked their plan, they were well prepared to deal with the shock seamlessly.

CHAPTER ELEVEN

Innovation and Technology

Innovation distinguishes between a leader and a follower.[1]

———

—STEVE JOBS

DIFFERENTIATE WITH DISRUPTIVE INNOVATION AND TECHNOLOGY

Innovation and technology are inextricably linked and thus are essential to building and sustaining an elite company. Innovation and technology are the antidote to the challenges brought on by disruptive events, which are occurring at an accelerating pace. No one is immune from the disruptive forces of change. Without innovation and technology, an organization will eventually wither away. Innovation and technology are so crucial that together they must be treated as a core principle under the foundational pillar of strategy. This fundamental principle transcends all business models and all end markets.

There are countless examples in the business media of how elite companies smartly apply innovation and technology throughout their businesses to derive a competitive advantage. Some of the leading nontech companies that are innovative and drive technology throughout the enterprise include Disney, Starbucks, and Mastercard. The need to differentiate and disrupt with innovation and technology is indispensable. This is because the Fourth Industrial Revolution is here. Companies that embrace and advance this digital revolution will be the winners.

For innovation to be successful, an organization must establish the right culture. In Walter Isaacson's wonderful book, *The Innovators*, he provides what I call the *innovation recipe* for a company to be successful: "The key to innovation ... was realizing that there was no conflict between nurturing individual geniuses and promoting collaborative teamwork. It was not either-or. Indeed, throughout the digital age, the two approaches went together. Creative geniuses ... generated innovative ideas. Practical engineers ... partnered closely with them to turn concepts into contraptions. And collaborative teams of technicians and entrepreneurs worked to turn the invention into a practical product. When part of this ecosystem was lacking ... great concepts ended up being consigned to history's basement. And when great teams lacked passionate visionaries ... innovation slowly withered."[2]

Steve Jobs had an interesting perspective on innovation too. This is what he said, "Innovation has nothing to do with how many R & D dollars you have. When Apple came up with the Mac, IBM was spending at least 100 times more on R & D. It's not about money. It's about the people you have, how you're led, and how much you get it."[3] As Steve Jobs proved, a strong innovation culture can drive disruptive innovation and elite performance.

EMBRACE AND ADVANCE THE TENETS OF THE FOURTH INDUSTRIAL REVOLUTION

The digital enterprise is here. Elite companies are in the vanguard of the Fourth Industrial Revolution, which is being driven by indispensable technologies that are disrupting markets and industries across the globe. Some of these technologies include artificial intelligence, robotics, big data, autonomous vehicles, electric vehicles, cloud computing, mobile computing, 3D printing, 5G networks, the Internet of Things, and quantum computing.

Experts on the Fourth Industrial Revolution believe that these technologies will affect business in four distinct ways: a change in customer expectations, product enhancements, collaborative innovation, and changes to organizational form and structure. Thus, companies that embrace the Fourth Industrial Revolution and focus on these four areas should see many opportunities for sustained growth. In addition to disrupting market segments, these technologies, I believe, can enhance business performance, mainly in the following areas: transportation and logistics; global supply chains; digital sales and marketing; automation of business processes; smart factories and offices; digital platform for R&D; mobile apps; and communications. By embracing these technologies, companies gain opportunities not only to be disruptive but also to transform how they do business. For example, automation of business processes and e-commerce are two areas of potential benefit to any company.

Building a digital enterprise can pay dividends. This was on display when the country was in lockdown during the COVID-19 pandemic. Companies that invested heavily in e-commerce, the virtual marketplace, and a modern information technology infrastructure operated seamlessly while many of their employees worked from home. Also, companies that invested heavily in robotics, artificial intelligence, and process automation in their factories and distribution centers fared much better than ones that weren't as advanced technologically.

INSTILL A CULTURE OF INNOVATION AND TECHNOLOGY

Innovation and technology are each a vital lifeline for any organization. If done or used right, innovation and technology can provide a competitive advantage in the marketplace. This can be achieved by instilling deeply in the culture of the organization the mindset that innovation and technology must touch all parts of the company. And there must be a strong passion for innovation and technology among the entire global leadership team. I believe that innovation and technology need to be broadly viewed. It means more than just simply developing new products and/or services. The modern view of innovation and technology needs to be more expansive to include disruptive innovation in the marketplace; ongoing innovation where new products and/or services are continuously developed; innovation as to how the company is organized; and innovation around all critical processes, especially the ones where there is interaction with the customer.

BEST PRACTICES FOR BUILDING A CULTURE OF INNOVATION AND TECHNOLOGY

Studies have shown that more innovation projects fail than succeed. Studies have also shown that these projects typically take longer to complete than expected. In an article in the *Wall Street Journal* on May 16–17, 2020, journalist Matt Ridley makes some insightful comments about innovation. Here is one of his salient points: "Innovation is nearly always a gradual process that proceeds by incremental steps." Mr. Ridley goes on to provide examples of how some innovations were developed in incremental steps. "It is a team sport: There is no individual who can be credited with inventing the computer or the internet." This is why a company must have an innovation culture that is deeply ingrained in the organization.

For a company to build a successful innovation and technology culture, it must first adopt industry best practices. These practices allow an innovation and technology culture to flourish. Following are some not too surprising practices that warrant consideration by anyone interested in building a world-class innovation and technology culture:

PRACTICE #1—USE A NEW MODEL FOR INNOVATION AND TECHNOLOGY

Creating a technology start-up environment within a large organization, one that fosters creativity, collaboration, and innovation, is difficult to achieve. However, a new model has emerged that has been successfully adopted by enterprises interested in infusing an entrepreneurial start-up culture into their organizations. This model utilizes some key innovative practices as the following directives indicate:

- Innovation and technology should begin with building the right culture. A culture that views innovation and technology broadly to include all aspects of the organization.
- The right innovation and technology culture requires an enterprise to scan the environment, both internal and external, for new ideas.
- Making innovation and technology as a core value can be a strong driver of high performance.
- Innovation workshops, innovation challenges, and idea pitch-parties are effective mechanisms for promoting creativity.
- 3M's 15 percent rule is a good mechanism that allows employees to experiment and pursue ideas that can ultimately be impactful.
- Creating an innovation lab can be an incubator of new ideas.
- Establishing workshops designed to speed up cycle time for developing prototypes of new ideas can be an effective mechanism.
- Coaching and teaching innovation and technology principles strengthens the culture.
- Holding failure conferences where people describe their worst mistakes can be a powerful way to avoid repeating these failures in the future.
- For larger companies, establishing an internal venture capital group to allocate funds for innovation and technology investments ultimately may result in the development of disruptive new products and/or services.

As part of this new model for innovation and technology, the company needs to instill the following habits:

OBSESS ABOUT CREATIVITY AND THE CONTINUOUS PURSUIT OF EXCELLENCE

Innovation and technology are usually driven by teams that obsess over creativity and the continuous pursuit of excellence. The continuous pursuit of exceptional products and customer service, for example, can help propel the company to new heights and is fundamental to building brand loyalty.

EXPLORE WITH ON-THE-EDGE INVESTMENTS

On-the-edge investments should be made to explore new ways of doing business and discovering new products and processes. These should be in the form of small bets; making one or several large bets should be avoided.

NURTURE EXTERNAL RELATIONSHIPS

Open innovation, joint ventures, acquisitions, and most importantly, customers all need to be used as essential mechanisms for developing and acquiring innovation and technology. There's much that can be learned from external parties, especially customers. Build trusted relationships with customers. Engage with them to better understand their innovation and technology needs and how they approach it in their organizations. Continuous feedback should be received from the customer as to what solutions he or she is looking for. Use that knowledge to develop innovative products and/or services. Customers can often provide leads and ideas not just on improvements to existing technology but also on transformative technologies.

CRITICALLY ASSESS INNOVATION AND TECHNOLOGY CAPABILITIES

The existing innovation and technology capabilities of the enterprise need to be critically assessed. It is vital that the leadership team properly understands the fundamental strengths of the organization. Also, current research and development projects, along with engineering projects, process reinventions, and transformation initiatives, must be closely reviewed to determine alignment with the company's strategy.

PROPERLY TRAIN ALL EMPLOYEES IN INNOVATION AND TECHNOLOGY

All employees in the organization should be trained to know the importance of innovation and technology and should be encouraged to bring forth ideas about anything from basic improvements to disruptive technologies. Celebrate, recognize, and reward innovation and technological achievements. Recognition of employee contributions needs to be part of your organization's culture.

UTILIZE CROWDSOURCING

Crowdsourcing should be utilized to tap into a global network of research scientists, entrepreneurs, and inventors to identify and accelerate development of new technologies. Research and development initiatives should be approached in multiple ways. Some should be done internally. Some should be outsourced to universities that are part of an established network. Some should be outsourced to independent labs that specialize in certain basic sciences.

INSTILL A LEARNING MINDSET

The principle of a learning entity should augment the innovation and technology principle because the former empowers the latter throughout the organization. The leadership team must ensure that there is a mindset of continuous improvement in the company. Lessons learned should be shared regularly.

INSTILL DISCIPLINE IN MANAGING INNOVATION AND TECHNOLOGY PROJECTS

Innovation and technology projects should not be open-ended; they need target dates for completion. The organization needs to have the mechanisms to terminate projects after a certain period so resources can be allocated to the next great idea. An example of this can be found at Google (Alphabet), where they allocate substantial sums to research and development. To better control its large investment in innovation, Alphabet has developed a disciplined process. One mechanism implemented includes limiting most projects to two years. The *Wall Street Journal* reported on this in April 1, 2015: "Most projects are limited to two years, after which they are killed, moved into Google, spun off into independent firms or licensed to others."[4]

UTILIZE KEY METRICS AND IMPLEMENT MECHANISMS

Develop and utilize the right metrics to properly monitor innovation and technology projects. Also, implement appropriate mechanisms that can help facilitate the building of an innovation and technology culture.

PRACTICE #2—BUILD A SUSTAINABLE BUSINESS

Building a sustainable business needs to be part of the innovation and technology strategy of all enterprises. In addition to benefiting the environment, sustainable business practices help accelerate innovation and technology. Organizations that excel at sustainable practices will, over the long run, outperform those that pay less attention to this component of strategy. Sustainable business practices include such elements as recycling of waste streams; reducing carbon footprint; reducing waste; using sustainable packaging; and ensuring responsible use of water. Since so much has been written about sustainability, I'm not going to repeat any of it here, but I will provide a personal example.

At a company that I led as CEO, we developed innovative environmental solutions for the global metals industry decades before *sustainability* became a household word. Steel is the most recyclable product in the world. We developed innovative technologies to extract valuable metal from waste streams generated by the steel production process. The recovered metal was then reused in the steelmaking process. What remained after recovering the valuable metal was a waste stream. We developed new usable products from this waste stream, including fertilizer, rail ballast, cement additive, and road aggregate. Our environmentally friendly solution essentially recycled 100 percent of the waste streams from the production of steel. Our sustainable solution was a win-win not only for us and our customer but also for us and the planet. We helped make the world better.

PRACTICE #3—APPOINT A DIGITAL ADVISORY BOARD

Elite companies recognize the value of having an effective digital strategy, which is truly indispensable. With the rise of transformative technologies, it's essential that enterprises develop and implement a digital strategy. Some of the biggest names in corporate America have embraced the value of a digital strategy and have accordingly appointed a digital advisory board. This group includes venerable names such as American Express and Target. In addition to an advisory board, leading companies are now focused on recruiting digital directors and establishing alliances with key technology partners. It is difficult to imagine how a major enterprise would be able to operate today without some form of a digital strategy.

When establishing a strong digital advisory board, you should consider some key elements. The advisory board should do the following:

- Have a clearly stated purpose.
- Set forth the responsibilities of all parties, including those retained to serve.
- Be informal, providing maximum flexibility to the company.
- Not have authority to vote on corporate matters.
- Not bear legal fiduciary responsibility.
- Provide nonbinding advice, insight, and perspective on digital matters.
- Be a key resource to the CEO, the management team, and the board.
- Be respected and valued.

- Appoint members to one-year terms; reappointment of each member should be at the sole discretion of the CEO.
- Be collaborative and engaged, and promote a healthy culture.
- Assess effectiveness annually, with key metrics established.

PRACTICE #4—DO NOT BE AFRAID TO FAIL, BUT FAIL FAST AND FAIL WELL

Edward Land, the famous US scientist and inventor, once said, "An essential aspect of creativity is not being afraid to fail."[5] However, in today's hypercompetitive economy, being unafraid to fail is no longer enough. Perhaps a modern version might be that it is vital to fail fast and fail well.

Speed has always been a critical factor in business, but it has never been more important than it is today. Speed is vital to maximizing any potential benefits derived from creativity and innovation. Enterprises that are smart about creativity and innovation clearly understand that if an idea is going to fail ultimately, that failure needs to happen quickly. In addition to acting with speed, failing well is just as important. What this means is that an enterprise must learn from its mistakes and must utilize any valuable parts from the failed project for future initiatives. The reasons for this are obvious: The enterprise benefits by using less money and less intellectual capital on a failed project. These salvaged resources can then be applied to benefit development of the next idea. The other benefit of this practice is that it instills a certain level of discipline into the employees of the organization.

Google offers an example of this mindset. In the book *How Google Works*, authors Schmidt and Rosenberg call it "fail well." Here is how their approach works: "To innovate, you must learn to fail well. Learn from your mistakes: Any failed project should yield valuable technical, user, and market insights that can help inform the next effort. Morph ideas, don't kill them: Most of the world's great innovations started out with entirely different applications. ... The timing of failure is perhaps the trickiest element to get right. A good failure is a fast one: Once you see that the project will not succeed, you want to pull the plug as quickly as possible, to avoid further wasting resources and incurring opportunity costs."[6]

PRACTICE #5—BUILD FORMIDABLE INTANGIBLE ASSETS

Elite companies are keenly focused on investing in and building important intangible assets because these are what drive performance. The valuable assets I am referring to include such things as superior brands, patents, knowledge-based solutions, trademarks, and copyrights. Disney is a shining example of a company that has invested in building formidable intangible assets. These intangible assets have given the company a dominant market position.

What Disney's former leader Robert Iger accomplished during his tenure in transforming the company was extraordinary. He successfully focused the venerable company on formidable intangible assets. In an article in the *Wall Street Journal* on June 9, 2015, Ben Fritz quotes a research analyst who accurately captures Disney's accomplishments and power in the marketplace because of the company's extraordinary franchises. In the article, the analyst points out that "Disney's collection of successful intellectual property is so vast that it's almost unfair to other players in the space."

As noted earlier in *Ascend to Greatness*, an unfair advantage is good in both the military and business. The same article goes on to say, "Over the past decade, Disney has primarily fostered franchises in its own animation divisions and at companies it bought. The takeover of Marvel ... [, and the] purchase of Lucasfilm ... [and] Pixar Animation Studios ... delivered a jolt of energy to Walt Disney Animation Studios." The brands mentioned here are just a sample of the superior brands that Disney has accumulated.

PRACTICE #6—HIRE SMART, CREATIVE PEOPLE

Extraordinary brands are built by smart, creative people, who are your greatest intangible asset. Likewise, new products and/or services are created by elite teams that are consistently innovative. Thus, the number one priority of elite leaders is to build teams throughout the organization that know how to win through collaboration, creativity, and innovation. Building teams that win starts with hiring the right people, namely, those who are creative and smart. Although this was covered extensively in section one of *Ascend to Greatness*, I believe it warrants a brief comment here.

Let's revisit Google's perspective on elite talent. Google calls its A players "smart creative." I believe that these two words capture perfectly and succinctly the type of people whom all organizations need in order to achieve enduring greatness. Such people are your ultimate intangible asset who will drive high performance.

PRACTICE #7—APPOINT A CHIEF INNOVATION OFFICER

Most companies operating today have the position of chief information officer. Other companies have a chief digital officer. Some elite companies have elevated these two positions and combined them into one: chief technology officer. There are also some companies that have created the position of chief innovation officer. I believe that the position of chief innovation officer is indispensable when a company undertakes a digital transformation.

The roles of both the chief information officer and the chief digital officer historically have been more narrowly focused. That's why these positions have, at times, been combined into the role of chief technology officer and elevated. As an outgrowth of this, a chief innovation officer has also emerged. Irrespective of the title, the recognition, expansion, and elevation of the role is what is important because this role should be responsible for discovering, developing, and implementing the right technologies for executing the strategy of the company. The role should also be responsible for identifying disruptive technologies that can provide the company a competitive advantage. In addition, this role is usually responsible for the information technology infrastructure and for digitally transforming key processes and digital initiatives that are customer-facing.

CHAPTER TWELVE

High-Performance Plan

I believe in the power of a positive, high-performance culture,
which begins with strong ethical values at the core.[1]

_____

—RON WILLIAMS

STRATEGIC PLANNING AND HIGH-PERFORMANCE PLAN

A high-performance plan consolidates all the key breakthrough objectives of the enterprise in both quantitative and qualitative terms. I like the term high-performance plan over the strategic plan because the former better aligns with the objective of ascending the summit of elite. A high-performance plan consistently focuses an enterprise on achieving superior year-over-year results. Superior performance over a long horizon is what separates the elite from all the others and ultimately leads a company to greatness.

Elite companies are exceptional at developing high-performance plans. There are several fundamental elements that are necessary for developing a plan that drives results. These elements include the following items:

- **Alignment with strategy.** The plan should be aligned with and descend from the core philosophy and overall strategy of the company. The focus of the plan needs to be on the vital element that truly matters, namely, achieving the vision of the company. As part of this focus, the plan must set forth the top strategic breakthrough objectives.

- **Reflective of decisions regarding the future.** The plan should reflect critical decisions made about creating a better future that emanated from scanning the environment.

- **Alignment within the organization.** The plan should align everyone in the company so that they all are working toward the same breakthrough objectives.

- **Has set priorities.** The plan should set forth all the priorities for the enterprise. It's about making the right decisions about what to do and what not to do. The company should set its top strategic breakthrough objectives for each plan cycle.

- **Allocation of resources.** The plan should allocate appropriate resources so that the strategic breakthrough objectives can be executed.

- **Agreement on outcomes.** The plan should reflect agreement on outcomes. First, there needs to be agreement between senior management and business segment leaders, and next there must be agreement between the CEO and the board of directors. The CEO is the person ultimately responsible and accountable for the plan.

- **Translation of agreements into financial targets.** The plan should translate agreements about any strategic breakthrough objectives into specific financial targets and metrics. These targets and metrics are translated into a three-year plan and into an annual operating plan. The three-year strategy needs to be updated annually with the development of the operating plan. These are the building blocks to achieving the stated vision of the company over an agreed period of time.

- **Sharing of the plan.** The plan should be shared within the organization—particularly with the global leadership team—and with the board of directors.

For a high-performance plan to be achieved, a company must first possess certain exceptional execution capabilities and implement robust mechanisms. A company must also have a deep understanding of enterprise risk. Elite companies understand well the implications of overall strategic risk elements and how essential it is to identify and mitigate these elements before they can cause harm to the organization. To do this requires a deep understanding of the strengths and weaknesses of the company, along with the ability to better predict and create the future. This capability, coupled with building a prodigious number of lifelines, is instrumental to the long-term success of the company.

DISRUPTIONS AND SHOCKS ARE THE NEW NORM

Our ability to predict the future, no matter how advanced we are, is fraught with risk and uncertainty. Planning scenarios may differ dramatically from reality mainly because of disruptions and shocks. In this section, we will first examine disruptions from innovation and technology and then review major economic, health, and geopolitical shocks.

When one thinks of innovation and technology disruptions, the first thought that comes to one's mind are new disruptive products and services. Innovation and technology disruptions have accelerated and have disrupted markets at a pace that has no historical precedent. I believe that disruptive innovation and technology will continue to upend markets at an ever-increasing rate. Enterprises that are slow to react to this trend will be left behind. Since so much has been written by the business media about disruptive innovation and technology, I will not repeat the stories here.

Let's now examine shocks. If one extrapolates global economic data from the past sixty years, one may develop a rough rule of thumb that says it's likely that there will be some form of major economic shock approximately once every decade. That's because no economic expansion since World War II has lasted much more than a decade. Amid these past economic cycles, we have experienced periods of relative calm, periods of violent turbulence, and periods that are a mix of the two. The shocks that have emanated from major economies of the world in recent years should cause all leaders some disquiet. Let's examine some of these shocks a little closer:

- The markets were completely upended with the Great Recession in 2008–9.
- In 2010–11, the markets were shaken to their core by the European sovereign debt crisis.
- During this period, we experienced an inordinate number of deadly outbreaks, including SARS in 2003, H1N1 virus (swine flu) in 2009, MERS in 2012, Ebola in 2014–2016, Zika in 2015, and COVID-19 in 2020–21.

I believe that China, more than other country besides the United States, has the ability to make an outsized impact on the world's economies. An argument can be made that volatility has increased in part because of the rise of China. That's because whatever happens in China adds further complexity to the overall global economic environment.

This new reality requires enterprises to better prepare and plan for future shocks. Consider the following points that leaders need to ponder as they reevaluate their future strategy: The rapid growth of China has accelerated the globalization of business, which adds to the potential for increased turbulence. These challenges include a concentration of supply chains, trade disputes, stock market volatility, and health risks. With the coronavirus pandemic, we saw the most dramatic effect on the global economy. The pandemic literally stopped the major economies of the world overnight. Retail, airlines, cruises, and numerous other market segments saw revenues drop precipitously, with some suffering as much as 90 percent to 95 percent decline. However, COVID-19 should not have been a complete surprise as it was somewhat foreseeable. This is because in recent years the world experienced two other viruses that emanated from Asia, SARS in 2003 and H1N1 in 2009. Including COVID-19, that is three outbreaks in about seventeen years, or one every six-plus years. Furthermore, during this period we also experienced additional outbreaks, including MERS, Ebola, and Zika, from other parts of the world. These trends should concern all CEOs and boards as they contemplate and plan for the future.

A NEW PARADIGM FOR DEVELOPING A HIGH-PERFORMANCE PLAN

The new reality of increasing frequency of disruptions and shocks needs to be considered when planning for the future. Companies need to rethink their assumptions about turbulence because we are now in uncharted territory. As a consequence, I believe that a new paradigm is needed; one that requires organizations to factor this reality into their strategic planning processes. Otherwise, leaders will be ill prepared for the next significant turbulent event. As part of this new thinking, it is my belief that the processes, practices, and assumptions that were used in the past for developing a high-performance plan are not going to be as effective in the future.

Like it or not, this is the new planning environment that leaders and boards need to confront and accept. So, what does the new model for planning look like? This model begins with reviewing my five sacrosanct rules that organizations need always to keep in mind with respect to planning for the future:

- Rule #1—Hope for the best, but plan for the worst.
- Rule #2—Know that plans always change.
- Rule #3—Always have a plan B.
- Rule #4—Always build ample lifelines.
- Rule #5—Always have a well-tested crisis response plan.

The first rule comes from mountaineering's rule number one. The second rule comes from the military, whose leaders have a strong belief in detailed planning with the knowledge that plans always change. The third rule relates to the first two rules. It is imperative always to have a plan B. Since plans always change, we need to be well prepared for any eventuality. The fourth rule comes from one of the core principles, namely that companies must build a prodigious number of lifelines if they are to survive any scenario. This is where the fifth rule comes in, the need to have a well-developed and well-tested response plan. If an enterprise follows these simple rules, it won't be caught off guard by unexpected turbulent events.

Companies need to perform various scenario analyses as part of the planning process. Critical and generative thinking needs to go into dialoguing about future trends and how they are going to impact the enterprise. Also, the company should have the ability to generate and analyze the right economic and market data. It's important that various planning scenarios be created, based on unimpeachable facts and assumptions that are validated, challenged, and tested as much as possible. Also, Monte Carlo simulation scenarios should be used to underpin the analysis of major projects. Finally, the plan should be stress-tested against accumulated lifelines to ensure that the company will survive even the worst-case scenario.

HIGH-PERFORMANCE PLAN BEST PRACTICES

Having served as CEO, CFO, and board member of several companies, and through my advisory practice, I have observed and experienced a number of strategic planning processes. Just as there are no two organizational structures that are alike, there are no two strategic planning processes culminating in the development of the high-performance plan that are alike.

However, there are some essential common sense best practices that are universally employed by leading companies. I believe some of these practices are vital to building and implementing a successful high-performance plan. Many of these elements have already been reviewed in *Ascend to Greatness*, but they warrant additional commentary here because they are indispensable to developing an elite-level plan.

#1. SCAN THE ENVIRONMENT IN REAL TIME
TO DETECT AND ASSESS TRENDS

Historically, a common practice for strategic planning at many companies was to complete a SWOT analysis. SWOT stands for "strengths, weaknesses, opportunities, and threats." Although a SWOT analysis is useful, I advocate for scanning the environment in real time. Continuously scanning the environment is crucial for properly detecting and assessing both positive and negative trends. Scanning the environment is an early warning mechanism that is utterly indispensable to planning a better future. This needs to be your so-called sentinel. By heeding early warnings, the leadership team can proactively respond to disruptions and shocks while also seizing potential opportunities.

Once this sentinel process is established and functioning well, an enterprise should properly segment identified trends between facts and assumptions. This is because facts are absolute, whereas assumptions are often based on attribution and unsubstantiated data. Each requires a different approach when making planning decisions. All these detected threats and opportunities need to be critically assessed and properly dialogued. As part of the deep understanding that results, important decisions made around threats and opportunities need to be appropriately reflected in the high-performance plan.

#2. ENSURE THAT PLANNING DESCENDS FROM
THE STRATEGY OF THE ENTERPRISE

Strategic planning needs to adhere to the objective of realizing the organization's vision, an action guided by the purpose of the company while strictly adhering to its core values. For a company to ultimately reach the summit of elite, they must break down their long-term vision into manageable and realistic three-year high-performance plans. It was common practice in the past to use a five-year time frame for strategic planning purposes, but more recently organizations have shifted to a more effective three-year model because of the increase in volatility and turbulence. The three-year cycle, which needs to include the current year's operating plan, is a major driver to arriving at the vision of the company. Each three-year block that is executed supremely gets the company closer to the summit.

#3. THE HIGH-PERFORMANCE PLAN MUST INCLUDE BREAKTHROUGH OBJECTIVES

The high-performance plan needs to be brilliantly developed. For a company to ultimately realize its vision, it has to have an exceptional going-forward plan. This means that the plan needs to include appropriate breakthrough objectives that are a stretch but that realistically can be attained by way of execution excellence. The going-forward plan needs to be underpinned with insight into the future, which is gained from scanning the environment. Please note that throughout *Ascend to Greatness*, I use the terminology *breakthrough objectives*, which comes straight from Danaher's DBS (Danaher Business System) presentation. DBS is detailed in chapter 13. This terminology is used for both the three-year plan and the annual operating plan. Using the term *breakthrough objectives* is compelling.

The breakthrough objectives of the plan need to be translated and distilled into specific targets that must be achieved within each one-year time frame. For year one of a three-year plan, a detailed annual operating plan should be prepared that includes three different scenarios: base case, upside case, and downside case. Also, a plan B or profit protection plan should be developed to underpin year one's base case. Developing a credible and substantive plan B is vital. Plans never play out as envisioned on account of uncontrollable and unpredictable variables, so it is imperative to have enough actions detailed in a plan B that can help deliver the base case scenario, hence the name of the profit protection plan. Both mountaineers and military officers know this well. As a US Army general once told me about an old military saying, "No battle plan survives first contact with the enemy." This is undoubtedly true, but planning is still critical to success.

#4. KNOW THAT A GROUND-UP APPROACH IS FUNDAMENTAL TO BUILDING A HIGH-PERFORMANCE PLAN

Building a high-performance plan must start at the business unit level. The global leadership team is who develops and builds the plan for the respective areas of responsibility. Although the CEO is ultimately accountable and responsible for overall results, it is the global leadership team who must execute the plan and deliver the expected results. The CEO, along with other senior corporate leaders, will weigh in and challenge each plan before it's finalized. As part of this process, the company must ensure total alignment of the business units and senior corporate management with regard to the final plan. There can't be any confusion.

The high-performance plan should establish and include appropriate three-year revenues, earnings, margins (gross and operating), and free cash flow targets. Both the annual and long-term incentive compensation should be linked in some manner to the plan. The ground-up approach to building a high-performance plan needs to include specific tactics that will be utilized to achieve the stated breakthrough objectives. The tactics always need to descend from the strategy. Thus, any elements that do not perfectly align with the overall strategy are eliminated, because these will unnecessarily waste resources.

#5. MAKE SCENARIO ANALYSIS AN INTEGRAL PART OF THE HIGH-PERFORMANCE PLAN

Mountaineering rule number one states, "Hope for the best, but plan for the worst." Mountaineering rule number two states, "Getting up the mountain is optional; getting down the mountain is mandatory." As a former CEO and an adviser to CEOs, I am a believer in routinely performing scenario analysis. All you have to do is experience recent events, both disruptive technologies and global shocks, to really appreciate just how essential scenario analysis is.

The importance of preparing a scenario analysis along with a plan to deal with any eventuality can't be overstated. It's especially critical today since we now have so many historical precedents showing what can really happen to end markets during extreme disruptions and shocks. Thus, it's imperative always to be adequately prepared to implement the two mountaineering rules mentioned earlier. No one wants to be stuck on the mountain and perish.

#6. CONTINUOUSLY MEASURE THE PROGRESS OF THE HIGH-PERFORMANCE PLAN

After a high-performance plan is agreed upon, the senior leadership and business segment managers should perform detailed monthly performance reviews. Forecasts or projections should be updated as frequently as practical so that appropriate proactive action can be taken to keep the plan on track. Many companies use a rolling forecast to project where the year is trending relative to the annual operating plan. All adjustments to the annual operating plan need to be seriously contemplated, including implementing a plan B.

Progress should also be reported and discussed at least quarterly with the board of directors. It's helpful and constructive to involve the business segment's senior managers in the quarterly dialogue with the board. This ensures that the information and message delivered to the board is directly from the people responsible and accountable for monthly results.

#7. ENSURE THAT THE HIGH-PERFORMANCE PLAN HAS A LASER FOCUS ON FREE CASH FLOW

Free cash flow should be the primary financial focus of the enterprise when developing a high-performance plan. Elite companies understand the power of generating substantial discretionary cash flow. Free cash flow is the so-called fuel necessary to sustain growth and create value. Moreover, free cash flow is the most complete metric because it touches all key aspects of a business.

An innovative business model can lead to the creation of prodigious free cash flow. Elite companies measure this through what is known as growth in free cash flow. The growth in free cash flow metric is fundamental to understanding the level of economic value being created. Within each component of a business, there are multiple levers that can be pulled to generate and enhance free cash flow. The main levers of focus should be net income, working capital components, and capital expenditures.

#8. KNOW THAT ASTUTE CAPITAL ALLOCATION IS AN ESSENTIAL PART OF A HIGH-PERFORMANCE PLAN

Astute capital allocation usually results in superior long-term performance. Capital allocation decisions will cumulatively determine the success or failure of an enterprise. When it comes to allocating capital, management needs always to be mindful of the impact any decisions will make on the health of the balance sheet. The following are the primary areas of capital allocation:

- investing in building lifelines and ample cash reserves,
- investing in capital expenditures to fund organic growth initiatives and sustain the current base of business,
- investing in inorganic growth initiatives,
- paying and increasing the dividend,
- investing in a major share repurchase program, or shares to offset the dilution from equity compensation, and
- paying down debt and funding pension plans.

When developing a high-performance plan, capital allocation should be broadly segmented into two categories: traditional capital for growth and sustaining the business, and investment dollars for building lifelines and the capabilities of the enterprise. No matter where capital is allocated, all decisions about capital allocation need to be executed with discipline.

#9. ALWAYS MAKE OPTIMIZING THE BALANCE SHEET PART OF THE HIGH-PERFORMANCE PLAN

The triple threat from the global shocks of the US financial crisis, the European sovereign debt crisis, and the COVID-19 pandemic severely damaged the balance sheet of some companies, particularly enterprises that were carrying elevated levels of debt before these events occurred. As a former CFO, I have a particular affinity for managing a balance sheet and knowing what actions are appropriate for its effective management.

Perhaps there's nothing more vital than having a strong balance sheet to "protect the house." This is a derivative of Under Armour's motto, "Protect This House," which is a concept that works well when thinking about maintaining a strong balance sheet. An exceptional balance sheet is indispensable if a company is to withstand shocks. It's a vital lifeline for a company. To illustrate the power of implementing balance sheet optimization initiatives, I am going to provide specific examples of things I utilized during my career. Here are some levers that are available to leaders to restore and/or enhance the health of their balance sheet:

SELL MISCELLANEOUS ASSETS

Take the opportunity to divest miscellaneous assets that are idle or unprofitable. Compile an inventory of all these assets, including land, buildings, small product lines, and even patents. Assign an executive to oversee this important project. At times, there are some valuable hidden assets that are not critical to operations that could be turned into cash. When I initiated this project at our company, we were able to generate $113 million in cash from these miscellaneous assets. It took a lot of hard work over many years to get this done, but the result was the creation of a sizable lifeline for the company.

REEXAMINE THE PORTFOLIO

Reexamine the portfolio with a long-term view, and possibly divest parts of the business that no longer fit with the vision of the enterprise. Hire outside experts to assist with this exercise, and involve the board. As part of this review, it is important to look into the future and try to predict what's going to happen. We did this well in our company, and we scored a substantial win for shareholders and the balance sheet. Let me explain: We looked into the future for one of our business segments that was struggling to fight off the commodity cycle and cyclicality. We determined that the future looked bleak. So, we shopped the business and, after a total team effort, sold the segment just before the Great Recession hit the United States. The business was sold for an amazing $300 million in cash. What makes this achievement even more spectacular is that after one year, the new owners of the company filed for bankruptcy protection. With this proactive action, we created one of the most consequential lifelines for the company.

REDUCE COSTS TO CONSERVE CASH

Conserving cash should always be top of mind for the leadership team. An effective way to reduce costs is to undertake a transformational program driven by an integrated management system. This is covered in section three but warrants a mention here. The best time to undertake such a transformational initiative is in good times. Don't wait until someone or some event dictates this action for the company. Reducing costs is the first action I took as a newly appointed CEO. Unfortunately, just as we were getting started with our transformation, we were engulfed in the twin storms of the US Great Recession and the European sovereign debt crisis, the latter following the former. Nonetheless, we were able to reduce of cost structure of the company during this period by approximately $230 million.

INVEST IN MAJOR PROJECTS WITH A PARTNER

Invest in major projects with a partner to reduce risk and the amount of capital investment. As I mentioned earlier, our company was particularly successful with joint ventures. We routinely invested with partners throughout the world with extraordinary success. This was one of the greatest strengths of the company. In fact, the most successful transaction in the history of our company was a joint venture we created in the defense business. Let me explain: During the 1990s, there was considerable consolidation of defense assets, and we were under severe pressure to divest our defense business because we were a relatively small player. However, instead of selling our defense segment, we smartly formed a strategic joint venture with an exceptional partner. Together, my company and our partner formed a premier global manufacturer of track vehicles for the military with revenues of approximately $1 billion. By any measure, including economic value created, cash flow, and return on invested capital, this business was an enormous success. The business was ultimately sold. We realized approximately $350 million in cash from the sale proceeds. That's on top of the substantial annual cash flows that were paid in the form of dividends while we owned the business.

RESTRUCTURE PENSION PLANS

Restructure pension plans to protect the balance sheet. Defined benefit pension plans can weaken the balance sheet and cause volatility with the income statement. For some companies, the best antidote is to freeze all defined benefit pension plans and convert these to defined contribution plans. Our company was particularly exposed to defined benefit pension plans because they had grown too large relative to the size of our company. These legacy plans were acquired over many decades through acquisitions. When I was CFO, this was one of the major projects that I undertook because of the elevated risk that these plans posed to the enterprise. After a robust internal dialogue, we decided that freezing the defined benefit pension plans was the right thing to do for the long-term health of the company. Symbolically, we started with the defined benefit plan that had been established for the executive officers. It sent a powerful message to the organization.

TAKE OTHER ACTION

There were other actions we took to strengthen the balance sheet. For example, we generated cash and income from royalties, licensing fees, and dividends from joint venture interests, particularly in emerging markets. Although these cash flow streams were not individually material, together they contributed tens of millions of dollars to improving the balance sheet.

SECTION THREE

Execution

Introduction

Excellence is never an accident. It is always the result of high intention, sincere effort, and intelligent execution; it represents the wise choice of many alternatives—choice, not chance, determines your destiny.[1]

—ARISTOTLE

WIN THROUGH EXECUTION EXCELLENCE

In this section, we will review the foundational pillar of execution, the final piece of the puzzle to ascend to greatness. Execution excellence means doing everything at an elite level in a disciplined manner. And this means that all tactical operational elements align perfectly with and descend from the strategy. There are no wasted actions and no actions that do not support the strategy. The ability to execute at the highest level is what propels an organization to elite status.

The foundational pillar of execution was captured well by Lawrence Bossidy when he said, "Execution is the ability to mesh strategy with reality, align people with goals, and achieve the promised results."[2] This quotation needs to be augmented by one from Morris Chang: "Without strategy, execution is aimless. Without execution, strategy is useless."[3] I believe that these two quotations capture the essence of disciplined execution.

When you think about execution excellence, who comes to mind? For me, it's organizations such as Apple, Danaher, Roper, Microsoft, and Disney. A leading example from history that comes to mind is the Roman Legion under the leadership of Julius Caesar. In the next section, we will briefly review why the Roman legions were so exceptional at execution because of the close parallel to the business world.

THE ROMAN LEGION'S EXECUTION EXCELLENCE

History books are replete with examples of how the Roman legions consistently executed at an elite level. They were disciplined, adaptable, innovative, and driven by a strong culture. An excellent summary of how the Roman legions were able to execute so superbly can be found on Wikipedia's website. Under the heading of "Factors in the legion's success"[4] in its entry "Roman legions," Wikipedia provides the following points that are insightful and applicable to the modern business world:

BEST PRACTICES AND ADAPTABILITY

"Having fought successively against all peoples, [the Roman legions] always gave up their own practices as soon as they found better ones." This is brilliant. The Romans were always scanning the environment for ways to continuously improve and to smartly incorporate best practices into their training and ultimately on the battlefield. The Roman legions were also very adaptable. "Roman organization was more flexible than those of many opponents. Over time, the legions effectively handled challenges ranging from cavalry, to guerillas, and to siege warfare."

DISCIPLINE

"Roman discipline, organization and systematization sustained combat effectiveness over a longer period. These elements appear throughout the legion in training, logistics, field fortification .... Strict, and more importantly, uniform discipline made commanding, maintaining, and replacing Roman legionaries a much more consistent exercise." The Romans clearly understood the link between discipline and execution excellence. Their level of discipline, considering the period in history when this occurred, was utterly amazing.

CULTURE

"The influence of Roman military and civic culture, as embodied particularly in the heavy infantry legion, gave the Roman military consistent motivation and cohesion." The Romans had purpose and many of the other elements necessary for building a strong culture. This gave the legions an advantage on the battlefield.

TECHNOLOGY AND INNOVATION

"Roman engineering skills were second to none in ancient Europe, and [the Romans'] mastery of both offensive and defensive siege warfare, specifically the construction and investiture of fortifications, was another major advantage for the Roman legions. Roman military equipment … was more withstanding and far more ubiquitous. … Soldiers … had a major advantage." Romans consistently demonstrated their superior innovation and technology capabilities, which often provided an advantage on the battlefield.

DISCIPLINED EXECUTION

Execution excellence is the economic engine that propels an organization to greatness. It's how elite companies win in the marketplace. Before execution excellence can be achieved, the other two foundational pillars need to be implemented at an elite level in a disciplined manner as the three pillars are all inextricably linked. Once the right people are in the right positions and the strategy is brilliantly developed, execution is what gets the company to enduring greatness. The driver of execution excellence is discipline. And discipline should be impelled by an effective integrated management system, such as Danaher's Business System (DBS).

IMPORTANCE OF DISCIPLINED EXECUTION

The importance of disciplined execution cannot be overstated. I personally experienced this challenge as a CEO. Just as the Great Recession was starting, I officially ascended to the position of CEO. The Great Recession was, of course, devastating to many industries, including that of the company I led. Our company was particularly vulnerable to a destructive economic shock because we were highly decentralized. Our company was a collection of numerous acquisitions that had been made over the span of many decades. For the most part, our business units operated independently at 475 different sites in 55 countries.

On day one, I knew that our challenge was going to be the cost structure of the company and the lack of standardization. To better prepare the company for the coming turbulent storm, we immediately started implementing key breakthrough objectives, several involving optimizing the cost structure. Here are the major initiatives that we started:

- Our first action was focused on a continuous improvement discipline. With assistance from outside consultants, we implemented Lean, with Kaizen breakthrough events and policy deployment.
- The second action was to enhance our supply chain. With assistance from outside experts, we built a strategic sourcing group to better capture supply chain savings across the enterprise.
- The third action was focused on the organizational structure and key processes. We reorganized the company into four reportable segments. We rebranded the company. We established a global shared services competency center in India. And we embarked on a

program to implement a one-instance ERP system for each segment, which is essential for standardization and optimization initiatives.

- We successfully commenced a commercial initiative to expand our business in Asia, winning some of the largest contracts in history. At some business units, we also undertook several commercial excellence initiatives such as value selling and pricing strategies. And, we embarked on an innovation initiative to regain our position as the industry leader in developing innovative environmental solutions.

While we were in the middle of these initiatives, we encountered a second economic shock—the European sovereign debt crisis. The European shock was even more devastating to our company than the financial crisis given our concentration in Europe. Looking back with total clarity on that turbulent period, I wish we had utilized an integrated management system similar to Danaher's DBS. What I have discovered is that there's no better tool than a DBS-type model to assist an organization in achieving execution excellence. An integrated management system could have perhaps been indispensable to us as we tried to do too much in too short a period of time.

EXECUTION OVERVIEW

In section three, we will explore the key principles under execution that are necessary to building and sustaining an elite enterprise. There are five core principles under the foundational pillar of execution; these are covered in chapters 13 through 17.

Here are the chapter titles indicating the most important principles necessary to execute at an elite level:

- Chapter 13. Disciplined Execution
- Chapter 14. Growth Engine
- Chapter 15. Commercial Excellence
- Chapter 16. Operational Excellence
- Chapter 17. Administrative Excellence

CHAPTER THIRTEEN

Disciplined Execution

There's only one sort of discipline, perfect discipline.[1]

——

—GEORGE S. PATTON

DISCIPLINED EXECUTION

Studies have shown that there is a high percentage of failure when it comes to supremely executing a good or even a brilliant strategy. Why is this? I believe that there are primarily two reasons why so many companies fail to skillfully execute their strategies. First, it's the people. Not having the right people, or not having enough of the right people in the right positions, is a sure way to fail at execution excellence. Second, the problem is the lack of a disciplined enterprise-wide integrated management system. A disciplined integrated management system is so indispensable to execution excellence that it is the focal point of this chapter. Some of the principal consequences of not having a robust integrated management system are less-than-optimal processes and lack of standardization across the enterprise.

The two elements of not having the right people and lacking an integrated management system, more than anything else, play a major role in contributing to a company's falling short of execution excellence. For a company to execute its people excellence and strategy development at an elite level, team members must be exceptionally skilled at disciplined execution. The same applies to the other execution principles, which are covered later in section three.

In this chapter, we will review what is required to achieve elite-level disciplined execution. We will also review some of the elements that drive superior results. Before we explore why an integrated management system is essential, let's start by reviewing a quotation that captures the essence of disciplined execution. In their extraordinary book *Execution*, the authors Ram Charan and Larry Bossidy state, "Execution is a specific set of behaviors and techniques that companies need to master in order to have competitive advantage. It's a discipline of its own."[2]

DISCIPLINED EXECUTION IS IMPELLED BY AN INTEGRATED MANAGEMENT SYSTEM

Superior execution is the driver of a high-performance culture. For a company ultimately to ascend to greatness, the leadership team should implement a disciplined integrated management system that is driven by continuous improvement and is linked to all three foundational pillars. This is because disciplined execution is a cumulative process; it just doesn't happen overnight. Every process and every daily activity that occurs in an organization in delivering its products and services, hiring and developing people, and building an exceptional strategy requires discipline and a mindset of continuous improvement. Thus, I believe that execution excellence cannot be completely achieved without having in place a disciplined integrated management system. When done well, such a system can be a game changer.

Two examples of a robust management system are Danaher's Business System, known as DBS, and Honeywell's Honeywell Operating System, known as HOS. The foundation to both systems is continuous improvement and operational efficiencies. Danaher's DBS system was formed using process improvement methodologies. It included Lean—along with Kaizen breakthrough events and policy deployment—and the world-renowned

Toyota Production System. In later years, Danaher expanded DBS to include growth and leadership. Honeywell took a similar path. Their HOS system included Lean (plus Kaizen), Six Sigma, and the Toyota Production System. Both Danaher and Honeywell continue to derive benefits from their respective management systems, which have been transformational.

I believe there's value in seeing how the company itself defines its management system. Here's what Danaher has to say about DBS on the company's website:

> Success at Danaher doesn't happen by accident. We have a proven system for achieving it. We call it the Danaher Business System (DBS), and it drives every aspect of our culture and performance. We use DBS to guide what we do, measure how well we execute, and create options for doing even better—including improving DBS itself.
>
> In the mid-1980s, a Danaher operating company faced with intensifying competition launched an improvement effort based on the then-new principles of lean manufacturing. The initiative succeeded beyond anyone's expectations— reinforcing the operating company's industry leadership and bringing forth the Danaher Business System.
>
> Fueled by Danaher's core values, the DBS engine drives the company through a never-ending cycle of change and improvement: exceptional *people* develop outstanding *plans* and execute them using world-class tools to construct sustainable *processes*, resulting in superior *performance*. Superior performance and high expectations attract exceptional people, who continue the cycle. Guiding all efforts is a simple philosophy rooted in four customer-facing priorities: Quality, Delivery, Cost, and Innovation.[3]

In addition, Danaher has stated in investor presentations, "DBS is our sustainable competitive advantage." They also state that with DBS they can "expand capabilities, drive consistent execution and sustain outstanding results." Most importantly, they state, "It is a mindset and it is our culture—DBS is who we are, and how we do what we do. DBS is constantly evolving: in the spirit of continuous improvement, we are always 'DBSing' DBS." It's quite clear from both Danaher's investor presentations and exceptional results that DBS has been truly transformational for the company.

The benefits that can be derived from having a strong integrated business system such as DBS can be transformative. Every company should implement a similar management system; otherwise, achieving execution excellence will likely be elusive. Some of the more notable improvements that can be derived from a disciplined integrated management system include productivity improvements, improved processes, waste reduction, lower inventory levels, cycle time reduction, logistics improvements, on-time delivery improvements, safer work environment, sustainability benefits because of lower energy and water usage, and world-class fill rates. There are other benefits of an integrated management system, including a positive effect on all the principles discussed in section three of *Ascend to Greatness*. The positive effect to both the income statement and cash flows can at times be dramatic.

For companies looking to implement their own disciplined integrated management system, they can use DBS as a model. Based on my experience, DBS is perfectly designed as it is currently constituted. It includes all the parts necessary to ascend to the summit. First, Danaher made continuous improvement a core value. Second, they decided to utilize many of the building blocks outlined below to drive continuous improvement. Third, they have incorporated leadership and growth into the system. In my mind, this is a perfectly built management system.

In the next section, we will review specific information about the various continuous improvement tools that are necessary for developing a disciplined integrated management system and achieving execution excellence. I call them the building blocks of an integrated management system. It's important to note, however, that these tools can't be implemented in isolation; they must be an integral part of a well-organized and comprehensive management system.

BUILDING BLOCKS OF AN INTEGRATED MANAGEMENT SYSTEM

When striving to ascend to greatness, an enterprise must employ a continuous improvement discipline that is underpinned with various tools. In addition, organizations need to have a culture that believes in and promotes continuous improvement. That's why, I believe, continuous improvement should be one of the core values of an organization.

It's important to emphasize that lean management tools need to be part of an integrated management system that is utilized across the entire organization and embedded in the culture of the company. Continuous improvement needs to be a mindset, a culture, and a potent driver of execution excellence. Let's now examine the Toyota Production System and the other two continuous improvement tools utilized in building an integrated management system, Six Sigma and Lean.

THE TOYOTA PRODUCTION SYSTEM (TPS)

TPS is world-renowned. With the development of lean manufacturing, Toyota was able to achieve best-of-class performance by improving cycle time, increasing productivity, and realizing significant efficiencies throughout the business. Many business people have traveled to Toyota sites to learn this highly effective discipline. Toyota's Lean principles have spread across the globe and have been adopted by many elite enterprises.

Here is how Toyota defines TPS: "A production system based on the philosophy of achieving the complete elimination of all waste in pursuit of the most efficient methods. The Toyota Production System (TPS) was established based on two concepts: 'jidoka' (which can be loosely translated as 'automation with a human touch'), as when a problem occurs, the equipment stops immediately, preventing defective products from being produced; and the 'Just-in-Time' concept, in which each process produces only what is needed for the next process in a continuous flow. TPS and its approach to cost reduction are the wellsprings of competitive strength and unique advantages for Toyota."[4]

Since TPS is based on the philosophy of achieving the complete elimination of all waste, it is helpful to review directly from Toyota how they describe this: "Waste can manifest as excess inventory, extraneous processing steps, and defective products, among other instances. All these 'waste' elements intertwine with each other to create more waste, eventually impacting the management of the corporation itself." This statement brilliantly captures the essence of why a discipline such as TPS is needed to improve all aspects of a business.

SIX SIGMA

Six Sigma is a continuous improvement discipline focused on reducing variability and improving business processes. It refers to 3.4 defects per 1 million opportunities, or 99.99966 percent, a level that is considered to represent world-class quality performance. Six Sigma was originally developed by Motorola in the 1980s. Six Sigma, just like Lean, is an effective mechanism for the CEO to use in changing and shaping the culture of the enterprise. In the early 1990s, I was fortunate to attend a Motorola Six Sigma class on improving the quality of the finance function. Our company utilized this tool very effectively to transform its global financial reporting process, reducing the number of days to close our books from sixteen to four.

LEAN

While Six Sigma's focus is on identifying and removing the root cause of defects, the focus of Lean is on eliminating waste. Lean traces its roots to the Japanese automobile industry in the 1980s and mainly the Toyota Production System. Unlike traditional cost-reduction initiatives, Lean is a robust tool that is not about doing more with less but is about doing more with existing resources. Eliminating waste and inefficiency frees up critical resources needed to scale the business without increasing overhead costs.

The Lean discipline is underpinned and driven by Kaizen breakthrough events and policy deployment. The vital process to executing the Lean discipline is rooted in the Japanese term *Kaizen*, which means "change for the good." Kaizen events typically take place over five highly focused days between extensive prework preparation and post-Kaizen sustainment. Kaizen events enable people from all parts and levels of the organization to participate. Most Kaizen recommendations are implemented immediately. Lean is a formidable tool that can be used in any part or process of the organization. It can be used with equal effectiveness in both manufacturing and service organizations.

When utilizing continuous improvement tools such as Lean and Kaizen breakthrough events, it's also essential to utilize policy deployment. Policy Deployment needs to be an integral part of Lean. Here's what the Lean Enterprise Academy has to say in a 2014 article about this important tool: "Policy Deployment … is an integral part of any lean implementation. It's a management process that aligns—both vertically and horizontally—an organization's functions and activities with its strategic objectives. A specific plan—typically annual—is developed with precise goals, actions, timelines, responsibilities, and measures."[5] In essence, policy deployment is a strong tool for executing the strategy of the company at an elite level. It turns the vision of the company into specific objectives. This is done with a policy deployment matrix known as an X-matrix.

I'm a passionate advocate of and believer in utilizing Lean—with Kaizen events and policy deployment—for achieving execution excellence. It's one of the most powerful tools available for eliminating waste, improving processes, reducing cycle times, unifying the culture, and realizing superior operating results.

OTHER ESSENTIAL PRACTICES OF DISCIPLINED EXECUTION

Under the principle of disciplined execution, there are additional indispensable practices that require elite-level performance. I've identified six practices that may augment the integrated management system; these are reviewed below:

- Build a data-and process-driven disciplined enterprise.
- Don't get blinded by the light of euphoria.
- Focus on only a handful of key goals.
- Know what to do and what not to do.
- Don't make one large bet; make small targeted investments.
- Don't make one large bet on acquisitions; make targeted smaller bets.

#1. BUILD A DATA-AND PROCESS-DRIVEN DISCIPLINED ENTERPRISE

Elite companies are disciplined in all aspects of decision-making. They build sound processes to ensure that good decisions are optimized and bad decisions are minimized. Leading companies painstakingly use big data and other analytical tools to make better decisions. They train their leadership team to think critically. They live by unimpeachable facts and empirical evidence. They are fanatical at avoiding what the great Andy Grove once said: "Altogether too often, people substitute opinions for facts and emotions for analysis."[6] How insightful and true. During my long career, I have unfortunately seen attribution rule major decisions. The outcomes of these decisions were usually very predictable; they tended to disappoint.

Robust processes that are underpinned by big data and analytics are imperative to making sound decisions and ultimately building an enduring elite company. These processes and tools are doubly important when it comes to making capital allocation decisions, such as investing in large projects and acquisitions. This is because there is compelling empirical evidence that project assumptions used in both acquisitions and large-scale capital projects are usually materially different from actual experience. Critical decisions made on either bad or incomplete information may cumulatively result in serious adverse consequences to the performance of an enterprise. Sometimes these consequences are so significant that they cause the company to fall from the summit or preclude it from reaching elite status in the first place.

#2. DON'T GET BLINDED BY THE LIGHT OF EUPHORIA

Too often, leaders become enamored by large investments. For a multitude of reasons, leaders sometimes minimize or even ignore inherent risks associated with these types of investments. This is particularly true when it comes to acquisitions. Sometimes these inherent risks are clearly visible, and other times they are hidden. It is management's responsibility to identify and flush out these risks. Unfortunately, this does not always happen because management becomes blinded by the light of euphoria.

This blind euphoria can ultimately lead to disastrous results. All one has to do is read the *Wall Street Journal* on a regular basis to see examples of this affliction. An excellent countermeasure to this blind euphoria is disciplined execution. Disciplined execution needs to be underpinned by implementing the previous practice of building a data and fact-driven enterprise. It also requires having a board of directors made up of seasoned and disciplined members who challenge vital assumptions and know how to identify inherent risks.

#3. FOCUS ON ONLY A HANDFUL OF KEY GOALS

Apple's Steve Jobs once said, "We try to focus and do very few things well. And focusing is hard because focusing doesn't mean saying yes, it means saying no. So we decide not to do a lot of things so we can focus on a handful of things and do them well."[7] I believe Steve Jobs perfectly captures the essence of discipline with this quotation.

Some enterprises make the mistake of trying to do too much, which usually stretches the resources of the organization to a point that the efforts sometimes become counterproductive. Also, focusing on too many objectives at the same time usually implies that the organization lacks proper discipline. To increase the probability of success and to instill a certain level of discipline, elite leaders know how to focus their organizations on two or three strategic breakthrough objectives. Elite leaders usually accomplish this by relying on their instincts and on unassailable facts to guide their decisions. Leaders also understand that saying no is sometimes more important than saying yes.

There are instances, however, where a company deems it necessary to focus on more than two or three objectives and ends up being successful at it. For example, I've seen organizations focus on four to five breakthrough objectives. Whenever there's a higher grouping of key objectives, such goals tend to be tightly linked and necessary to accomplish for a company to achieve its vision. When that happens, the breakthrough objectives also tend to span multiple years.

#4. KNOW WHAT TO DO AND WHAT NOT TO DO

The great Steve Jobs once said, "I'm actually as proud of the things we haven't done as the things I have done."[8] Knowing what to do and what not to do are equally important. CEOs are constantly being faced with choices. It is vital that CEOs choose wisely because bad choices regarding goals for either the enterprise or the teams, or even bad personal habits, can take a leader down a dangerous path that can lead to dire and irreversible consequences. Developing a "stop doing" list that clearly identifies ineffective personal and enterprise activities is also critical to the long-term health of the organization.

Thus, successful leaders utilize their uncanny ability to know what to do and what not to do. Importantly, elite leaders unplug the many "doing" habits that naturally form in an organization over time. Before obsessing over a long to-do list for the enterprise, leaders should focus on a "stop doing" list. Cutting out extraneous things that do not add value to the overall organizational objective of realizing its vision will unleash resources that can be used to build an elite company.

#5. DON'T MAKE ONE LARGE BET; MAKE SMALL TARGETED INVESTMENTS

When leading enterprises make significant strategic investments such as expansion in new territories, introduction of new products, or development of new products through innovation, they usually approach these projects with a laser-like focus and discipline. Moreover, they usually do not make one large bet; they make a series of small bets. Often, these small bets are on the edge, exploratory, and innovative in nature.

Many examples abound of exceptional companies that have taken this approach. Apple again offers a good leadership example in the launching of its retail stores. Apple first did a significant amount of preparatory work and then launched only one store. They knew that initially launching multiple stores was not the right approach. As they gained more experience with the concept and the format, they expanded slowly, store by store, until a broad network of stores was ultimately put in place.

Conversely, JC Penney and Target took the opposite approach. Around 2012, JC Penney decided to radically transform its retail store format across the company without first testing the idea in a more focused way. The results of JC Penney's large bet were significantly different from expected; the rollout sent revenues plunging as customers fled to the competition. Target's expansion into Canada in 2013 offers a similar lesson. As was expressed in a *Fortune* magazine article at the time, "Rather than launching new stores in carefully selected spots and building slowly, Target acquired 124 locations in 2013 in one fell swoop by buying all the outlets from a defunct discounter called Zellers. Never mind that one of the causes of Zeller's demise was the poor location of its stores. Or that the spaces were designed to enable a different strategy from Target's. Throw in supply-chain problems that yielded empty shelves and high prices, and it added up to an unmitigated disaster."[9]

Google, on the other hand, completely understands the importance of making targeted bets. In an official August 10, 2015, blog post concerning the reorganization of the company into Alphabet Inc., cofounder and CEO Larry Page reiterated what he and his cofounder had previously said about the need to make smaller bets in areas that may seem very speculative. Then he went on to say, "We did a lot of things that seemed crazy at the time. Many of those crazy things now have over a billion users, like Google Maps, YouTube, Chrome, and Android."[10]

The same habit of making small bets also works well when engaging elite outside consultants. Companies will usually hire elite outside consulting firms to assist with major transformations, portfolio reviews (strategy), and numerous other projects. The elite consulting firms are expensive, but they often achieve strong results. An effective way to ensure that a firm can deliver results is to start with a small targeted project. If the consultants demonstrate exceptional execution abilities and there's a good cultural match, then the company can move forward with a larger project. I've seen this practice successfully utilized at several companies. It works!

#6. DON'T MAKE ONE LARGE BET ON ACQUISITIONS. MAKE SMALLER TARGETED BETS

This habit is identical to number 5 above, but it warrants a separate discussion because it ties in well with disciplined growth. Elite leaders know and understand that making large acquisitions is a high-risk proposition. Often, large acquisitions either fail completely or don't live up to expectations. A better approach is to be disciplined by making smaller targeted acquisitions.

This approach requires patience and discipline, along with a strong pipeline of acquisition targets that fit the parameters set by the company. I've seen companies that follow this habit achieve exceptional results. There's no need to take outsized risks with one large acquisition when a targeted growth strategy can still be achieved, albeit more slowly, by acquiring relatively smaller enterprises.

CHAPTER FOURTEEN

Growth Engine

There are no great limits to growth because there are no
limits of human intelligence, imagination, and wonder.[1]

———

—RONALD REAGAN

GROWTH ENGINE

The equity markets truly value growth. That's because growth is widely
viewed as the lifeblood of an organization, and it's what ultimately gets
an enterprise to the summit. I would, however, slightly modify these
statements by inserting the word *disciplined* in front of *growth* because it
is disciplined growth that the markets value over the long term.

Disciplined growth, of course, is one of the most difficult challenges
that all leaders face. Without discipline, an enterprise at some point will
likely stumble and possibly even fall from the summit of elite. That's
because without discipline, it's likely that some bad investment decisions
will be made, which cumulatively can have a significant adverse effect on
the performance of the company. As we learned in the previous chapter,
sustained excellence can only be achieved with disciplined execution.
Disciplined execution optimizes the organization so that it operates as

efficiently as possible. When optimization is combined with disciplined growth, it can be a powerful engine for creating value.

There are essentially two ways to grow a business: organically and inorganically. Inorganic growth is straightforward because it means you grow through acquisitions. Organic growth is more complicated because it involves numerous paths that can be taken to achieve success. In this chapter, we will review both organic and inorganic growth excellence and the exceptional capabilities that must be built to achieve disciplined growth. In addition, we will review some important practices for achieving disciplined growth.

Growth initiative duties at most organizations are usually widely distributed among many executives, including the CEO, the COO, group CEOs or group presidents, and several others within the senior management ranks, including the chief revenue officer, chief commercial officer, and chief marketing officer. For a company to achieve consistent disciplined growth, it must execute at an elite level. To that end, here is a list of some of the more fundamental disciplined practices that are utilized by leading companies to build their growth engines:

- Maintain disciplined growth.
- Develop a growth engine.
- Pursue an organic growth strategy that wins.
- Target strategic acquisitions.
- Establish a growth team.
- Seek out joint ventures and strategic alliances.
- Identify frontier markets.
- Unleash the power of scalability.
- Invest and grow niche businesses.
- Build an internal ventures group.

MAINTAIN DISCIPLINED GROWTH

Disciplined growth is difficult to achieve, but it is absolutely necessary when a company is striving to reach the summit of elite. Disciplined growth allows a company to avoid many of the pitfalls and traps associated with inconsistent or erratic growth. This point is captured well in Packard's law and the 20 Mile March. These two insightful growth concepts are described in Jim Collins's seminal works *Good to Great* and *Great by Choice*, respectively.

Packard's law, named after the great David Packard (cofounder of Hewlett-Packard Company) states, "No company can grow revenues consistently faster than its ability to get enough of the right people to implement that growth and still become a great company. If your growth rate in revenues consistently outpaces your growth rate in people, you simply will not—cannot—build a great company."[2] Packard's law proves that there's outsized risk in uncontrolled growth. That's why disciplined growth should be the imperative.

A way to achieve disciplined growth is to utilize the 20 Mile March mechanism. Companies that grow in a controlled and disciplined manner over a long horizon typically outperform enterprises that grow erratically. The 20 Mile March "requires hitting specified performance markers with great consistency over a long period of time. It requires two distinct types of discomfort, delivering high performance in difficult times and holding back in good times."[3]

What I discovered over the years in selecting an appropriate 20 Mile March is that it's best to use a range of revenues. When selecting a range of revenue streams that the company aspires to grow annually, your overarching objective must be to fill key positions with the right people. For a company that can successfully fill positions, I recommend a range of about 5 percent to 9 percent annually. When using a range, I recommend that, at least internally, the company break the target number down into organic and inorganic growth rates. No matter what range is chosen, in the end it is consistent growth that matters.

When I was CEO, with the assistance of Jim Collins at one of our lab sessions, other executives and I engaged in considerable dialogue about trying to decide on our 20 Mile March. As we discovered, the 20 Mile March is a relatively easy concept to understand but is a difficult thing to implement. This is because it takes piercing insight to arrive at the right metric that is meaningful and impactful and is one that the entire global leadership team can commit to and deliver every year.

DEVELOP A GROWTH ENGINE

Leading companies know that disciplined growth is truly the lifeblood of any organization. That's why elite enterprises develop their growth engines through two key building blocks: inorganic (acquisitions) and organic growth initiatives. Inorganic growth and organic growth need to be part of the overall equation when developing a disciplined and balanced growth engine. The rate of targeted growth for each category needs to be well strategized. Both inorganic growth and organic growth need to be value creating, which can be achieved through discipline and elite-level execution. As part of this disciplined approach, it's important to closely track and measure growth.

Enterprises that can develop and execute both inorganic and organic growth capabilities at an elite level are usually rewarded with a higher stock price and sustainable value creation. However, it's essential to understand that each exceptional capability requires a very different skill set. These two elite-level growth capabilities will be discussed next.

PURSUE AN ORGANIC GROWTH STRATEGY THAT WINS

For a company to ascend to greatness, it must pursue an organic growth strategy that wins. The responsibility for organic growth usually rests with the management team running each business unit, but the process is usually overseen by senior corporate management.

Organic growth by its nature is slower than inorganic growth, but it's less risky. Leading companies invest considerable resources in building their capabilities to grow organically. Although organic growth takes a different type of skill set from what's required for inorganic growth, there are some common attributes that the two share, including establishing a disciplined process, having the process managed by an elite group of individuals, and implementing effective mechanisms and metrics. Enterprises have numerous levers they can pull to build an organic growth engine. Some of the more effective include the following:

INNOVATION

Development of new products and services that are powered by innovation propels and sustains an organic growth engine. Innovative development of new products and services must also be driven by an entrepreneurial culture, exceptional research and development capabilities, technological prowess, and elite-level engineering.

SCALING

Successfully scaling a business platform can produce new revenue streams, which can be a major growth engine. This growth can be accomplished by winning new customers in existing markets and expanding in different markets.

PRICING

When an enterprise has the ability to successfully increase prices, it gains pricing leverage. Pricing leverage can be a powerful source of additional revenues and earnings for an enterprise.

PRICING STRATEGIES

Companies that launch pricing studies have demonstrated improvement in their results. Pricing decisions need to be disciplined and augmented with analytics and tools. More disciplined pricing decisions can help a company generate additional revenue streams and improve margins.

STRATEGIC GROWTH INITIATIVES

These are specifically targeted initiatives to grow certain business units or product lines. Strategic growth initiatives can be more effective when the company teams up with the right outside consultants. The top consulting firms are exceptional at assisting organizations in rethinking their businesses and identifying new paths for growth.

ADJACENT MARKETS

Successfully developing adjacent markets can create new revenue streams. This is an excellent source of growth. The premiere consulting firms are exceptional at assisting enterprises in identifying adjacent markets.

STRONG BRAND DEVELOPMENT

Strong brand development of products that attract loyal customers can provide a steady stream of recurring revenues and can create new sources of revenue as well.

VALUE SELLING

The ability to sell value can create a win-win scenario with customers. Value selling is normally accomplished by demonstrating to the customer the value that is being added to his or her business, which in turn can provide the company with higher selling prices and incremental orders.

CROSS-SELLING

Elite companies that possess a wide-ranging portfolio of product platforms have an opportunity to collaborate internally to cross-sell products. For this to be successful, the company must have a collaborative culture. When team members are free to connect and collaborate in creative ways, this can result in incremental sales that help fuel growth.

ROBUST MACROECONOMIC ENVIRONMENT

Never underestimate the power of a robust macroeconomic environment, as it is always a major tailwind for growth.

REPURPOSING PRODUCTS

Several companies that I worked with during the COVID-19 pandemic successfully repurposed products. This is a new source of revenue that can't be ignored. Companies don't have to wait until there's a global shock to repurpose a product. This is something that should be reviewed regularly as part of innovation initiatives.

LUCK

As was demonstrated during the COVID-19 pandemic, certain parts of the economy, such as high tech and streaming services, benefited immensely because of the shift to working from home. Some of these companies saw revenues grow dramatically.

TARGET STRATEGIC ACQUISITIONS

Acquisitions provide new and accelerated avenues of growth and can be a powerful engine. Inorganic growth by nature is faster than organic growth, but it's also riskier. Leading companies, however, clearly understand the elevated risk associated with acquisitions. As a consequence, they invest considerable resources in building strong inorganic growth capabilities.

Capital allocation effectiveness is vital for acquisitions. That's because acquisition decisions are even riskier than organic growth initiatives given the relative size and complexity of the former. Allocating capital for acquisitions requires a superior level of skill to generate long-term positive economic value. Included with this skill is the ability to decide which companies to acquire and which ones to pass on. Deficiencies in this skill perhaps partially accounts for the high failure rate of acquisitions.

Companies that excel at successfully executing acquisitions, such as Roper and Danaher, are usually rewarded with growing free cash flows, revenues, and profitability, as well as a higher stock price. Also, properly targeted acquisitions can accelerate the development of technology and innovation. Developing an elite acquisition process is not easy; it requires a host of organizational skills. All aspects of the acquisition process must be effective, including sourcing transactions, valuations, negotiations, definitive agreements, due diligence, integration planning and execution, and post-acquisition reviews. Leaders must also be disciplined and refrain from overpaying.

Enterprises that have a well-developed acquisition playbook and strong execution abilities have the ability to create shareholder value. Also, it's vital to smartly integrate acquisitions into the acquiring company's organizational structure and culture. Integration plans need to be put in place before the deal closes. A senior-level executive should be appointed to develop and oversee the plan. Smartly integrating an acquisition doesn't always mean destroying the existing structure of the acquired company. It means ensuring that the company's integration is consistent with the acquiring enterprise's business model and culture.

ESTABLISH A GROWTH TEAM

An innovative approach to organic growth can be found at Facebook with their "growth team" concept. This was highlighted in a *Fortune* article of

December 1, 2016, by Adam Lashinsky. The article provides insight into Facebook's leader's management style: "One of Facebook's key business innovations is a 'growth team' ... that designs tactics for various parts of the company, relying on a rigorous set of metrics to gauge success. The growth unit has broad latitude to weigh in on any aspect of Facebook's business."[4]

The article goes on to say that the growth team essentially is responsible for removing obstacles that prevent Facebook from growing. This growth concept is being replicated across Silicon Valley, and I believe that this creative concept has broad applicability to most enterprises as well. Lean and after-action reviews can be helpful and valuable tools to the team empowered to assist with growth.

SEEK OUT JOINT VENTURES AND STRATEGIC ALLIANCES

Leading organizations ensure that joint ventures and strategic alliances are a core competency of the enterprise. These vehicles can be value creators if they are conceived and executed well. They can also spell disaster if executed poorly. Developing this skill internally takes considerable resources. Once this capability is well-developed within the organization, organic growth can be accelerated and shareholder value can be created. Joint ventures and strategic alliances have the potential to reduce the amount of cash invested in projects, which spreads the risk between the parties. In addition, they provide an enterprise with the potential to penetrate new markets that it may have found difficult to expand to on its own.

Two of the most successful business investments of my career involved joint ventures. One was in the defense business and the other in the metals business. In both cases, we created a formidable global leader with scale and prodigious technical capabilities. As a result, the joint ventures created significant shareholder value. Here are some lessons that I learned from these two successful joint ventures:

- Enterprises must remember my three sacrosanct rules of successful joint ventures: you must select the right partner, you must have a strong governance framework, and you must have a clearly defined exit strategy.
- The joint venture must have a purpose, core values, and a vision, and the business model must be clearly defined.
- It's preferable, but not imperative, to have a controlling interest. In my two successful joint ventures, one was a controlling interest and the other was a minority interest. What's more important is who the partner is and what the purpose of the venture is.
- Considerable due diligence is required to ensure that the venture partner adheres to similar core values and conducts business to the highest ethical standards.

IDENTIFY FRONTIER MARKETS

Another exceptional capability that should be developed by an organization is finding new areas for profitable growth, including frontier markets. That is, how can the business create incremental value in the future by investing in areas that perhaps competitors are not seeing? For example, when I was CEO, we started with a mechanism to internally identify the "next UAE." This was a reference to when the United Arab Emirates was virtually an unknown market but came to prominence because of its great energy wealth. The UAE embarked on a massive infrastructure spend, and the companies that identified the market early (which we did) were rewarded with healthy contracts. In addition to being welcomed to do business with the UAE, our company was one of the first in our market sectors to enter places like Russia, Saudi Arabia, China, Brazil, India, and Egypt, among many other emerging markets. All these early moves were strategically important and generated some of the highest returns on invested capital.

So, the question is, where is the next market that offers significant upside potential for strongly positioning the company? The emerging market does not have to be a physical location; it can be a virtual opportunity using e-commerce. This mechanism requires scanning the environment in real time and using generative thinking, considerable dialogue, lots of data, and due diligence. It also requires being close to the customer because the customer is the one who can provide valuable information and intelligence on various emerging markets. What is important in the process, however, is not to make large bets. The approach must be to make many smaller bets to test various markets that improve performance, all without taking outsized risks.

UNLEASH THE POWER OF SCALABILITY

Scalability can provide a competitive advantage to a company. Scaling a business platform requires elite-level skills. The development of these skills is absolutely necessary because scaling a platform can be a strong growth engine. It simply cannot be ignored. There are many models that are used for properly scaling a business. The models are largely dependent on the organizational structure of the company, its unique practices, and its technology. Some models require a relatively large investment, while others require a much more limited amount.

No matter what model is used to scale a business, the objective is, of course, to have as much of every incremental dollar of revenue as possible flow to the bottom line. This number can be calculated; it's a metric that should be closely monitored. Enterprises that can skillfully scale their business model by keeping their fixed costs relatively flat and their variable costs minimal have an opportunity to create considerable shareholder value. This is especially true when scaling a new, innovative product. All those incremental revenue dollars that flow to the bottom line can make a significant impact on key metrics, including return on invested capital, gross margins, and operating margins.

INVEST AND GROW NICHE BUSINESSES

Leaders and boards of diversified companies routinely ponder this question: should we invest and nurture for the long-term potentially higher-margin, higher-return niche business opportunities, or is it better to continue with the more traditional path of balancing and improving the current mix of businesses in the portfolio? I believe that the more appropriate question to ask is, how do we do both?

There's no question that an organization must learn to properly balance and improve its portfolio of businesses. This is normally an ongoing process. As part of this balancing and improvement effort, capital must be allocated effectively to sustain the current revenue streams while generating new growth opportunities. At the same time, it's also prudent for enterprises to make small bets in nurturing niche opportunities. Niche businesses can ultimately turn into powerful platforms that may blossom and generate higher returns and substantial free cash flows. Numerous examples of this approach can be found at leading companies, particularly in the tech sector with Alphabet (Google).

BUILD AN INTERNAL VENTURES GROUP

An effective practice utilized mainly by larger companies for growth and innovation is building an internal ventures group. An internal ventures group provides an organization the ability to expand its reach by accelerating innovation, which in turn can propel revenue growth. An added benefit of an internal ventures group is that this can be an excellent mechanism to explore and learn new business models. The group can also help accelerate bringing new products and services to market.

Some of the more prolific elite US companies in this category include Alphabet, Apple, Facebook, Microsoft, UPS, Campbell Soup, Coca-Cola, and General Mills. Through their internal ventures group, elite companies invest in partnerships and, at times, even acquisitions. I believe that the internal ventures model can be adapted to and utilized across most industries. Given the hypercompetitive global marketplace, developing this exceptional capability, particularly with a focus on accelerating innovation, can help an organization fuel its growth engine.

CHAPTER FIFTEEN

Commercial Excellence

Leadership and greatness comes to those who follow-
through. Who stand for near-flawless execution.[1]

—ROBIN S. SHARMA

COMMERCIAL EXCELLENCE

We have just reviewed two important principles under the foundational
pillar of execution: disciplined execution and growth engine. In the
remainder of section three, we will tackle the final three principles that,
when put into practice, are also responsible for delivering extraordinary
results, starting with commercial excellence. Commercial excellence is
inextricably linked to the principle of growth engine.

Commercial excellence includes a multitude of critical elements that
are necessary to achieving greatness. We will review some of the most
impactful in this chapter. Through commercial excellence, an enterprise
can deliver new products and services; optimize pricing strategies to realize
the highest revenues possible; deliver extraordinary customer experience;
build strong brand loyalty; optimize sales channels; and excel at contract
negotiations that positively impact terms, pricing, and growth.

Responsibility for commercial excellence is usually vested in several key executive positions. These responsibilities are normally assigned to the chief operating officer, chief commercial officer, and chief revenue officer. Some enterprises will assign these responsibilities to various other executives, such as the chief customer officer. Furthermore, these responsibilities will usually rest with each business segment or group leader and his or her direct reports. All these individuals are responsible for overseeing the essential elements that are reviewed in this chapter.

For a company to achieve execution excellence, it must excel at commercial capabilities. Here is a list of some important things related to commercial capabilities that a company must execute at an elite level:

- Excel at product innovation.
- Center the digital transformation on the customer.
- Make each customer touch extraordinary.
- Know your customer through value selling.
- Focus on pricing strategies.
- Excel at contract negotiations.
- Dictate favorable terms on commercial agreements.
- Increase prices to offset inflation.
- Focus on brand management.
- Optimize sales and distribution channels.
- Utilize customer profitability management to improve performance.

EXCEL AT PRODUCT INNOVATION

Product innovation, a crucial lifeline for all organizations, includes improving existing products and creating completely new ones. For a company to excel at product innovation, it must consistently invest in the future to develop exceptional capabilities. These investments are the engine that drives the creation of new products. Without these investments, it's impossible to sustain an elite company. This is where the principle of building lifelines and the principle of innovation and technology—under the foundational pillar of strategy—come into play.

In addition, the principle of culture—under the foundational pillar of leadership—is likewise an important factor. Companies with entrepreneurial cultures are more focused on customer excellence and are thus more likely to create new innovative products. Amid an entrepreneurial culture, organizations passionately embrace product innovation. This level of commitment to innovation can drive differentiation in the marketplace. This in turn creates growth and sustainment for the enterprise.

CENTER THE DIGITAL TRANSFORMATION ON THE CUSTOMER

Elite companies, now more than ever, are accelerating their transformation to digital enterprises. The central focus of this digital transformation is the customer. The value of a digital transformation centered on the customer was on full display during the COVID-19 crisis. Based on numerous reports in the *Wall Street Journal* throughout the pandemic, companies that were more digitally advanced relative to the customer performed better than those that were less prepared. In some cases, the results were dramatically better.

As part of this digital transformation, leading companies smartly utilize technology to seamlessly serve the customer and drive market growth, while at the same time securing vital data about customer habits. There are certain indispensable technologies that leading companies are focused on to improve the overall customer experience. These technologies include the following: e-commerce websites, artificial intelligence, mobile apps, big data, cybersecurity, cloud computing, and social media.

MAKE EVERY CUSTOMER TOUCH EXTRAORDINARY

Making every customer touch extraordinary should be the goal of all enterprises. However, before a company can be successful at this, it must first understand how many times a customer interacts with the enterprise. What I discovered throughout my career is that some organizations don't always have a precise understanding of what happens in various situations when a customer interacts with the company. This is where the continuous improvement discipline can help a company map out the various scenarios and touch points.

Another essential element of making every customer touch extraordinary is a workforce who, when empowered, can be responsive to customer needs. Implementing this key mechanism is indispensable to making the customer experience truly exceptional. Companies that excel at understanding all the touch points and making the customer experience extraordinary will likely build brand loyalty.

There are many elite companies that make every customer touch extraordinary. Two of the leading enterprises on this list include Apple and Disney. When customers interact with these companies, they find overwhelmingly that the company's total focus is on making every customer touch simply special.

KNOW YOUR CUSTOMER THROUGH VALUE SELLING

In the business world, pricing power is nirvana. Elite organizations are exceptional at taking advantage of pricing power to improve operating results. Companies with true pricing leverage have the ability to invest additional earnings and cash flow into innovation and hiring the best people. The end result is that these companies build prodigious lifelines while improving their overall operating performance. Although most companies do not have elite-level pricing power, they can still develop many of the exceptional capabilities that can help an organization overcome some pricing obstacles. One key skill is the use of value selling.

Perhaps there's nothing more important in business than truly knowing the customer. A strong mechanism a company can use to achieve this deep knowledge of a customer is value selling, which is simply a focused approach on the customer. Ideally, the sales force should know more about the customer than the customer knows about himself or herself. This is a completely different mindset from that needed for traditional selling. It requires gaining a deep understanding of the customer's challenges and needs so that you can develop innovative solutions and sell on value. Selling solutions that add value provide an organization with the ability to generate higher revenues because there's usually more pricing leverage.

For a company to utilize value selling to transform how it sells solutions to a customer, it needs to develop some fundamental capabilities. These exceptional capabilities, which must be driven by a customer-centric culture, include the following: implementing a customer relationship management software platform to properly manage customer data and interaction; utilizing big data to gain insight into customer habits; training sales personnel on the need to sell solutions that create value; and implementing other technologies that improve sales force effectiveness.

When I was CEO, we undertook a value-selling initiative in one of our business segments. With the assistance of an outside firm, we achieved excellent results. It was amazing to see the transformation of the sales team and how they approached selling value based on solutions, as opposed to the past approach of just landing an order.

FOCUS ON PRICING STRATEGIES

A key strength of elite companies is the ability to optimize the pricing of products and services. This is an area where some companies have opportunities to improve margins and profitability. When I was CEO, we undertook a review of our pricing policies and strategy in some of our businesses. With the assistance of outside experts, we discovered that we were leaving some margin on the table with each order. We also discovered that policies sometimes were not clear and, at times, were even conflicting and confusing. Launching a commercial pricing initiative usually begins by engaging outside consultants to undertake this complex but vital program to spur growth. Several large and some smaller consulting firms excel at assisting companies with these types of initiatives. Pricing review engagements can be expensive, but when done right they are well worth the investment dollars.

When used effectively, consultants can help an enterprise make smarter pricing decisions, avoid leakage, and eliminate inconsistent policies. Added benefits from this type of initiative include the development of tools and the provision of accountability on pricing decisions. Probably the most important benefit is the discipline that is instilled in the process. Cumulatively, all these benefits will pay extra dividends as the company expands its markets and scales up its business.

For a pricing strategy and policy review to be successful, I recommend the following guidelines:

- Use outside experts to assist with this complex undertaking. Do not attempt this with just internal resources. Make sure that the outside consultants come highly recommended. Start small. Do not initially implement enterprise-wide.
- Train all appropriate people who are involved with the customers. I have discovered that extensive training and good communication are vital to obtaining a good outcome and for sustainment.
- Use Lean to improve processes, and utilize technology to gather and analyze data.
- Develop potent tools that provide discipline, crucial pricing information, and other relevant data that makes the sales force more productive.
- Ensure that the key outcomes are sales force effectiveness, pricing discipline, practical tools, and sound policies.

EXCEL AT CONTRACT NEGOTIATIONS

Companies need to excel at contract negotiations. It is fundamental for an organization to develop the exceptional commercial capability of negotiating and executing contracts that truly add economic value. This is especially vital if a major portion of the business is reliant on long-term contracts. In addition to long-term commercial agreements, contract negotiations may also make an outsized impact in the area of mergers and acquisitions.

During my career, I was exposed to long-term contracts in the defense industry, steel industry, and infrastructure construction industry. The length of many of our contracts in these businesses was in the range of three to ten years, with some contracts exceeding fifteen years. What I learned in dealing with long-term contracts is that you need to put your best people on these immensely important negotiations. Your best people need to be supported by an elite team that is normally composed of exceptional talent from such disciplines as engineering, legal, risk, and finance. As part of this review is an in-depth economic analysis of the specific terms and conditions underpinning the contract.

Some essential value-adding terms and conditions that can make an outsized economic impact include, but are not limited to, the following: inflation protection, risk transfer, cash advances, timing of cash payments and cash receipts, pricing, exit clauses, termination clauses, and intellectual property protections. A badly negotiated long-term contract can have a particularly adverse effect on the company and, in some cases, may result in permanent damage to the enterprise.

A disciplined approach to contracts should also apply to medium-term commercial arrangements. The length of medium-term contracts is usually in the range of one to three years. A focused approach is necessary because, cumulatively, these commercial arrangements can also have an adverse effect on the performance and risk profile of the company.

When dealing with material contracts, leading companies implement the key control mechanism of proper dialogue and approval. Elite companies ensure that all material commitments—both financial and terms—are talked about with and approved by the CEO and CFO. In some cases they also need board approval. From the financial commitment standpoint, all contracts over a certain preestablished threshold should be reviewed, dialogued, and approved. Any significant contractual terms that either individually or cumulatively pose a risk to the enterprise need to be subjected to the same process.

Once commercial arrangements and contracts are signed, they must be managed properly. This is where superior contract administration skills come into play. If the contract is not monitored, managed, and implemented effectively, then significant economic leakage may follow.

DICTATE FAVORABLE TERMS ON COMMERCIAL AGREEMENTS

Above, we examined the significance of understanding the true economic value embedded in both long-term and medium-term contracts. In this section, we will examine daily arrangements and short-term commercial arrangements with a duration of less than a year. Elite companies excel at negotiating strong terms and conditions for contractual obligations such as sales orders and accounts payable, just to name a couple. Favorable payment terms (both on sales and purchases) can affect the working capital and thus the cash flow of the company. In some cases, the amounts are material when both accounts receivable and accounts payable terms are effectively negotiated and managed.

A robust metric utilized by leading companies is the cash conversion cycle. The cash conversion cycle measures the speed of cash and working capital efficiency. The formula is as follows:

accounts receivable days + inventory days – accounts payable days = the cash conversion cycle

Some businesses make a notable effort to receive advance payments from customers—an excellent practice to follow, if possible. However, if advance payments are received, the calculation must be modified to include these advances. In such cases, the enterprise would have to deduct (–) the advance payment days and accounts payable days (–) from accounts receivable and inventory days to determine (=) the cash conversion cycle number. The objective, of course, is to arrive at the lowest number possible, with the best-case scenario being a negative number.

When Dell first developed its innovative online ordering business several decades ago, the computer giant was posting a negative cash conversion cycle number. The customers were funding working capital for the company. More recently, in 2019, Roper Technologies achieved this amazing milestone with an outstanding –5.3 percent revenue number. While this scenario is ultimately nirvana, for most organizations it is impractical to expect to achieve a negative cash conversion number. Nonetheless, the CEO should not accept the working capital status quo and should set improvement targets that are monitored closely. Effective tools such as Lean can help improve working capital efficiency, which in turn generates incremental cash. Since cash is essential to the health of an enterprise, the cash conversion cycle is a lifeline that can't be ignored.

INCREASE PRICES TO OFFSET INFLATION

There are some businesses where the commodity cycle has a severe adverse effect on their performance and their long-term viability. I've seen industries where vital input costs rose so dramatically and so fast that they had an outsized disruptive effect on the operations and financial performance of the company. This was on full display in 2021. To manage this risk, a company's executives require the ability to quickly raise prices to offset the rapid inflation as much as possible.

A practical way to manage this risk is to closely track all input costs while simultaneously implementing a comprehensive strategy to increase prices. Both input cost trends and price increases need to be graphed and scrutinized. It is crucial to see where the respective curves are trending. Excellence occurs when the curve indicating price increases crosses the curve indicating input inflation costs. Just as you need elite people negotiating long-term contracts, you need elite people to engage in ongoing negotiations with short-cycle customers. Successfully passing on price increases may lead to the generation of substantial economic value. This is an exceptional capability that all companies need to possess.

FOCUS ON BRAND MANAGEMENT

Whenever a customer interacts with a company it is vital that his or her experience be extraordinary. Providing exceptional customer service is fundamental to building a valuable and venerable brand. Strong brand development begins with the CEO and then flows to all team members who interact with customers and the community. Innovative brand engagement models can assist organizations in building better customer experiences, which can help promote and build the brand.

A brand is usually built through a positive and well-developed customer experience underpinned by such elements as innovation, product quality, design, functionality, and service level. Moreover, the entire customer experience has to be consistently world-class. Besides these fundamental drivers of brand performance, other critical factors can enhance the brand. These factors include brand awareness, reputation, integrity, sustainability initiatives, community involvement, and perhaps even the financial strength of the organization.

Companies that build strong brands with loyal customers often have more pricing leverage. Clearly, one of the branding gurus is the late CEO of Apple, Steve Jobs, who passionately believed that building a brand needs to be reflected in everything a company does: marketing, design, packaging, functionality, and customer interaction. Apple has actually achieved something few companies can claim: they are viewed as a luxury brand.

OPTIMIZE SALES AND DISTRIBUTION CHANNELS

Leading companies understand the economic power that comes from building optimized sales and distribution channels. They also understand that building these channels requires a long-term commitment to investing in such areas as people, technology, training, infrastructure, and supply chain. Optimized sales and distribution channels can provide a company with a competitive advantage. As was demonstrated during COVID-19 pandemic, digital sales channels that were supported with efficient distribution facilities proved to be an effective strategy. Companies with well-established digital channels generally outperformed organizations that were underinvested. Many companies that found themselves unprepared to deal with the rapid shift to e-commerce struggled with their performance and had to accelerate their digital initiatives so they could compete.

An excellent example of a company with strong sales and distribution channels is Amazon. All one has to do is examine how Amazon excels and sets the standard—such a company is truly elite. Amazon's marketplace e-commerce site, their one-day delivery process, their return process, the Whole Foods network, and many other vital aspects of the company's digital sales and distribution channels are difficult to compete against.

UTILIZE CUSTOMER PROFITABILITY MANAGEMENT TO IMPROVE PERFORMANCE

Elite companies focus intensely on all aspects of their customers. One valuable area of this engagement is customer profitability management. In a 2010 publication, the Institute of Management Accountants (IMA) provided some insight into customer profitability management:

Managing profitability requires not only a customer-centric focus but also a thorough understanding and effective management of customer profitability. Customer profitability management (CPM) is a strategy-linked approach to identifying the relative profitability of different customers or customer segments to devise strategies that add value to most-profitable customers, make less-profitable customers more profitable, stop or reduce the erosion of profit by unprofitable customers, or otherwise focus on long-term customer profitability. Managers are often surprised to find out that a small percentage of customers generate substantially more than 100% of profits, and the remaining customers are either breakeven or unprofitable. Using a customer profitability management system replaces intuitive impressions of customer profitability with fact-based information and supporting analysis.[2]

Another source on CPM is the groundbreaking research paper "Customer Profitability Management," written by Robert S. Kaplan and V. G. Narayanan and published in May 2001 by Harvard Business School Publishing. This is a must-read for anyone interested in developing this exceptional execution capability. For CPM to operate properly, a costing system must be developed that accurately assigns and allocates costs to each customer. This is the major challenge in accurately measuring customer profitability. Activity-based costing, or ABC, was developed to address and underpin a CPM system. ABC systems can range from complex to simple. It takes resources to develop a strong ABC system that accurately captures customer profitability. No matter the level of sophistication, a CPM system is indispensable.

CHAPTER SIXTEEN

Operational Excellence

Success doesn't necessarily come from breakthrough innovation but
from flawless execution. A great strategy alone won't win a game
or a battle; the win comes from basic blocking and tackling.[1]

—NAVEEN JAIN

OPERATIONAL EXCELLENCE

World-class operational excellence is the norm at elite companies. Certain
universal characteristics are typically evident when examining the
operational excellence of organizations that have ascended the summit of
greatness. These performance characteristics are usually manifested in the
following ways: continuous improvement discipline, exceptional technical
and engineering skills, highly optimized supply chain, and extraordinary
levels of customer service.

Operational excellence capabilities include a multitude of essential
elements that we will review in this chapter. Some enterprises appoint a chief
operating officer to oversee all or some of these critical components. Some
enterprises will assign these responsibilities to various other executives,
such as vice president of manufacturing, vice president of global supply
chain, and vice president of engineering.

For a company to achieve operational excellence, it must implement certain best practices consistently and at an elite level. These are in addition to having in place an integrated management system. Here is a list of some of the more fundamental practices necessary for achieving operational excellence:

- Implement standardized processes.
- Utilize sales, inventory, and operations planning.
- Consistently deliver a superior product.
- Optimize the global supply chain.
- Manage inventory effectively.
- Optimize the operational footprint.
- Utilize value engineering and design.
- Develop engineering and technical capabilities.
- Execute a product management strategy.
- Implement a variable cost model.
- Develop exceptional program management skills.
- Rationalize assets.

IMPLEMENT STANDARDIZED PROCESSES

In my private equity work, I have had the privilege of meeting several elite CEOs. One CEO in particular stood out because of his amazing ability to turn companies around. When I spoke to him, he was on his third successful turnaround and getting ready to move on to his fourth assignment. I asked him, "If you had to distill your success down to one element in your playbook for turning troubled businesses around, what would that be?" Without hesitation, he emphatically stated, "Standardized processes!"

Standardized processes are fundamental in all areas of the enterprise. In order to implement effective processes, a company must infuse technology and utilize a continuous improvement discipline. There are many benefits derived from having well-designed standardized processes that operate efficiently. A standardized process normally improves productivity, reduces costs, eliminates any confusion about what to do and what not to do, and improves overall quality. Standardized processes bring discipline to the organization. This is likely the single most important element to optimizing an organization. It's also the necessary foundation when rapidly scaling a business.

UTILIZE SALES, INVENTORY, AND OPERATIONS PLANNING

Sales, inventory, and operations planning (SIOP) is a robust tool utilized by elite companies to better balance demand and supply. A key requirement for an effective SIOP process is to have in place a one-instance ERP system. SIOP requires teamwork and discipline across the enterprise. The sales team is at the front end of the system, the finance team is responsible for forecasting, and the operations team is responsible for inventory levels and supply chain. All these areas require exceptional coordination.

Companies will often use outside consultants to implement SIOP. There are numerous benefits of a compelling SIOP process, including lower inventory levels, which improves cash flows; more accurate forecasting, which improves decision-making; and improved capacity and resource planning, which lowers costs and increases efficiency.

CONSISTENTLY DELIVER A SUPERIOR PRODUCT

If a company does not consistently deliver a superior product and/or service, then it will eventually fall from the summit of elite and become irrelevant. All seventeen principles outlined in *Ascend to Greatness* either directly or indirectly make an impact on the product and/or service quality. Obviously, some principles are more influential than others. Probably the most critical to improving both product and service quality is disciplined execution.

There are several other principles that warrant further mention because of their outsized impact on quality, namely, culture and the right people. Since these principles are covered elsewhere in *Ascend to Greatness*, they won't be repeated here. However, the important takeaway from the discussion about this best practice is that an enterprise must never forget just how vital it is to consistently deliver the highest-quality product and or/service to the customer and to know that disciplined execution is the best way to realize this objective.

OPTIMIZE THE GLOBAL SUPPLY CHAIN

A modern company cannot survive without a quality strategic sourcing group, talented and empowered people to run it, and a potent global supply chain software system to manage the function. In that it facilitates development of strategic relationships with suppliers, a strong global supply chain group can create formidable economic value for an enterprise. The importance of having an effective global supply chain was on full display in 2021. It is essential that the senior officer who oversees this function report directly to the CEO or at least to either the COO or the president (when separate from the CEO position). For large companies, the person who oversees the supply chain usually has the title of chief operating officer, executive vice president of strategic sourcing, or executive vice president of global supply chain. There are several other titles as well.

Apple is an excellent example of a company that uses its global supply chain to drive input costs down, find the best partners, and deliver a superior product. In the book *Inside Apple*, author Adam Lashinsky provides some revealing insight into how Apple manages and benefits from its supply chains. "Apple doesn't own the saw, and it doesn't own the company that owns the saw," Lashinsky writes. "It also doesn't staff the factory where the saw will be used. But it absolutely has an opinion as to which saw its supplier will use. It's a new form of vertical integration; where once a manufacturer would own every step of the process, Apple now controls each step without owning any of it." Another advantage of this virtual vertical structure is that costs now become variable as opposed to fixed.

The global supply chain typically includes sourcing, procurement, logistics, and transportation. An exceptional supply chain can provide a company with a competitive advantage. Information technology is crucial to building a dynamic global supply chain. The strategic benefits of building and executing an innovative supply chain are numerous. Here are some important benefits:

- elimination or reduction of production disruptions,
- elimination or reduction of excess inventory,
- an ensured higher level of product availability,
- elimination or reduction of premium freight charges,
- reduction in the cost of sourcing,
- leverage of the supplier base for innovation,
- the building of strategic relationship with key suppliers,
- reduction in cycle time, particularly when speed is vital, and
- improvement on the return on invested capital.

MANAGE INVENTORY EFFECTIVELY

Supremely managing inventory is paramount to success. Inventory impacts the business in numerous ways, but there are three very specific ways it can be material. First, a company must have the right inventory in the right place at the right time to fulfill orders to a high standard of customer satisfaction (fill rates). Second, inventory can be a major cash drain on the enterprise because it is a meaningful component of working capital. Too much inventory ties up crucial cash, and not enough inventory can adversely affect customer service and loyalty. Third, the buildup of inventory obviously impacts plant operations, distribution centers, and supply chains and logistics. All these elements have to be managed well in order to operate at an elite level.

SIOP, ERP computer systems, manufacturing automation technologies, greater visibility of supply chains, highly trained teams, standardized processes, automated systems, and critical apps are all necessary to properly plan and manage inventories. The objective is to turn inventory planning and management into a competitive advantage, as opposed to being a negative force on operating performance.

OPTIMIZE THE OPERATIONAL FOOTPRINT

The ability to optimize and streamline manufacturing plant operations, warehouses, branches, distribution centers, and offices can provide a company with a several advantages, including a reduction in fixed costs and improved customer service levels. Elite companies ensure that they operate at an optimum level by minimizing the number of locations they employ to deliver their products and/or services. This is an area where I have observed excellence in leading enterprises.

With respect to manufacturing plant operations, for example, I've seen leading organizations reduce the number of plants they operate without any adverse effects on delivery performance. I've seen plants that previously operated on only one shift begin to run on three shifts, without compromising fill rates or overall quality of the product. Also, elite enterprises ensure that their warehouses, distribution centers, branches, and offices are optimized as much as possible. These companies employ automated warehouses and/or smaller warehouses that are strategically located, and they ensure the company is not overburdened by large, inefficient distribution centers. Finally, these organizations consolidate office locations by centralizing administrative functions and creating shared services centers.

Streamlining and optimizing operations starts with having skilled teams of people who are well trained and exceptional at execution. These teams are adept at using a wide array of robust tools, particularly the company's integrated management system. The efficiencies realized from an integrated management system augmented with other practical tools can be notable. Such supportive tools include optimization software, artificial intelligence, robotics, and enabled sensors. Important insights and benefits can be derived from utilizing these tools, including the following:

- the ability to monitor equipment and identify potential maintenance issues before they arise and thus reduce downtime,
- the ability to reduce or eliminate waste, and
- the ability to reduce fixed costs and improve productivity.

UTILIZE VALUE ENGINEERING AND DESIGN

Elite-level value engineering and design requires world-class processes for both enhancing existing products and developing new ones. Leading companies utilize their integrated management system tools to map out and improve every step of this vital process. When value engineering is combined with strong product design, a company can create a formidable competitive advantage in the marketplace.

The main objective of value engineering is to efficiently reduce all unnecessary costs while either maintaining or improving the quality of the product. A key practice of value engineering is qualifying alternative materials that can be utilized in the manufacturing of the product. The purpose of alternative materials is to reduce costs and also to allow the company to develop other sources in the supply chain. Product design, on the other hand, can benefit the customer experience in several ways, including improving the attractiveness of the product as well as its functionality and ease of use.

DEVELOP ENGINEERING AND TECHNICAL CAPABILITIES

Elite companies possess remarkable engineering and technical support skills. These capabilities are indispensable when positioning and maintaining products and/or services in the marketplace. Enterprises sometimes find themselves in a position where they need to augment these skills. More and more companies are looking outside the organization to fill this need. Companies have been successful at identifying exceptional engineering and technical support skills through acquisitions.

The old practice of acquiring companies principally for the purpose of growth is no longer a valid one. The new model is that acquisitions not only provide growth but also bring much-needed skills and capabilities into the organization. This is particularly true in the tech sector, which is on the vanguard of this trend. It is common practice today for exceptional companies to routinely acquire other enterprises to augment and strengthen their own technical, software, and engineering capabilities.

The need to acquire and enhance skills through acquisitions has grown in importance in recent years. This is evident in the artificial intelligence (AI) space. In the December 27, 2019, edition of the *Wall Street Journal*, Asa Fitch writes about AI: "Tech giants … have made acquisitions in recent years to strengthen their ability to apply complex algorithms to improve the performance of everything from delivery robots to self-driving cars." The article goes to say, "Many of the deals are driven as much by buyers wanting to land talent as to acquire a specific product." This approach is creative, and it applies to all industries, not just the tech sector.

In addition to acquisitions, some companies turn to countries such as India to establish centers of excellence, particularly on account of their strong engineering and technical skills. India has a well-educated technical workforce that can be utilized to fill gaps or even be developed into the main center of excellence. When I was CEO, we utilized India and found the workforce to be talented and keen to work for US companies.

EXECUTE A PRODUCT MANAGEMENT STRATEGY

A sound product management strategy consolidates the power of and responsibility for the product life cycle under one person, as opposed to being fragmented across multiple functions. When a product executive is given decision-making responsibility and accountability for pricing, innovation, design, and other critical elements, this usually culminates in stronger results. Note that it is paramount for the product executive to be an A player with exceptional leadership abilities, deep product knowledge, and an ability to work across functions.

Google is a good example of a company that is structured around its products. In 2015, they reorganized and formed Alphabet as the parent company, with all the other businesses—including Google—organized as separate product platforms. The product-focused business groups are all separate entities. These include Google, Calico, Nest, Life Sciences, and Fibers, along with several others. Each executive of a product group has responsibility and accountability for results. Although Google still accounts for the majority of Alphabet's revenues and profitability, the reorganization has allowed the smaller entities to better focus on their respective businesses. Whenever an organization undertakes a significant reorganization or restructuring similar to Alphabet's, it is always helpful to study companies that have already implemented a successful model. By benchmarking against best-of-class performers, key mistakes can possibly be avoided or at least minimized.

IMPLEMENT A VARIABLE COST MODEL

A variable cost model is essential for enterprises that operate in cyclical markets. It's even more crucial when a company is also required to invest substantial sums in capital expenditures in order to sustain its business model. When an enterprise is exposed to both these conditions, its risks are amplified. Even when a company operates in a more stable and predictable market, it is still vital to reduce the amount of fixed costs in the business. This is an indispensable lifeline that could benefit a company during extreme shocks.

During severe turbulence, it is not unusual to see a precipitous drop in revenues. That's why enterprises need a flexible and variable cost model that will allow them to quickly reduce costs as markets turn down. Also, long-term contracts need to be negotiated with flexibility built in so that in the event of a downturn, the company can take immediate action to reduce personnel and other operating costs. In periods of rapid decline, the ability to proactively take these vital countermeasures can mean the difference between survival and failure. When designing a variable cost model, companies should know that operating leverage is the key. An aversion to bricks and mortar should be entrenched in the culture of a company in order to provide such operating leverage. Business models that are variable not only are a true lifeline but also can provide a sustained competitive advantage.

DEVELOP EXCEPTIONAL PROGRAM MANAGEMENT SKILLS

When executed at an elite level, program management can consistently deliver projects on time and within budget. For projects to be properly managed and delivered successfully, the enterprise must develop effective tools, utilize robust software, and implement efficient processes. All these parts must be put in the hands of an elite manager who has been highly trained in project management and has a history of delivering results.

Some examples of internally focused projects that require exceptional program management skills are as follows:

- a major restructuring or transformative initiative,
- managing through a major shock or disruption,
- a greenfield start-up site for a new plant,
- a new enterprise resource planning system implementation,
- managing a large contract with significant deliverables,
- managing an acquisition integration,
- establishing a new joint venture,
- establishing a new shared services center in other parts of the world,
- entering a new market in a foreign country, and
- developing new products and/or services.

Enterprises that can execute these types of projects flawlessly and consistently can also create appreciable value. Some projects are so vital that leading companies create key positions for them, such as chief restructuring officer or chief transformation officer. Note that sometimes it may make sense simply to outsource a program if the project is exceptionally complex or large in scale.

RATIONALIZE ASSETS

An important part of operating an elite company is having the courage and skill to rationalize assets that are either nonperforming or underperforming. Nonperforming assets are those that are making no appreciable contribution to the overall profitability of the company and are destroying economic value. The common denominator of underperforming assets is that they do not typically earn their cost in capital. Although these assets may be making some contribution to earnings, they are destroying economic value because their returns are below the overall cost of the enterprise's invested capital.

Nonperforming and underperforming assets include such things as individual products, services, product lines, business lines, a plant, a warehouse, and even an entire business unit. If possible, a company should first try to fix the problems causing these assets to be nonperforming or underperforming. If in the end it is not possible to salvage these assets, then the company should rationalize them for the overall benefit of the organization.

In addition to nonperforming and underperforming assets, an enterprise needs to rationalize idle assets. This includes such items as an idle plant, an idle office building, and idle equipment. Rationalizing nonperforming, underperforming, and idle assets can generate substantial cash for an organization. These assets can be a vital lifeline for a company. During my career, when working with several companies on similar initiatives, we identified assets in these three categories worth hundreds of millions of dollars. The cash realized from these initiatives proved to be a valuable lifeline to these organizations because it strengthened their respective balance sheets. In one particular case, this lifeline ended up saving the company from being severely crippled.

Administrative Excellence

Excellence is doing a common thing in an uncommon way.[1]

———

—BOOKER T. WASHINGTON

ADMINISTRATIVE EXCELLENCE

Administrative execution excellence can add value to an organization. Unfortunately, this is an area that does not get as much attention as the other principles covered in this section of *Ascend to Greatness*. I believe that exceptional administrative execution can improve efficiencies and allow the company to grow faster and deliver products and/or services more productively. The responsibility for administrative excellence is usually distributed among many senior officers, including the chief financial officer, chief information officer, general counsel, chief people officer, chief administrative officer, chief risk officer, chief technology officer, and chief sustainability officer, as well as several others within the management ranks.

People excellence responsibilities normally fall under the leadership of the chief people officer. They are covered extensively in section one of *Ascend to Greatness* and thus will not be discussed again in this chapter. Administrative excellence, which is required in managing commercial contracts, was also briefly reviewed earlier in section three and thus won't be discussed in this chapter. The following is a list of some important administrative excellence tasks that need to be executed at an elite level in order to ascend to greatness:

- Manage risks well.
- Utilize zero-based budgeting.
- Establish global shared services.
- Maintain a nimble governance framework.
- Embrace environmental, social, and governance.
- Build a strong information technology infrastructure.
- Minimize or eliminate lengthy presentations.
- Close your books fast.

MANAGE RISKS WELL

Businesses, just like mountaineers, face a multitude of perils. These perils normally range from clearly identifiable known risks to completely unknown risks. Unknown risks, such as global shocks and disruptive innovation, can pose unmanageable threats to an enterprise. On the other hand, known risks such as foreign currencies, commodity cycles, cyberattacks, compliance matters, and acquisitions can all be managed with the right strategy, the right mechanisms, and strong execution.

For a company to manage risks well, it must first understand the various types of risks that could adversely affect it. As part of this understanding, it is helpful to separate and segment manageable known risks from unknown risks. Managing known risks typically includes the use of a standard tool kit with such items as transfer of risk, sharing of risk, acceptance of risk, and minimization of risk. Some risks can also be transferred and managed through insurance. Some risks can be shared through joint ventures. For example, insurance can be purchased to protect against cyberbreaches; hedges can be put in place to protect against currencies; and exceptional capabilities can be developed to achieve more consistent outcomes with acquisitions.

Unknown risks, however, require a different type of skill set because they first need to be identified early. An indispensable mechanism for identifying early on any unknown risks requires scanning the environment in real time. The ability to closely monitor external events is much easier today thanks to big data capabilities, the use of outside experts, and development of strong internal capabilities. The early identification of any unknown risks can provide an enterprise some precious time to develop and implement countermeasures to manage risks well before they become unmanageable.

Tool kit for managing risk. We just reviewed some tools for managing known risks and identifying early on any unknown risks. In addition, an organization should have other key risk mitigation capabilities in its tool kit, which we will now review. It starts with, first, the CEO possessing a risk mindset. Proactive leaders focused on various risks and risk mitigation strategies force these excellent habits down through their organizations. This is an area where the CEO can drive the risk culture of the company. Second, an enterprise should either form a risk committee or appoint a risk officer who is responsible for overseeing and managing certain risks. Third, an enterprise should use a complete tool for managing risk, such as enterprise risk management, or ERM. ERM has been around for years. Elite companies have sophisticated ERM processes in place that are guided by integrated risk maps.

UTILIZE ZERO-BASED BUDGETING

How should leaders approach budgeting in their organization? With the rise of activism, global shocks, and digital disruptions, a leader must maintain a relentless focus on expenses no matter how well he or she perceives the organization to be performing. Leaders who do not have a proactive and relentless focus on productivity and efficiency will most likely find themselves in a future situation where someone else takes the initiative for them. Think activist investor.

Leaders need to have a laser focus on costs. This means that they need to do a deep dive into their cost structure. No expense should be spared for this action. I believe a good place to start is with the cost of sales category and the SG&A (selling, general, and administrative) category. A productive tool that organizations can use to assist with their cost reduction measures is zero-based budgeting.

Zero-based budgeting was the brainchild of Pete Pyhrr, a Texas Instruments Inc. accounting manager, who introduced the concept about five decades ago as a way to significantly reduce costs for his company. In recent years, the concept was reenergized by 3G Capital Partners LP, a private equity group in Brazil. The firm enthusiastically embraced the tool and has used it to transform the cost structure and reduce the costs of its portfolio companies operating in the US food industry. To illustrate the power of this tool in the hands of 3G, let's examine an excerpt from an August 7, 2015, *Wall Street Journal* article titled "Big Food Sees Big Changes." The article compares the cost reduction efforts of 3G's Heinz business with those of Mondelez. The article points out that Heinz used 3G's tool to improve its profit margin by seven hundred basis points, as compared to Mondelez's announced three-hundred-basis-point improvement. Plus, Heinz reached its improvement goal in half the time frame announced by its competitor.

In its simplest form, zero-based budgeting requires managers to plan each year's budget as if they were starting from scratch. This practice forces discipline in an organization. It requires managers to break down spending to the lowest level of detail. Decisions are then made about proposed expenditures. It's important to note, however, that following this practice annually can be very time-consuming for the organization.

When our company faced the onset of the US financial crisis and later the European sovereign debt crisis, we implemented a simpler cost reduction approach. In our case, we examined all major spend categories and then asked the following question: Is it a nice-to-have expense or an absolutely critical expense? If the expense was absolutely required, then it had to be justified—through a robust dialogue—with unimpeachable facts. Otherwise, the expense was eliminated from the budget. Any cost of something that was merely nice to have was automatically eliminated. Although this was a painstaking and lengthy process to arrive at what was truly a critical cost, we discovered that many of the items initially deemed to be necessary were in reality not so vital.

Leaders can learn a great deal from successfully implementing zero-based budgeting. Although it may not be possible to implement zero-based budgeting with the same skill that 3G has brought to the table, any company operating in today's turbulent environment should not ignore this tool's potential impact. This is especially true for a proactive company seeking to lower its breakeven point and improve its competitive position. However, it's important always to balance the need to reduce costs with the objective of investing for the future.

ESTABLISH GLOBAL SHARED SERVICES

A global shared services center is an important capability for a multinational firm. India is currently the ideal place for these services, especially if a company needs services in engineering and information technology. The move to India not only should lower the overall cost of doing business but also may improve overall capabilities of the company given the highly educated and talented labor pool in the country.

In addition to India, there are several other shared services hot spots throughout the world, particularly where there is a high English literacy rate and a business-friendly atmosphere. Note that it's sometimes desirable to maintain two centers to avoid disruptions in business that may arise because of instability and other unforeseen changes in a key resource country. The global shared services center should report to the CIO, the CFO, or an executive vice president responsible for enterprise services.

Notwithstanding everything that I just said about establishing a shared services center offshore, I recommend that companies seriously consider repatriating their most strategic centers to the United States. This is particularly important when it comes to critical services. As we learned with the COVID-19 pandemic, being over-reliant on offshore locations brings risks.

MAINTAIN A NIMBLE GOVERNANCE FRAMEWORK

Elite companies have an established and well-functioning governance framework. For a governance framework to be effective, it must be built on ethical business conduct, strong enterprise internal controls, and pragmatism. When establishing and sustaining a strong governance framework, it's imperative that the policies and processes established do not overburden the organization. This is where being nimble and practical is critical.

Leading companies know how to balance the need for strong governance while at the same time avoiding the pitfalls of excessive regulation and bureaucratic policies. This is where culture and having the right people in the right positions is essential. Under a healthy culture, the right people understand that they are accountable and responsible. They understand that there's no value in excessive and burdensome policies and procedures that suffocate an organization.

EMBRACE ENVIRONMENTAL, SOCIAL, AND GOVERNANCE

Environmental, social, and governance—which is referred to as ESG— is something that elite companies fully embrace. ESG initiatives are paramount to a company's ascending to the summit of greatness. ESG is so critical that there's a separate class of investing called "sustainable investing," and it is now a focal point in activist campaigns. Leading CEOs clearly understand the importance of ESG and they receive regular reports and metrics on their effectiveness. We will cover all these elements in this section, starting with environmental.

Leading companies ensure that they are respectful of the environment in everything they do throughout their business. They are committed to sustainable practices that are designed to improve the planet. These companies take substantive actions to minimize adverse environmental effects, and they conserve natural resources through practical engineering design and processes. They focus on reduction of carbon emissions, on increasing renewable energy, and on recycling materials. They also develop innovative product solutions that support environmental sustainability. This means recyclable packaging and materials that minimize waste, product designs that reduce energy use, and reduction of water consumption and waste. It also means improving air quality by installing new equipment and redesigning manufacturing processes.

The other two parts of ESG—social responsibility and corporate governance—are also vital to the overall success of an organization. Social policies include diversity, equity, and inclusion. This means that the company is focused on fostering and supporting diversity efforts throughout the enterprise. Social responsibility also includes excellent employee health and safety practices. Elite companies ensure that their employees are protected to the highest standard possible. This means they have ongoing robust training programs, supply the right protective equipment, conduct risk assessments, and design work processes that incorporate health and safety measures. It also means empowering employees to stop their own work when a hazard is detected, actively enforcing accident prevention and reporting policies, and promoting lifestyle choices through wellness programs.

With respect to governance, this includes policies on board diversity, integrity and ethical business conduct, independence of directors, and many other important elements that help build an exceptional company.

BUILD A STRONG INFORMATION TECHNOLOGY INFRASTRUCTURE

An organization's current state of digital readiness is paramount to achieving elite status. That's why leading companies consistently invest in building a robust information technology infrastructure. It is essential that organizations, at a minimum, keep pace with changing technologies and markets. A strong information technology infrastructure is the backbone to running an elite company. This vital capability was front and center with the coronavirus pandemic as armies of workers were sent home to perform their duties and markets shifted to e-commerce. The companies that invested heavily in this capability operated and functioned well.

Building a strong information technology infrastructure means implementing a one-instance ERP global computer system (if possible) to run the business. It also means providing employees with the most up-to-date technology needed to execute prongs of the company strategy; having the appropriate cybersecurity tools available to prevent or at least detect intrusions; having an appropriate computer disaster recovery process in place; and having in place numerous other support functions necessary to smooth operation.

MINIMIZE OR ELIMINATE LENGTHY PRESENTATIONS

One of my favorite mechanisms covered in section four is Amazon's narrative or six-pager. Honeywell used a similar mechanism under its former CEO David M. Cote, who called it a three-to-four-page executive summary. When I was CEO, I started using a similar process as Mr. Cote. I still use this process today as an adviser. The reason I started the practice of an executive summary is because over the years I found lengthy PowerPoint presentations to be ineffective. On the other hand, the executive summary mechanism turned out to be very helpful. For example, I learned more about how the executives think in those summaries than perhaps I would have if we had stayed solely with the presentations. The executive summaries often revealed the critical thinkers and exposed those who were not.

In his insightful book *Winning Now, Winning Later*, Mr. Cote perfectly captures my sentiment about the lengthy presentations driven by bullet points that are the standard at most organizations: "Each July our businesses made presentations to the CEO. ... Rather than choosing goals thoughtfully, they picked ambitious targets they thought would please their bosses, without regard for whether the business could realistically achieve them. ... They threw around lofty language and piled on hundreds of pages of charts and tables … without much critical analysis. … One of my top priorities as CEO was to eradicate the BS and reinvent planning. … I required teams presenting to me to write a three-to-four-page executive summary that highlighted the basic plan. That document would allow us to cut through the pages of obfuscating charts and bullet points."[2]

Amazon follows a similar approach as Honeywell. Here is what the narrative or six-pager is all about: It starts with Amazon banning all PowerPoint presentations—a great move! In place of these, they have implemented the potent six-pager mechanism for making meetings more productive, focused, and constructive. At the beginning of an important meeting to review a proposed project, attendees sit and carefully read and study a six-page written document prepared by the sponsor. The objective is to have attendees absorb, understand, and reflect on the project before engaging in a robust dialogue about it.

I recommend that companies consider either curtailing lengthy presentations or completely eliminating them. The presentations should be replaced by some form of document as mentioned above. For companies that want to continue using PowerPoint presentations for critical projects, I recommend a paradigm shift. Use shorter presentations that are more focused. These presentations should be augmented with an executive summary. This forces the presenters to clearly articulate their position on the topic, and it instills a certain discipline in the organization.

CLOSE YOUR BOOKS FAST

The world-class standard for closing the books of an enterprise is one day. Although it's not imperative that all enterprises close their books in one day, there are compelling reasons to close the books as fast as possible, for example, in five days or less. The current best practice for closing the books is two to three days. With tools such as Lean, global consolidation software, modern ERP systems, artificial intelligence, and numerous other powerful technologies, a company has no substantive excuse for not closing its books in five days or less. This should include producing financial statements and performing high-level analysis of results.

Closing the books efficiently can reduce the amount of time that the finance group has to devote to this administratively burdensome task. Furthermore, it allows these resources to be more productively utilized in improving and growing the business. Another benefit is that senior management will have the right information about performance in their hands earlier so that appropriate actions can be taken. The ability to accelerate the closing process has never been easier with standard processes and new technologies now available in the marketplace.

Metrics and Mechanisms

Introduction

Building mechanisms is one of the CEO's most powerful but
least understood and most rarely employed tool.[1]

———

—JIM COLLINS

JIM COLLINS AND MECHANISMS

The great author and business guru Jim Collins brought mechanisms to
the forefront in his extensive body of work. In an article on his website
titled "Forget Strategy, Build Mechanisms Instead," Mr. Collins stresses
the importance of mechanisms. Of course, Mr. Collins is not literally
saying to forget strategy; he's simply emphasizing that it is vital to build
and implement powerful mechanisms.

I was first exposed to mechanisms as a CEO when I attended three
Good to Great dialogue sessions at Jim Collins's lab in Boulder, Colorado.
Mr. Collins is a thought leader on mechanisms and how potent they can be
in helping an organization realize its vision. He has consistently stressed
his main point about mechanisms: they help enterprises turn their goals
and objectives into concrete results. More specifically, in his article on
mechanisms, he talks about "the task that the CEO is uniquely positioned
to do: designing the mechanisms that reinforce and give life to the

company's core purpose and stimulate the company to change." He goes on to write, "Building mechanisms is one of the CEO's most powerful but least understood and most rarely employed tools. Along with figuring out what the company stands for and pushing it to understand what it's really good at, building mechanisms is the CEO's role—the leader as architect."[2] All CEOs need to take to heart the insightful words of Jim Collins, because without the right mechanisms, the journey to sustained greatness gets even more arduous.

I'd like to make a couple of additional salient points on mechanisms. First, it's not necessary to implement hundreds of mechanisms. What's more critical is that any mechanisms you choose are very specific to the organization, that they are powerful and can't be easily subverted, and that they are enforced. I would recommend that the senior leadership team, along with input from the global leadership team, develop what works best for the enterprise. There's no right number of mechanisms, thus it's difficult to provide specific guidance. What's important is to ensure that that there are enough of the right mechanisms implemented to effectively drive performance.

Mr. Collins also advocates patience, because mechanisms sometimes have unintended consequences. Some mechanisms may need to be changed or even eliminated if they don't achieve their intended purpose.

METRICS AND MECHANISMS NEED TO DRIVE THE FOUNDATIONAL PILLARS AND RELATED CORE PRINCIPLES

Metrics and mechanisms need to underpin and drive the three foundational pillars and the seventeen core principles. I would argue that it's impossible to properly implement my elite enterprise model and achieve enduring greatness without the proper metrics and mechanisms. Section four includes some valuable metrics and mechanisms that I believe should be considered by organizations intent on climbing to the summit of elite. You will find many of these metrics and mechanisms at elite companies.

Metrics are well understood and are utilized extensively in just about everything that occurs in the business world. Mechanisms, however, are another matter. My experience and research has shown that some CEOs do not use mechanisms as frequently as perhaps they should. Enterprises that underutilize mechanisms are likely losing out on some important benefits that could be derived from both a performance and culture viewpoint.

In this section, we will explore some essential metrics and mechanisms related to the three foundational pillars. It's important to note that the metrics and mechanisms outlined in this section are not meant to be an all-inclusive list; the purpose is simply to illustrate some that I have used and observed in use. In addition, with respect to metrics, it is imperative that the trajectory of the enterprise be assessed over a specific time frame, usually matching that of the high-performance plan and the vision. Knowing the trends is critical to determining the effectiveness of implementing my elite enterprise model.

Each chapter in this section is segmented into two parts. Part A covers metrics, and part B covers mechanisms, both of which are reviewed in chapters 18 through 20. The following chapters underpin the three foundational pillars:

- Chapter 18. Leadership Metrics and Mechanisms
- Chapter 19. Strategy Metrics and Mechanisms
- Chapter 20. Execution Metrics and Mechanisms

CHAPTER EIGHTEEN

Leadership Metrics and Mechanisms

The secret to my success is that we have gone to exceptional lengths
to hire the best people in the world. And when you're in a field
where the dynamic range is 25 to 1, boy, does it pay off.[1]

———

—STEVE JOBS

PART A: LEADERSHIP METRICS

The right metrics are indispensable when building an enduring elite
company. Here are some essential metrics relative to the foundational
pillar of leadership:

- percent of key positions filled by the right people
- talent acquisition success rate and failure rate (percent)
- leadership development success rate and failure rate (percent)
- thought leadership ranking among peers
- talent turnover rate (percent)
- talent retention rate (percent)
- employee satisfaction rating
- ranking among best places to work

- CEO ranking
- percent of employees who can repeat verbatim the core philosophy.

PERCENT OF KEY POSITIONS FILLED BY THE RIGHT PEOPLE

For the executive leadership team (ELT), the percent of key positions filled by the right people needs to be consistently at 100 percent. That should be the benchmark. For some enterprises, this may be difficult to achieve. However, given that the ELT tends to be relatively small—somewhere in the range of eight to twelve people—the goal of 100 percent is not unrealistic.

With respect to the global leadership team where all positions of the members are deemed to be key, that number needs to be at least 90 percent, preferably greater. This is a critical metric; if not enough of the key positions are filled by the right people, the organization will have difficulty achieving and sustaining elite status.

TALENT ACQUISITION SUCCESS RATE
AND FAILURE RATE (PERCENT)

As was discussed earlier, in section one, employee selection and hiring must deliver strong results. A key metric in this regard is to monitor both the percent of success rate and percent of failure relative to new hires. The trend lines of these numbers need to be closely monitored.

Each organization will have to establish parameters for what it considers to be a best-of-class success rate when it comes to talent acquisition. It will have to do the same with failures. When analyzing both success and failure, groups should be segmented by type of position, for example, executive, vice president, director, manager, various professional ranks, and entry level.

LEADERSHIP DEVELOPMENT SUCCESS RATE
AND FAILURE RATE (PERCENT)

The leadership development success and failure rates are just as important as the hiring rates. To achieve enduring greatness, a company must execute the talent management and leadership development principle at a world-class level. Remember, the people you are dealing with here represent the pipeline of future leaders. In addition, the company should pay special attention to individuals identified on the watch list as being high-potential talent.

The trend lines here also need to be closely monitored; it is vital to understand the effectiveness of training, development, and the succession planning processes. Each organization will have to establish parameters for what it considers to be a best-of-class success rate when it comes to leadership development. It will have to do the same for failures. When analyzing both success and failure, each group should be segmented by type of position, for example, executive, vice president, director, and manager.

THOUGHT LEADERSHIP RANKING AMONG PEERS

This industry-specific metric may not apply to some enterprises. The main thing to understand on this metric is where the leadership team stands relative to peers. What boards do the team members serve on? What national conferences have invited them to speak? What technical papers and/or books have they published? In the professional services industry, this can be an important metric.

TALENT TURNOVER RATE (PERCENT)

This standard metric has been employed for generations. Turnover can be either voluntary or involuntary. When it comes to measuring your employee turnover rate, it is fundamental to understand the reasons why people leave voluntarily. This insight is invaluable to improving both the talent acquisition process and talent development process.

Each organization will have to establish parameters for what it considers to be a world-class low turnover rate of team members. When doing this, groups should be segmented by type of position, for example, executive, vice president, director, manager, various professional ranks, and entry level.

TALENT RETENTION RATE (PERCENT)

Commensurate with understanding talent turnover is the knowledge of what drives talent retention rates. Obviously, these two metrics work together to help the company understand turnover and retention. The talent retention rate is a standard metric that has been employed for generations. When it comes to measuring your employee retention rate, it is vital to consider the reasons why people stay. This insight is invaluable to improving both the hiring process and the talent development process.

Each organization will have to establish parameters for what it considers to be a best-of-class success rate when it comes to talent retention. When doing this, each group should be segmented by type of position, for example, executive, vice president, director, manager, various professional ranks, and entry level.

EMPLOYEE SATISFACTION RATING

Employee happiness or employee satisfaction is critical to the success of an organization. Happy employees are usually productive and committed to the cause. There are proven methods for measuring employee satisfaction and happiness, including third-party surveys. What's important when choosing one for your company is to design a satisfaction survey that provides an appropriate level of insight into what is actually transpiring inside the organization.

RANKING AMONG BEST PLACES TO WORK

Rankings of this nature have become popular over the past decade. Some companies invest considerable resources to ensure they are included in the rankings. They do this because talented people usually want to work for great organizations. Although these rankings can be beneficial, what is really crucial is the culture of the company and how people are treated.

CEO RANKING

CEO rankings are difficult to measure. One source to consider is Glassdoor.com, where employees rank their CEO. Another way to measure CEO ranking is to determine what other boards the CEO serves on. Is the company for which he or she works an elite company? Institutional investors also can provide feedback on how they rank CEOs.

When ranking a CEO, however, one must carefully guard against attribution, which can provide inaccurate or biased information. Through attribution, studies have shown that some CEOs get either too much credit or not enough credit. The same goes for negative feedback. So, do not fall into the attribution trap. When ranking a CEO, base your ranking on facts. CEO ranking criteria need to be both quantitative and qualitative. Again, each organization will have to set the parameters for how it is going to measure its CEO.

PERCENT OF EMPLOYEES WHO CAN REPEAT VERBATIM THE CORE PHILOSOPHY

Although this may sound like a simple expectation, I find it amazing that some employees in certain companies are unable to repeat verbatim and without hesitation their organization's purpose, core values, and vision. This is something that can be easily measured and also easily fixed if it's a problem. The result should always be 100 percent.

PART B: LEADERSHIP MECHANISMS

Just as the right metrics are indispensable to building an enduring company, key mechanisms are vital for the same reason. It is imperative that enterprises have in place an adequate number of mechanisms designed to improve the company, provide early warning signs, and help keep the organization on the right path to excellence.

Here are some examples of essential mechanisms that enterprises should consider implementing relative to the foundational pillar of leadership:

- objectives and key results
- hiring around the core values
- linking core values to performance appraisals
- a "future leaders" watch list
- a code of ethical business conduct
- after-action reviews
- Google's 70/20/10 rule
- Google's rule of seven
- a quarterly report on the state of the business
- a business watch list
- Amazon's fictional press release
- a CEO internal blog
- allowing for a period of inner reflection
- Wegmans' Ask Bob initiative
- awards in recognition of excellence.

OBJECTIVES AND KEY RESULTS

My favorite mechanism, one that applies across all three foundational pillars, is objectives and key results (OKRs). OKRs have their origins in the tech sector; specifically, they are attributed to Andy Grove of Intel. Google uses OKRs extensively. In the book *How Google Works*, the authors provide examples of how Google uses OKRs. They also provide guidelines on how OKRs should be established, including the following advice and statements:

- OKRs should marry the big-picture objective with a highly measurable key result, that is, a strategic goal measured against a concrete goal.
- OKRs should be a stretch to achieve and should be practically unachievable. Almost everyone does them. Doing them allows people or teams to judge their performance honestly.
- OKRs are not comprehensive; they are reserved for areas that need special focus and that won't be reached without extra effort.
- As the company grows, the most important OKRs shift from individuals to teams. This doesn't mean that individuals stop doing them, but rather that team OKRs become the most important means to maintaining focus on big tasks.
- An OKR-driven culture helps keep people from chasing competitors. If employees are focused on a well-conceived set of OKRs, they know where they need to go and don't have time to worry about the competition.

In addition to the above guidance, it's important to remember that the objectives part of an OKR needs be a qualitative statement that is pithy and inspirational. The key results part of an OKR needs to be quantitative, that is, must be measurable. OKRs are a powerful mechanism that can be implemented to propel an enterprise to the summit. I have developed some clear examples of OKRs that I utilized during my career, as well as several others that I have identified from other companies. Here is a list of some relevant OKRs that should be considered:

- **Increase equipment utilization rate from x percent to y percent or by x basis points.** This OKR is relevant in the equipment rental business or in businesses that have a high concentration of equipment that is necessary to carry out a service or produce a product. Incremental utilization rates usually translate to higher profitability.

- **Increase rental rates from x percent to y percent or by x basis points.** In businesses where the economic engine is the rental rates, this is a vital OKR to utilize because of its potential sizable impact on profitability.

- **Increase labor utilization rate from x percent to y percent or by x basis points.** This is relevant in professional services. Higher labor utilization rates normally translate to increased profitability.

- **Grow free cash flow by x percent or from x dollars to y dollars.** Ultimately, an enterprise needs to be measured by its ability to continuously generate free cash flows and grow its cash reserves. This is a wonderful team goal.

- **Reduce the cash conversion cycle by x days or from x days to y days.** The cash conversion cycle measures the speed (velocity) of cash and working capital efficiency. The lower the number, the better. Nirvana is achieving a negative number. Any improvement (less days) generates cash for the organization. The formula is outlined in chapter 15. This is an incredible mechanism that really works!

- **Improve the time to complete a customer installation from x hours, days, or weeks to y hours, days, or weeks.** In the construction and home improvement markets, this is a critical driver of profitability and customer satisfaction, and it can provide a competitive advantage. Thus, if you can reduce the number of hours, days, or weeks—and for some large projects even months— then you can improve your company's profitability and customer satisfaction. The large home construction companies continuously strive to reduce the number of days to build a home, and they have made notable progress in reducing the time it takes to complete one. If tailored properly, this type of OKR can be applied to just about any business.

- **Raise employee satisfaction scores by x percent (Google).** There is usually a direct correlation between high employee satisfaction and performance. Thus, a key OKR is to strive to improve the overall score by a stated percent. This OKR applies to all businesses.

- **Roll out a product in a specific number of countries (Google).** This is a straightforward OKR that can be easily measured yet is very effective in scaling a business.

HIRING AROUND THE CORE VALUES

Leading organizations use the mechanism of hiring around the core values to sustain a healthy culture. People who align well with the core values of the company will ultimately help drive exceptional performance.

LINKING CORE VALUES TO PERFORMANCE APPRAISALS

Just as it's important to hire around the core values, it is likewise vital to link them to performance appraisals. Once people are hired, it is crucial that they reflect the same values day by day. This mechanism helps sustain the core values and culture of the company.

A "FUTURE LEADERS" WATCH LIST

An indispensable component of the leadership development program should be the early identification of outsized talent. An excellent mechanism to use for identifying such high-potential individuals is a watch list of future leaders. Once these individuals have been identified, the company should put a robust development plan into place for these people as part of the succession planning process. These potential future leaders need to be closely monitored and mentored.

A CODE OF ETHICAL BUSINESS CONDUCT

It is hard to imagine a company operating in today's global business environment without some type of business conduct policy (code). Elite companies separate themselves from perhaps all other enterprises by focusing intensely on this particular mechanism to ensure it has teeth. There should be zero tolerance for any violations of the code—regardless of the position of the violator—and action must be swift. Leading companies devote substantial time and resources to embedding the code in the DNA of the organization because this is the cornerstone of a strong governance framework and a healthy culture.

AFTER-ACTION REVIEWS

After-action reviews are a potent mechanism for learning, taking action, and guarding against attribution. The clear objective of using this mechanism is simply to discover what happened and then to take action to ensure lessons learned are implemented. Such a review ensures that failures are not repeated and that the factors leading to success are sustained.

GOOGLE'S 70/20/10 RULE

In the book *How Google Works*, Eric Schmidt and Jonathan Rosenberg explain how the 70/20/10 rule works: "Our rule for resource allocation: 70 percent of resources dedicated to the core business, 20 percent on emerging, and 10 percent on new. ... While the ... rule ensured that our core business would always get the bulk of the resources and that the promising, up-and-coming areas would also get investment, it also ensured that the crazy ideas got some support too, and were protected from the inevitable budget cuts."[2] This is a marvelous mechanism that instills discipline and focus in the organization.

GOOGLE'S RULE OF SEVEN

In *How Google Works*, Schmidt and Rosenberg also note just how hard organizational design is, particularly when a company grows in size. To put aside some preconceived notions about how a company should be organized, they stress adherence to a few key principles: "First, keep it flat. ... Smart creatives ... want to get things done and need direct access to decision-makers." The authors go on to discuss the importance of the rule of seven in terms of the way they organized the company: "The Google version suggests that managers have a *minimum* of seven direct reports. ... We still have formal organizations charts, but the rule (which is really a guideline, since there are exceptions) forces flatter charts with less managerial oversight and more employee freedom. With that many direct reports—most managers have a lot more than seven—there's simply isn't time to micromanage."[3]

A QUARTERLY REPORT ON THE STATE OF THE BUSINESS

Sometimes the most basic mechanisms are the most critical. One such mechanism that stands out is the quarterly report to the board on the state of the business that's prepared by the CEO. As soon as I was appointed CEO, I implemented this mechanism. That's because I see it as essential for a CEO to provide his or her perspective and insight regarding the state of the enterprise. This report should capture succinctly the state of the company as seen through the eyes of the CEO. It puts together in one place everything that truly matters. During periods of high turbulence, I recommend doing a monthly report.

Ideally, the report should be in two parts: a written section that summarizes all salient points augmented by a charts and graphics section. Some CEOs prefer that this report be entirely text with no graphics. They believe that the financial information is self-evident in all the various reports provided to the board. No matter which format is adopted, what is critical is that the CEO captures the essence of the current state of the enterprise and makes sound predictions for the future. From the board perspective, this is an indispensable document that can assist them in better assessing the performance of the CEO and senior team. Sometimes boards can obtain insight into how a CEO thinks and approaches the job by reviewing this report.

An example of this mechanism can be found at Google. In the book *How Google Works*, the authors Schmidt and Rosenberg emphasize just how important the quarterly report is to the management, the board, and employees. They go on to say that the prepared slides are presented at company-wide meetings and that most of the board letter is communicated in an email.

A BUSINESS WATCH LIST

This mechanism has broad applicability. The watch list is a mechanism utilized to monitor underperforming business units, branches, and product lines, and/or whatever other part of the business that needs special attention from the CEO and possibly even the board. When a business unit is added to the watch list, its members fall under intense scrutiny, including having to meet with senior management and, at times, even with the board. You only get off the watch list by performing.

AMAZON'S FICTIONAL PRESS RELEASE

This is another wonderful mechanism that I have used in my career. Amazon uses it well with their six-pager mechanism. Amazon employees are asked to write a fictional press release that accurately describes the project they are presenting. The fictional release forces employees to really think about the project and how to communicate their vision.

I first learned about this mechanism back in 2008 when I attended a *Good to Great* dialogue session with Jim Collins at his lab in Boulder, Colorado. I was there with my executive leadership team to develop and implement our *Good to Great* framework to transform and modernize our company. Collins asked each participant to select a newspaper and to write a headline and the corresponding article about something some twenty years out in the future. This was very helpful in developing our long-term vision for the company. I recommend using it for both near-term projects (as Amazon does) and developing a long-term vision.

A CEO INTERNAL BLOG

CEOs are increasingly receiving comments from employees through various platforms. This is in addition to the traditional channels. With the digital transformation of enterprises, a new mechanism is available today for direct feedback: the CEO internal blog. A *Wall Street Journal* of February 3, 2020, captures this well: "At Kimberly-Clark ... employees can address Chief Executive ... via his internal blog, a mechanism set up by his predecessor. ... According to the company, ... none get deleted as long as they follow a few ground rules: Posters must name themselves, refrain from disclosing confidential information and be real, but be nice."

ALLOWING FOR A PERIOD OF INNER REFLECTION

Take the time on a regular basis for a sustained period of inner reflection. It is imperative for a leader to have meaningful time for critical thinking. The period allocated for inner reflection needs to be meaningful too, usually several days per month. It is vital to step back and see the bigger picture through a different lens and then use that insight to take the crucial next steps. The result of inner reflection should be new perspectives gained and immediately actionable decisions. For this mechanism to be effective, the leader needs to be disciplined. It is best to preplan the days, block them off on your calendar, and stick to your plan.

WEGMANS' "ASK BOB" INITIATIVE

The elite grocery chain Wegmans has a mechanism called the Ask Bob initiative. As explained earlier in *Ascend to Greatness*, this mechanism is an open line of communication between the company's fifty thousand employees and its senior vice president of operations, Bob Farr. Farr takes pride in reviewing every email he gets from employees and personalizing every response he sends back.

AWARDS IN RECOGNITION OF EXCELLENCE

Great companies take the time to recognize excellence through a high-profile internal awards ceremony. I've seen this mechanism work well at several companies. It is a strong practice that centers on having an annual awards dinner that is high on energy and enthusiasm. Some of the more common recognition awards are for innovation, the best-performing business, perseverance, continuous improvement, and collaboration. An important benefit of this mechanism is that it reinforces the culture of the company.

CHAPTER NINETEEN

Strategy Metrics and Mechanisms

Simple can be harder than complex. You have to work hard to get your thinking clean to make it simple. But it's worth it in the end because once you get there, you can move mountains.[1]

—STEVE JOBS

PART A: STRATEGY METRICS

The right metrics are indispensable to building an enduring company. Many of the metrics outlined in this chapter equally apply to the foundational pillar of execution. For ease of discussion and reference, and to avoid duplication, the metrics that are covered under strategy will not be replicated later under execution.

Here are some essential metrics under the foundational pillar of strategy (and execution) that need to be closely monitored:

- return on invested capital
- free cash flow
- year-over-year sales growth percentage
- year-over-year earnings before interest and taxes (EBIT) growth percentage

- year over-year EPS growth percentage
- year-over-year earnings before interest, taxes, depreciation, and amortization (EBITDA) growth percentage
- EBITDA conversion ratio
- compound growth rate
- margin growth rate
- planning and forecasting accuracy rate (percentage)
- stock price relative to the S&P 500
- stock price relative to peer group
- price/earnings ratio and expansion trend
- net capital expenditure (CapEx)-to-sales percentage
- enterprise value/revenues multiple
- enterprise value/EBITDA multiple.

RETURN ON INVESTED CAPITAL

The return on the amount of capital invested in the business must exceed the cost capital in order to generate positive economic value. If the cost of capital exceeds the return on invested capital, then economic value is being destroyed. Thus, this is a fundamental metric that every company needs to utilize because consistently destroying economic value is not sustainable. Whereas, generating positive economic value can take a company to new heights, particularly when it's done consistently over a long horizon.

Generating high returns on invested capital can be even more difficult when the business requires substantial investment in capital expenditures to grow and sustain the business. Likewise, if a company relies heavily on acquisitions for growth, cumulatively generating high returns can also be challenging. Under these scenarios, capital allocation strategies and execution must be exceptional to achieve and sustain returns on invested capital that exceed the cost of capital.

FREE CASH FLOW

Free cash flow should be the primary focus of all enterprises, there's nothing more important. In the end, free cash flow is what drives valuations. Free cash flow is calculated by taking cash flow from operations, less capital expenditures, and less dividends. However, if the dividend has a highly discretionary element to it, it can be excluded from the calculation.

Free cash flow as a percent of sales should also be measured. In addition, the incremental growth in free cash flow is vital and it should be measured annually as well as over a certain time period.

YEAR-OVER-YEAR SALES GROWTH PERCENTAGE

If a business is not growing, it will eventually become irrelevant and possibly even disappear in the future. Thus, year-over-year growth in sales is important to the long-term viability of an enterprise.

When measuring sales growth, it's important to analyze the number and separate all its key components. First, the difference between organic and inorganic must be determined, both are vital. It's also relevant to know the effect of foreign currency translation. As a subset of organic growth, the various elements within this category need to be also understood. These elements of growth include such items as price increases, product mix, and volume.

YEAR-OVER-YEAR EBIT GROWTH PERCENTAGE

Just as growth in sales is important, so is the relative growth of EBIT or operating income. One aspect of this metric, is to determine what percent of incremental sales from scaling the business are actually translating to earnings growth. If a greater percent is achieved, it can demonstrate the earnings power of scaling strategies. Other key aspects of operating income growth include: price increases, product mix, foreign currency translation, contribution between organic and inorganic growth, cost control initiatives, and various other elements that have a bearing on profitability and its year-over-year growth.

YEAR-OVER-YEAR EPS GROWTH PERCENTAGE

Earnings per share (EPS) growth is a particularly crucial metric for public companies. This is what analyst use to set expectations for the quarter and the year. It's a main driver of stock price. Even for private companies this should be viewed as an important metric, along with margins and free cash flow growth.

YEAR-OVER-YEAR EBITDA GROWTH PERCENTAGE

Earnings before interest, taxes, depreciation, and amortization (EBITDA) is a key cash flow metric used by commercial and investment bankers in viewing the financial health of an organization. The growth in EBITDA as a percent is vital in establishing both valuations for enterprises as well as determining their ability to cover debt.

EBITDA CONVERSION RATIO

As just stated, EBITDA is extensively used in valuations. Equally important is how much of the EBITDA is converted into cash flow. The formula is: cash flow from operations/EBITDA. This conversion ratio measures the efficiency of a company to turn EBITDA into cash. A low number usually means that the company is inefficient with such things as working capital.

COMPOUND GROWTH RATE

In addition to measuring annual growth in revenues, earnings, and free cash flow, it's equally vital to also measure their compound growth rate over an established period of three years, five years, ten years, and even longer. Consistent stream of growing revenues, earnings, and free cash flow typically means that the enterprise is being successful in its markets. It means that its flywheel is gaining momentum.

MARGIN GROWTH RATE

Margin growth is critical to generating long-term shareholder wealth. Margin expansion often results in greater cash flow growth, a higher price/earnings ratio, and a higher stock value. Thus, it's essential to calculate the growth in gross margins, operating margins, and net margins.

PLANNING AND FORECASTING ACCURACY RATE (PERCENTAGE)

The actual performance to plan metric is universally used. It's one of the most basic but yet necessary metrics that needs to be closely monitored. That's because the current year operating plan is an integral part of the three-year strategic plan, which is a building block to achieving the vision of the company over a stated time frame. Planning and forecasting accuracy is critical to the success of a leader, especially to a CEO of a public company. Poor planning and forecasting have been the demise of many CEOs because of their inability to project future earnings with a certain level of confidence. Missing analyst estimates is usually a good way to have investors and the board lose confidence in a leader. That's why the accuracy rate of the planning and forecasting system must be monitored quarterly, annually, and over a long horizon.

STOCK PRICE RELATIVE TO THE S&P 500

A robust metric for measuring the performance of an enterprise is the comparison to the S&P 500 over a certain time horizon. This should be viewed annually and cumulatively over a period of time, preferably ten years.

STOCK PRICE RELATIVE TO PEER GROUP

In addition to comparing the enterprise to the S&P 500, the other comparison is to the peer group. The relative performance to the peer group is obviously critical to measuring success of the company.

PRICE/EARNINGS RATIO AND EXPANSION TREND

Elite companies usually are assigned best-of-class price/earnings (PE) ratio. The higher the ratio, the more shareholder value is created. It's essential to not only examine the current PE ratio but also the trend over a stated time period. Obviously, an increasing ratio shows that market is rewarding the performance of the company and believes it has a bright future.

NET CAPEX-TO-SALES PERCENTAGE

Measuring what percent of sales or revenues goes to CapEx is an excellent indicator of the capital intensity and capital efficiency of the enterprise. This metric needs to be combined with the free cash flow metric to better understand what impact CapEx is having on the financial performance of the enterprise. In addition, the long-term trend of this percent needs to be monitored as well.

ENTERPRISE VALUE/REVENUES MULTIPLE

The enterprise value to revenues multiple is often used to determine the potential value of a company in connection with the acquisition process. It's also used as a benchmark ratio to measure performance against peer companies in the same industry.

ENTERPRISE VALUE/EBITDA MULTIPLE

The enterprise value to EBITDA multiple is a popular valuation tool that is used extensively by investors, especially when comparing companies within the same industry.

PART B: STRATEGY MECHANISMS

Just as the right metrics are indispensable to building an enduring company, key mechanisms are equally critical for the same reason. It is essential that enterprises have in place mechanisms that are designed to improve the company, provide early warning signs, and help keep the organization on the right path to excellence.

The following are some examples of mechanisms that enterprises should consider relative to the foundational pillar of strategy:

- objectives and key results
- new products to total revenues
- innovation challenge
- 3M's 15 percent innovation rule
- protecting the house
- Jim Collins's red flag mechanisms
- Roper's cash return on investment
- Honeywell's tech symposium
- Honeywell's practice of holding fixed costs constant
- investing in the future.

OBJECTIVES AND KEY RESULTS

As was outlined in chapter 18, my favorite mechanism, one that applies across all three foundational pillars, is objectives and key results (OKRs). OKRs have their origins in the tech sector; they are specifically attributed to Andy Grove of Intel. OKRs are a powerful mechanism that can be implemented to propel an enterprise to the summit. Following is a list of some relevant OKRs that should be considered:

- **Improve the planning/forecasting accuracy rate from x percent to y percent or by x basis points.** As explained earlier, planning/ forecasting accuracy is paramount in today's environment, particularly if the enterprise is public. A critical OKR would focus the organization on improving the accuracy rate either by a certain percent or by x number of basis points.

- **Improve the percent of new products to total revenues from x percent to y percent or by x basis points.** New products are the lifeblood of an organization. For some companies, consistently achieving a certain percentage of new products to overall revenues is vital to their very existence. This OKR focuses the enterprise on achieving an improvement, something over a historically achieved percent. This OKR demonstrates a commitment to both innovation and continuous improvement.

- **Improve the company's investment grade rating by one notch.** The three rating agencies—S&P, Moody, and Fitch—all use a rating system to grade a company's debt. Using S&P as an example, a one-notch improvement could be to go from a BBB+ rating to an A–. This falls under the "protect the house" type of mechanism (see below).

NEW PRODUCTS TO TOTAL REVENUES

A strong mechanism for stimulating product innovation is to target a certain range of revenues that need to be derived from new products every year. This can be accomplished by establishing a range, from x percent to y percent, that needs to be contributed to total revenues. This mechanism requires a focused effort on innovation and the customer—all good things.

INNOVATION CHALLENGE

Innovation is a must for a company if it is to endure for generations. A mechanism that gets strong results in this area is the annual innovation challenge. I've seen this mechanism generate some amazing ideas that ultimately paid huge dividends for the company. With an innovation challenge, the various teams in the organization are each challenged to present their innovation idea in a shark tank type of setting. Winners are rewarded in various ways, including with recognition, stock awards, and most importantly, funding for their winning idea. Using the innovation challenge creates energy in the organization and stimulates ideas that can, at times, truly benefit the enterprise.

3M'S 15 PERCENT INNOVATION RULE

3M is an innovative company, and their 15 percent rule is a reason for this. The company invites employees to devote approximately 15 percent of their time to experimenting or working on projects they want to pursue. This mechanism has yielded numerous innovative products. The 15 percent rule also benefits the company in another way by promoting the strong innovative culture of the company. 3M's rule is similar to Google's, which was covered under the 70/20/10 leadership mechanism.

PROTECTING THE HOUSE

Enterprises that value their investment grade rating need to utilize this mechanism. The "protect the house" mechanism requires the company to set a target investment grade rating. When doing so, the organization needs to select either a specific rating, such as A− (using S&P) or a range from BBB+ to A− (using S&P). A wider range can also be used. The fundamental point is that if the mechanism is to be effective, it must have teeth. That is, once the rating is set, it must be sacrosanct.

JIM COLLINS'S RED FLAG MECHANISMS

Jim Collins uses the term *red flag mechanisms* in his *Good to Great* diagnostic tool. Here is what he says about red flag mechanisms: "We have red flag mechanisms that bring brutal facts to our attention, and force us to confront those facts, no matter how uncomfortable."[2] I believe that a strong red flag mechanism is achieved by building enterprise risk indicators that alert the enterprise to coming storms as early as possible. These risk indicators must then force the company to confront those facts and take proactive countermeasures.

ROPER'S CASH RETURN ON INVESTMENT

Roper Technology utilizes a powerful mechanism called cash return on investment, or CRI. As explained earlier in *Ascend to Greatness*, Roper's performance has been world class, as good as that of any of the top-tier companies. Their CRI mechanism is one of the reasons for their extraordinary performance. CRI-based principles pervade everything the company does. It instills discipline in the organization and keeps the entire workforce well aligned with the company's business model recipe elements.

HONEYWELL'S TECH SYMPOSIUM

In his insightful book *Winning Now, Winning Later*, former CEO of Honeywell David M. Cote talks about the company's effective tech symposium. He states that as part of Honeywell's efforts to promote growth and improve their innovation processes, he and his executive team created a global event called a tech symposium. Annually, hundreds of Honeywell's top marketing and technology executives throughout the company gather to network and collaborate on innovation and technology. Such a symposium can be a potent mechanism if utilized properly. Just like the global leadership team meeting, the tech symposium should have a stated purpose and be well organized, and outcomes should be tracked and measured.

HONEYWELL'S PRACTICE OF HOLDING
FIXED COSTS CONSTANT

Another mechanism that Mr. Cote talks about in his book is holding fixed costs constant while growing sales. Holding fixed costs constant is no easy task. As Mr. Cote explains, continuous process improvement initiatives are required to achieve constant costs while growing the sales of the company. This can generate notable economic value because of the benefits to both earnings and cash flows.

INVESTING IN THE FUTURE

This is an essential mechanism that instills discipline and helps build lifelines. Leading companies implement this mechanism to ensure that a consistent level of earnings within a preestablished range is invested annually into the business. A range is recommended so that a minimum and a maximum amount will be established as guidelines, depending on the economic environment and the performance of the enterprise.

Execution Metrics and Mechanisms

It takes a lot of work to make something simple, to truly understand the underlying challenges and come up with elegant solutions.[1]

———

—STEVE JOBS

PART A: EXECUTION METRICS

The right metrics are indispensable to building an enduring company. As mentioned in the previous chapter, many of the metrics outlined in this chapter equally apply to the foundational pillar of strategy. For ease of discussion and to avoid duplication, the metrics that are covered in this chapter were not first expounded on under strategy.

The following are some essential metrics that a company should monitor relative to the foundational pillar of execution:

- product line contribution margin
- business unit–specific metrics
- gross profit as a percentage of sales
- SG&A expenses as a percentage of sales
- customer profitability contribution
- success rate percentage on "A" accounts

- customer return percentage and dollar value
- cash conversion cycle
- net promoter score on customer satisfaction
- capacity utilization rate
- contract renewal or customer retention rate
- plant fill rates
- labor utilization rate
- cost of waste
- days to close the books
- backlog and sales cadence.

PRODUCT LINE CONTRIBUTION MARGIN

This is a meaningful metric, particularly if a company has numerous product lines. It's imperative that the company at least understands the contribution margin of each product line. Ideally, it's better if a product line's operating margin can be ascertained. Any identified underperformers need to be highlighted and proactive actions should be taken by management.

BUSINESS UNIT–SPECIFIC METRICS

Some businesses more than others lend themselves to be measured not only at the enterprise or segment level but also at the site, branch, or individual unit level. A good example of this is where I spent about three decades, serving the global steel industry. In this environmental solutions business, it's all about the performance of each customer site that is being served. Some of the key metrics that we monitored, included: liquid steel tons produced by the customer; site level return on invested capital; and, revenues, operating income, and free cash flow. For enterprises that have a large branch network, similar types of metrics should be utilized to measure performance.

GROSS PROFIT AS A PERCENTAGE OF SALES

Gross profit percent is essential in all businesses, but especially so in manufactured products. The objective is to continuously work on improving the overall gross margin percent. This is usually viewed in terms of x basis points improvement in gross margins. That means, maximizing selling price and minimizing cost of goods sold. This is a good metric to measure the company against its peer group.

SG&A EXPENSES AS A PERCENTAGE OF SALES

SG&A expenses have a direct impact on operating income and margins. Thus, the obvious challenge is to strive to continuously lower SG&A as a percent of sales. This is usually viewed in terms of x basis points improvement (reduction) in SG&A costs.

CUSTOMER PROFITABILITY CONTRIBUTION

Customer profitability contribution requires understanding the relative profitability of each customer. Insight into customer profitability is critical to devising value-adding strategies for the best customers and in determining appropriate strategies for less profitable ones. The ultimate goal is to eliminate as many unprofitable customers, while simultaneously optimizing profitable ones.

SUCCESS RATE PERCENTAGE ON "A" ACCOUNTS

A vital metric to measure commercial excellence, is closely monitoring the win rate on key accounts. Often, these accounts are referred to as "A" accounts because they are the most desirable relative to pricing and terms. These accounts are indispensable to realizing superior results because they normally contribute the most to profitability.

CUSTOMER RETURNS PERCENTAGE AND DOLLAR VALUE

It's essential to measure customer returns as a percent of sales and in dollars. Returns are normal in some businesses, such as retail. What's important is to separate normal from abnormal because they require different approaches. For normal returns, the goal is to continuously improve and strive to reduce the returns through various strategies. Abnormal returns usually indicate serious issues with the products, the sales team, or other aspects of the business. This usually requires a more urgent and radical approach than normal returns.

CASH CONVERSION CYCLE

This is also covered under leadership OKRs but warrant a repeat because it's both a metric and mechanism. The cash conversion cycle measures the speed of cash and working capital efficiency. All businesses should put a significant effort in having the lowest number of days possible.

NET PROMOTER SCORE ON CUSTOMER SATISFACTION

"The Net Promoter Score is an index ranging from −100 to 100 that measures the willingness of customers to recommend a company's products and/or services to others. It is used as a proxy for gauging the customer's overall satisfaction with a company's product and/or service and the customer's loyalty to the brand. Customers are surveyed on one single question. They are asked to rate on an 11-point scale the likelihood of recommending the company or brand to a friend or colleague. On a scale of 0 to 10, how likely are you to recommend this company's product or service to a friend or a colleague? Based on their rating, customers are then classified in 3 categories: detractors, passives and promoters."[2]

CAPACITY UTILIZATION RATE

Capacity utilization rates are important in manufacturing businesses due to a relatively high fixed costs structure. Running a higher utilization rate usually translates to improved financial performance. There are certain levers that companies can pull to improve utilization rates, including processing more customer orders without increasing fixed costs.

CONTRACT RENEWAL OR CUSTOMER RETENTION RATE

Businesses that operate on long-term contracts monitor their renewal rates closely. This is particularly important when it involves high-performing contracts. However, there are many businesses that don't operate on long-term contracts. These businesses need to instead monitor customer retention rates. Retention rates of customers that make a significant contribution to profitability need to be closely monitored.

PLANT FILL RATES

The ability to efficiently fill a customer order is paramount to the success of an enterprise. The objective is to achieve at or near 100 percent rate on a consistent basis. Poor service levels can have severe adverse consequences on an enterprise, including higher costs and possibly losing customers to the competition.

LABOR UTILIZATION RATE

High labor utilization is important in just about every business, particularly in professional services. A highly utilized workforce usually translates to strong financial performance. This metric is crucial where labor is one of the highest costs of a service or product.

COST OF WASTE

Costs incurred from waste and poor quality need to be measured and monitored, with appropriate actions taken to rectify issues. In some industries, the cost of waste and poor quality can be significant. This is where tools such as Lean and/or Six Sigma can be effective at reducing and even possibly eliminating the problem by fixing inefficient processes.

DAYS TO CLOSE THE BOOKS

An often overlooked opportunity under administrative processes is the time it takes a company to close its books, which includes preparing a full set of financial statements. Streamlining the closing process can benefit a company in numerous ways, including allowing financial personnel more time to better support the operations.

BACKLOG AND SALES CADENCE

A potent sales cadence and backlog process is an essential lifeline. It's important for an organization to establish a process that ideally captures the sales cadence on daily basis, with appropriate metrics and trend lines. Organizations that have this daily visibility in their order flow can take proactive actions more quickly. The sales cadence process builds the backlog. A backlog that contains estimated gross margins is even more critical. Ultimately, a strong sales cadence process, along with backlog information, provides an organization with the ability to better forecast future results.

PART B: EXECUTION MECHANISMS

Just like the right metrics are indispensable in building an enduring company, so are key mechanisms. It is imperative that enterprises have in place numerous mechanisms that are designed to improve the company, provide early warning signs, and help keep the organization on the right path to excellence.

The following are examples of mechanisms that enterprises should consider relative to the foundational pillar of execution:

- objectives and key results
- Facebook's growth team
- Jim Collins's 20 Mile March
- Nucor's pay for high performance
- the growth conference
- after-action reviews for acquisitions
- identification of "the next UAE"
- thirty-day risk-free trial
- Amazon's narrative
- major contracts approval.

OBJECTIVES AND KEY RESULTS

As was outlined in chapter 18, my favorite mechanism, one that applies across all three foundational pillars, is objectives and key results (OKRs). OKRs have their origins in the tech sector; they are specifically attributed to Andy Grove of Intel. OKRs are a powerful mechanism that can be implemented to propel an enterprise to the summit. Following is the list of some relevant OKRs that should be considered:

- **Improve gross margins from x percent to y percent or by x basis points.** As explained earlier, gross margins need to be a focus of all businesses, particularly companies that make products.
- **Improve the percentage of the selling, general, and administrative expense from x percent to y percent or by x basis points.** An effective OKR is to challenge the organization to reduce the SG&A percentage so that operating margins are improved.

- **Improve the maintenance CapEx percentage of revenues from x percent to y percent or by x basis points.** In businesses with heavy CapEx spending, you will often find the need for replacement or maintenance CapEx to sustain the current revenue stream base. An effective OKR is to challenge the organization to reduce that percentage.

- **Improve the number of hours or days to resolve a customer issue.** A key customer metric is to capture the time it takes to completely resolve a customer issue, no matter what it is. An improvement in the cycle time to resolve all customer issues is imperative to maintaining happy customers and building the brand.

- **Improve the customer satisfaction star rating from x percent to y percent or by x basis points.** Another valuable customer metric is the star rating posted online. This should be improved. An improvement in the star rating is important not only to promoting the company but also to maintaining happy customers and building the brand.

FACEBOOK'S GROWTH TEAM

An innovative approach to growth can be found at Facebook, with their "growth team" concept. The growth team is empowered and responsible for designing tactics to remove any obstacles that prevent the company from growing. The growth team must have broad latitude to weigh in on any aspect of the company's business.

JIM COLLINS'S 20 MILE MARCH

This mechanism can be utilized to set parameters for growing in a consistent and disciplined manner. The 20 Mile March "requires hitting specified performance markers with great consistency over a long period of time. It requires two distinct types of discomfort, delivering high-performance in difficult times and holding back in good times."[3]

NUCOR'S PAY FOR HIGH PERFORMANCE

Nucor's commitment to pay employees for high performance, while at the same time not guaranteeing incentives or retiree benefits, is a powerful mechanism that has worked well for the company. With this mechanism, Nucor is saying that everyone in the organization will benefit from the reward when performance is high. Conversely, if the workforce does not perform at a high level, then incentives may not be paid. Not only does this mechanism promote performance, but also it turns some of Nucor's cost structure into variable as opposed to fixed.

THE GROWTH CONFERENCE

This mechanism is similar to the innovation challenge mechanism discussed under strategy. At a growth conference, business units are challenged to come prepared to present growth initiatives that are consistent with the enterprise's strategy. Each team is allotted a certain amount of time to present growth initiatives to both the corporate senior management team and all business unit leaders. Presenters are challenged to bring their best ideas forward. The ideas need to be sound, well thought out, and well presented. The best ideas are ultimately selected for funding. An added benefit of a growth conference is that it reinforces the culture of the company.

AFTER-ACTION REVIEWS FOR ACQUISITIONS

Another mechanism that I have utilized is the after-action review for every acquisition, along with reporting the results annually to the board of directors. The after-action review is necessary to help executives gain a clear understanding of what went right and what went wrong. As part of the mechanism, we had to take specific action to incorporate these lessons learned into our acquisitions process. On the reporting side, we then compared the performance of each acquisition to the projections used in the base case. Then we analyzed and summarized the results for the board.

We had to report each major acquisition until there was demonstrable evidence of either success or failure. Sometimes the reporting would span a period of three to five years.

IDENTIFICATION OF "THE NEXT UAE"

This was explained earlier under the growth engine principle. The question posed by this mechanism is, where is the next market that will offer significant upside potential for strongly positioning the company? The market does not necessarily need to be a physical location; it can be virtual. This mechanism requires generative thinking, dialogue, lots of data, and due diligence. It also requires being close to the customer. What is important in the process, however, is not to make large bets. The approach must be to make many smaller bets to test various markets for improvement in performance without taking outsized risks.

THIRTY-DAY RISK-FREE TRIAL

This mechanism is utilized by enterprises in the retail industry. The policy is straightforward. If a customer is unhappy with the product, he or she can simply return it for any reason during the thirty-day period. If the company truly believes in its products and customer service, then this can be a potent mechanism to ensure that the organization does not lose its way.

AMAZON'S NARRATIVE

This was explained earlier under the administrative excellence principle. Here is what the narrative or six-pager is all about: It starts with Amazon banning all PowerPoint presentations. As a replacement, they implemented the narrative mechanism for making meetings more productive, better focused, and more constructive. At the beginning of a meeting to review an important project, attendees sit and carefully read and study a six-page written document prepared by the sponsor. The objective is to have attendees absorb, understand, and reflect on the project before engaging in a robust dialogue about the project.

MAJOR CONTRACTS APPROVAL

This was explained earlier under the commercial excellence principle. Elite companies ensure that material commitments—both financial and contractual terms—are dialogued and approved by both the CEO and CFO, and in some cases even the board. From the financial commitment standpoint, all contracts over a certain preestablished threshold should be reviewed, dialogued, and approved. And from the standpoint of contractual terms, any significant terms that either individually or cumulatively pose a risk to the entire enterprise need to follow same approval process.

The Journey Never Ends

After climbing a great hill, one only finds that
there are many more hills to climb.[1]

———

—NELSON MANDELA

It is fundamental for leaders to understand that the journey to climb the summit of elite never ends! To achieve enduring greatness, an organization must climb a multitude of summits over a long horizon. Each summit must equate to the bold vision of the company. As each vision is realized over the stated time frame, a new vision is established. This cycle is then repeated.

To successfully ascend to greatness and ultimately add your company to the ranks of the elite, it's paramount that you implement the elite enterprise model outlined in *Ascend to Greatness*. By successfully implementing this innovative framework is how an enduring enterprise is created. Even if you are lucky enough to reach that ultimate summit where the air is thin, it will take determination, focus, and discipline to continue to perform at an elite level.

During the quest to join the relatively small group of elite companies, you will certainly face challenges, make missteps, and encounter unforeseen events that can slow or temporarily impair your progress or even terminate the quest. It is important that you ensure that your leadership team is steadfast in its objective of ascending to the summit of elite. Everyone on the team must have unwavering faith in their ability to overcome all obstacles.

Once an enterprise reaches the summit, it remains vitally important to sustain this elite status, which arguably is even more difficult. Sustainment will likewise take discipline and a strong will to succeed. It is imperative that the leadership team avoid the trap of hubris or complacency, because falling into such a trap will likely undermine, or possibly even end, the journey.

The takeaway message from *Ascend to Greatness* is that achieving elite status is difficult, but sustaining it for a long horizon is even more challenging. I truly believe that companies have the potential to reach and maintain elite status by rigorously following the Holy Grail elite enterprise model outlined in *Ascend to Greatness*. So, what's important is to persevere and keep climbing!

ACKNOWLEDGMENTS

Elite leaders build great teams. Elite teams build great companies.

—SALVATORE FAZZOLARI

There is no better expression of appreciation than a sincere and heartfelt thank-you. So, I want to thank all the elite leaders I have met throughout my career who have provided their insight, perspective, and wisdom, which was instrumental in my professional development. I am especially grateful to the leaders who believed in me. These leaders gave me the opportunity to grow by providing me with indispensable experiences that ultimately helped me ascend to the CEO position.

A special thank-you goes to my mother and father for having the courage and perseverance to embark on a great new adventurous journey to the United States when I was nine years old. They truly changed my life for the better. I'm deeply grateful to them for their sacrifice, their love, and for providing me with the opportunity to live my dream.

I'm blessed to have such a loving wife, a loving family, and supportive friends. Without their encouragement and inspiration over many years, *Ascend to Greatness* would not have been possible. I'm honored and humbled to have had my small focus group of colleagues and family members contribute so much to making this book possible. The following contributors provided invaluable insight: Frank C. Sullivan, Thomas S. Gross, Michael Feuer, Michael Fazzolari, and Salvatore V. Fazzolari.

ABOUT THE AUTHOR

Salvatore D. Fazzolari is the founder of Salvatore Fazzolari Advisors LLC. He has professional experience spanning almost four and a half decades, including having held positions as CEO, president, and chairman; management adviser; and board member. He is a thought leader on how to build an enduring elite company. His innovative *elite enterprise model* provides a comprehensive framework for visionary leaders who aspire to reach the ultimate summit of greatness.

Salvatore is both a CPA (inactive) and a CISA (inactive). He is fluent in Italian and has deep experience in both industrial and consumer markets, including metals, steel, engineering, construction, defense, rail, energy, building products, coatings, specialty chemicals, and headwear. He also has wide-ranging public speaking experience.

Salvatore is currently a board member of RPM International Inc. (NYSE: RPM), a world leader in specialty coatings, sealants, building products, and related services serving both industrial and consumer markets; Gannett Fleming Inc., a leading engineering company; Bollman Hat Company, a world-leading designer, manufacturer, and distributor of men's, women's, and children's headwear and accessories.

Salvatore also provides management advisory services to companies, and partners with private equity firms. Salvatore is the former chairman, president, and CEO of Harsco Corporation.

Salvatore has published *CEO Lifelines—Climb On: Exceptional Habits of Elite Companies* (2017); *CEO Lifelines: Nine Commitments Every Leader Must Make* (2014); an article in *Management Accounting* magazine (1988);

and a short essay in Dr. Richard A. D'Aveni's book *Strategic Capitalism: The New Economic Strategy for Winning the Capitalist Cold War* (2012). Salvatore is currently working on a fourth book, on the inimitable Italian culinary culture inspired by the traditions of his native provinces of Calabria and Liguria. He is also acknowledged by Jim Collins in two books: *Great by Choice* and *How the Mighty Fall*.

NOTES

AUTHOR'S NOTE

1   Alan Mulally, Brainy Quotes, accessed June 9, 2021, https://www.brainyquote. com/quotes/alan_mulally_903271?src=t_leadership.

INTRODUCTION

1   Jim Collins, *Great by Choice* (New York: HarperCollins, 2011), 182.

SECTION ONE INTRODUCTION

1   Oxford Learners Dictionary, s.v. "Veni, vidi, vici," https://www. oxfordlearnersdictionaries.com/us/definition/english/veni-vidi-vici.

CHAPTER 1. LEADERSHIP CORE CHARACTERISTICS

1   Henry Kissinger, https://www.brainyquote.com/quotes/henry_kissinger_ 130663?src=t_leadership.
2   "Apollo's $433 Billion Makeover Man," *Wall Street Journal*, October 31– November 1, 2020, B2.
3   Jim Collins, *Turning the Flywheel* (New York: HarperCollins, 2019), 32.
4   Aristotle, https://www.passiton.com/inspirational-quotes/7103-we-are-what -we-repeatedly-do-excellence-then.

CHAPTER 2. THE RIGHT PEOPLE IN THE RIGHT POSITIONS

1   Steve Jobs, https://wisdomquotes.com/steve-jobs-quotes/.

2   http://www.greatthoughtstreasury.com/m-h-mckee/quote/integrity-one
-several-paths-it-distinguishes-itself-others-because-it-right-path-and.

CHAPTER 3. TALENT ACQUISITION

1   https://www.brainyquote.com/quotes/ray_kroc_100366.

2   Eric Schmidt and Jonathan Rosenberg, *How Google Works* (New York: Grand
Central, 2014), 95.

CHAPTER 4. TALENT MANAGEMENT AND
LEADERSHIP DEVELOPMENT

1   https://wisdomquotes.com/steve-jobs-quotes/.

2   Charles Rogel, "What Is a Leadership Derailer?," DecisionWise, accessed June 4,
2021, https://decision-wise.com/what-is-a-leadership-derailer/#:~:text=A%20
leadership%20derailer%20is%20a,are%20to%20realize%20our%20potential.

CHAPTER 5: DISTINCTIVE CULTURE

1   https://www.brainyquote.com/quotes/tricia_griffith_852303.

2   Stanley McChrystal, *Team of Teams* (New York: Penguin, 2015), 99–100.

CHAPTER 6. LEARNING ENTITY

1   https://www.brainyquote.com/quotes/jack_welch_173305.

2   Mark F. Twight and James Martin, *Extreme Alpinism: Climbing Light, Fast,
and High* (Seattle: The Mountaineers Books, 1999), 25.

3   George   Bernard   Shaw,   https://www.brainyquote.com/quotes/george_
bernard_shaw_121841.

4   Walter Isaacson, *Steve Jobs* (New York: Simon & Schuster, 2011), 461.

5   Michael Den Tandt, "Cry in the Dojo, Laugh on the Battlefield," *Fudoshindojo*
(blog), July 21, 2012, https://fudoshindojo.wordpress.com/2012/07/21/cry-in
-the-dojo-laugh-on-the-battlefield/#:~:text=Here%20is%20what%20we%20
most,level%20of%20discomfort%20is%20controlled.

SECTION TWO INTRODUCTION

1   https://www.brainyquote.com/quotes/sun_tzu_155751?src=t_strategy.

CHAPTER 7. PURPOSE, VALUES, AND VISION

1   https://www.brainyquote.com/quotes/eleanor_roosevelt_100940.
2   Simon Sinek, *Start with Why* (New York: Penguin, 2009, 2011), 65–66.
3   Ibid., 66.

CHAPTER 8. UNIQUE PRACTICES

1   https://www.brainyquote.com/quotes/angela_duckworth_837114.

CHAPTER 9. ORGANIZATIONAL STRUCTURE

1   https://wisdomquotes.com/steve-jobs-quotes/.
2   Ibid.
3   Boston Consulting Group, May 2013, 2.
4   Walter Isaacson, *The Innovators* (New York: Simon & Schuster, 2014), 277.
5   https://wisdomquotes.com/steve-jobs-quotes/.

CHAPTER 10. BUILDING LIFELINES

1   https://www.azquotes.com/quote/720328.
2   Anatoli Boukreev and G. Weston DeWalt, *The Climb: Tragic Ambitions on Everest* (New York: St. Martin's Griffin, 1997), 17.
3   Jim Collins, *Turning the Flywheel* (New York: HarperCollins, 2019), 34–35.
4   https://www.aei.org/carpe-diem/only-52-us-companies-have-been-on-the-fortune-500-since-1955-thanks-to-the-creative-destruction-that-fuels-economic-prosperity/.
5   Jay Yarrow, "Google CEO Larry Page Spoke at TED, and Everyone Freaked Out over His Ideas," *Business Insider*, March 19, 2014, http://www.businessinsider.com/larry-page-at-ted-2014-3.
6   https://www.azquotes.com/quote/118559.
7   Jim Collins, *How the Mighty Fall and Why Some Companies Never Give In* (New York: HarperCollins, 2009), 20–21.

8   https://yourstory.com/2016/03/50-quotes-visionary-andy-grove?utm_
    pageloadtype=scroll.

9   Ibid.

10 Satya Nadella, "Businesses Are Being Pushed to Evolve," *Wall Street Journal*,
    January 30–31, 2021.

CHAPTER 11. INNOVATION AND TECHNOLOGY

1   https://www.brainyquote.com/quotes/steve_jobs_173474?src=t_innovation.

2   Walter Isaacson, *The Innovators* (New York: Simon & Schuster, 2014), 134.

3   https://wisdomquotes.com/steve-jobs-quotes/.

4   Alistair Barr, "Google Lab Puts a Time Limit on Innovations," updated March
    31, 2015, *Wall Street Journal*, April 1, 2015, B6.

5   https://www.brainyquote.com/authors/edwin-land-quotes.

6   Eric Schmidt and Jonathan Rosenberg, *How Google Works* (New York: Grand
    Central, 2014), 238–39.

CHAPTER 12. HIGH-PERFORMANCE PLAN

1   https://www.brainyquote.com/quotes/ron_williams_902906.

SECTION THREE INTRODUCTION

1   https://www.goodreads.com/quotes/search?utf8=%E2%9C%93&q
    =excellence&commit=Search.

2   https://www.wiseoldsayings.com/execution-quotes/#ixzz6RLh05lYW.

3   https://www.wiseoldsayings.com/execution-quotes/#ixzz6RLiP8jJt.

4   Wikipedia, s.v. "Roman legion," last modified May 25, 2021, 23:15, https://
    en.wikipedia.org/wiki/Roman_legion.

CHAPTER 13. DISCIPLINED EXECUTION

1   https://www.brainyquote.com/quotes/george_s_patton_145012?src=t_
    discipline.

2   https://www.khorus.com/blog/14-inspirational-quotes-strategy-execution/.

3   Danaher Business System, accessed June 4, 2021, https://www.danaher.com/how-we-work/danaher-business-system.

4   Toyota Production System, accessed June 4, 2021, https://global.toyota/en/company/vision-and-philosophy/production-system/.

5   David Brunt, "Deploying Policy," Lean Enterprise Academy, August 5, 2014, http://www.leanuk.org/article-pages/articles/2014/august/05/deploying-policy.aspx.

6   https://yourstory.com/2016/03/50-quotes-visionary-andy-grove?utm_pageloadtype=scroll.

7   https://wisdomquotes.com/steve-jobs-quotes/.

8   Ibid.

9   *Fortune*, March 1, 2015, 92.

10 googleblog.blogspot.com/2015/08/google-alphabet.html.

CHAPTER 14. GROWTH ENGINE

1   https://www.brainyquote.com/quotes/ronald_reagan_183770.

2   Jim Collins, *Good to Great* (New York: HarperCollins, 2001), 54.

3   Ibid., 65.

4   Adam Lashinsky, "The Unexpected Management Genius of Facebook's Mark Zuckerberg," *Fortune*, November 10, 2016, https://fortune.com/longform/facebook-mark-zuckerberg-business/.

CHAPTER 15. COMMERCIAL EXCELLENCE

1   https://www.brainyquote.com/quotes/robin_s_sharma_857673?src=t_execution.

2   http://www.imanet.org/docs/default-source/thought_leadership/management_control_systems/customer_profitability_management.pdf?sfvrsn=2.

CHAPTER 16. OPERATIONAL EXCELLENCE

1   https://www.brainyquote.com/quotes/quotes/n/naveenjain416008.html.

CHAPTER 17. ADMINISTRATIVE EXCELLENCE

1   https://www.brainyquote.com/quotes/booker_t_washington_382201?src=t_excellence.
2   David M. Cote, *Winning Now, Winning Later* (HarperCollins Leadership, 2020), 39–40.

SECTION FOUR INTRODUCTION

1   https://www.jimcollins.com/article_topics/articles/forget-strategy.html#articletop.
2   Ibid.

CHAPTER 18. LEADERSHIP METRICS AND MECHANISMS

1   https://wisdomquotes.com/steve-jobs-quotes/.
2   Eric Schmidt and Jonathan Rosenberg, *How Google Works* (New York: Grand Central, 2014), 223.
3   Ibid., 42–44.

CHAPTER 19. STRATEGY METRICS AND MECHANISMS

1   https://wisdomquotes.com/steve-jobs-quotes/.
2   https://www.jimcollins.com/tools/diagnostic-tool.pdf.

CHAPTER 20. EXECUTION MEASURES AND MECHANISMS

1   https://wisdomquotes.com/steve-jobs-quotes/.
2   https://www.medallia.com/net-promoter-score/.
3   Jim Collins, *Great by Choice* (New York: HarperCollins, 2011), 65.

CONCLUSION. THE JOURNEY NEVER ENDS

1   https://www.brainyquote.com/quotes/nelson_mandela_178785.

INDEX

A

acquisitions
 making small targeted bets on,
  not one large bet on, 179
 targeting strategic acquisitions,
  186–187

acting fast, when a change needs to be
 made in a critical position, 42

adjacent markets, as lever to build
 organic growth engine, 185

administrative excellence
 overview, 215–216
 as principle of execution, xvi,
  215–224
 building a strong information
  technology infrastructure,
  221–222
 closing your books fast, 223–224
 embracing environmental, social,
  and governance (ESG),
  220–221
 establishment of global shared
  services, 219–220
 maintaining a nimble governance
  framework, 220

managing risks well, 216–217
minimizing or eliminating
 lengthy presentations,
 222–223
utilization of zero-based
 budgeting, 217–219

adversity, forms of, 119

after-action reviews
 for acquisitions, as execution
  mechanism, 263–264
 as leadership mechanism, 239
 as one of seven fundamental
  components to building a
  successful and high-impact
  learning organization, 62,
  66–67, 69
 treating them as indispensable, 31

AI (artificial intelligence), 211, 223

Alphabet Inc. *See also* Google
 (Alphabet)
 formation of, 179, 212
 as having internal ventures
  group, 191

Amazon
 as example of reimaging business
  model, 113

as exceptional at building
strength and positioning
themselves to
dominate market and
competition, 68
exemplary purpose statement
of, 81
fictional press release, 241
hiring practices, 33–34
leadership principles of, 47–50
narrative or six-pager, 222, 223,
241, 264–265
"Amazon Takes Over from GE as
CEO Incubator" (*Wall Street
Journal*), 33, 48
Apollo Global Management Inc., 9
"Apollo's $433 Billion Makeover Man"
(*Wall Street Journal*), 9
Apple
as best example of successful
integrated enterprise
model, 108
as example of execution
excellence, 164
as example of strong balance
sheet, 123
as example of winner, xv
examples of exceptional unique
practices, 99–100
as exceptional at building
strength and positioning
themselves to
dominate market and
competition, 68
as gold standard regarding strong
balance sheet, 124

as having internal ventures
group, 191
impact of iPod, 116
internal university, 64–65
leadership team at, 4–5
unique practices of, 94
use of global supply chain by, 207
Aristotle, 13, 163
artificial intelligence (AI), 211, 223
Ask Bob initiative
as innovative approach to
employee engagement,
40–41
as leadership mechanism, 242
assets
building formidable intangible
assets, 143
rationalization of, 214
selling of miscellaneous
assets, 156
awards, in recognition of excellence,
as leadership mechanism, 243

B

backlog and sales cadence, as
execution metric, 260
balance sheet
building a strong one as essential
lifeline, 123–124
optimization of as part of high-
performance plan, 156–159
BE 2.0 (Collins and Lazier), 78, 88
behaviors, of CEO and leadership
team as impacting culture, 54
Berkshire Hathaway, 123

best places to work, ranking
among, 234
Beyond Entrepreneurship (Collins and
Lazier), 78
big data, use of in scanning
environment, 128–129
"Big Food Sees Big Changes" (*Wall
Street Journal*), 218
big hairy audacious goal (BHAG), 78,
79, 88–89
blind euphoria, 176
board of directors
described, 20
governance and nominating
committee of, 21
as important team, 16
in selecting and appointing
CEO, 17
succession planning process for,
20–21
ways board behaves, thinks,
and acts as impacting
culture, 59
books, closing your books fast,
223–224
Bossidy, Lawrence, 163, 169
Boston Consulting Group, 110
Boukreev, Anatoli, 115
brand development, strong brand
development as lever to build
organic growth engine, 185
brand management, focusing on,
200–201
breakthrough objectives
inclusion of in high-performance
plan, 152

use of term, 152
"Building Your Company's Vision"
(Collins and Porras), 78
Built to Last (Collins and Porras), 78
business model, reimagining of, 109,
113–114
business unit-specific metrics, as
execution metrics, 256
business watch list, as leadership
mechanism, 241
"Businesses Are Being Pushed
to Evolve" (*Wall Street
Journal*), 130

C

Calcbench, 124
Calico, as Alphabet product
group, 212
calls to action, in response to
disruptive events and
devastating shocks, 120–121
Campbell Soup, as having internal
ventures group, 191
capacity utilization rate, as execution
metric, 259
capital
allocation effectiveness of as vital
for acquisitions, 187
astute capital allocation of as
essential part of high-
performance plan, 155
efficient allocation of as essential
lifeline, 129–130
return on invested capital as
strategy metric, 245

disruptive innovation, 116

disruptive innovation and technology
    as category of severe external
        forces of change, 119
    differentiating with, 133–144
    as threat, 120

distinctive culture
    culture as cornerstone of
        enduring greatness, 51–52
    leadership excellence as needing
        to underpin, 54

diversity, embracing of, 41

Duckworth, Angela, 93

E

earnings before interest, taxes,
    depreciation, and amortization
    (EBITDA), 247

earnings per share (EPS), 247

EBITDA conversion ratio, as strategy
    metric, 247

elite, use of term, xiv

elite company examples
    Amazon hiring practices, 33–34
    Google (Alphabet) hiring
        practices, 32–33

elite enterprise model
    foundational pillars of, x
    overview, xiii–xiv
    elite leaders
    as building great teams, 7
    new breed of, 8

ELT (executive leadership team)
    composition of, 17–18
    as key position, 22

as needing five core leadership
    characteristics, 18
    percent of key positions filled by
        right people, 231

employee engagement program
    innovative approaches to, 40
    necessity of robust one, 40

employee satisfaction rating, 233

employee surveys, use of, 40

empowerment, of team members, 41

engineering and technical capabilities,
    development of, 210–211

enterprise performance, as correlated
    with exceptional succession
    planning process, 42

enterprise resource planning (ERP),
    106, 108, 206, 208, 222, 223

enterprise risk management
    (ERM), 217

enterprise value/EBITDA multiple, as
    strategy metric, 250

enterprise value/revenues multiple, as
    strategy metric, 249

entrepreneurialism
    building entrepreneurial
        culture, 127
    ways of promoting of as
        impacting culture, 56

environmental, social, and governance
    (ESG), embracing of, 220–221

EPS (earnings per share), 247

ERM (enterprise risk
    management), 217

ERP (enterprise resource planning),
    106, 108, 206, 208, 222, 223

instilling discipline in management of, 139–140

as principle of strategy, xvi, 74, 133–144

proper training for all employees in, 139

using a new model for, 136–137

innovation challenge, as strategy mechanism, 252

innovative business model, parts of, 93–94, 102–103

The Innovators (Isaacson), 111, 134

Inside Apple (Lashinsky), 207

Instagram, exemplary purpose statement of, 81

instinct, as core personal characteristic, 3, 10, 11–12

instinctive leader, described, 11–12

Institute of Management Accountants (IMA), 202

integrated management system

building blocks of, 172–174

as impelling disciplined execution, 169–172

use of, 75

integrated model of organizational structure, 102, 103, 107–109

interaction, ways of as impacting culture, 55

internal university

as one of seven fundamental components to building a successful and high-impact learning organization, 61, 63–64

as vital for talent development, 39

internal ventures group, building of, 191

interviewing

conducting effective exit interviews, 31

need for exceptional skills in, 29, 33

inventory, managing it effectively, 208–209

investing in future, as strategy mechanism, 254

investments

exploring with on-the-edge investments, 138

making small targeted investments, not one large bet, 178–179

Isaacson, Walter, 65, 108, 111, 134

J

Jain, Naveen, 204

JC Penney, large bet of, 178

Jobs, Steve, 4–5, 14, 25, 35, 46, 53, 65, 102–103, 108–109, 111, 133, 134, 176, 177, 201, 230, 244, 255

joint ventures and strategic alliances

as one of seven fundamental components to building a successful and high-impact learning organization, 62, 66

seeking them out, 188–189

journey (to climb summit of elite), as never ending, 267–268

Julius Caesar, 3–4

K

Kaizen, 86, 166, 169, 170, 174
Kaplan, Robert S., 202
Kimberly-Clark, CEO internal
    blog, 242
Kroc, Ray, 25

L

labor utilization rate, as execution
    metric, 259
Land, Edward, 142
Lashinsky, Adam, 188, 207
Lazier, Bill, 78, 88
leadership
    overview, 5–6
    principles of, xvi, 1–70
    building team for the future, 4–5
    disciplined leadership, 5
    elite leaders as building great
        teams, 7
    few people as natural-born
        leaders, 42
    as foundational pillar of elite
        enterprise model, x, xiii,
        xiv, xvi
    Julius Caesar, 3–4
leadership core characteristics, as
    principle of leadership, xvi
leadership development, success rate
    and failure rate (percent), 232
leadership mechanisms
    after-action reviews, 239
    allowing for period of inner
        reflection, 242

Amazon's fictional press
    release, 241
awards in recognition of
    excellence, 243
business watch list, 241
CEO internal blog, 242
code of ethical business conduct,
    238–239
"future leaders" watch list, 238
Google's 70/20/10 rule, 239
hiring around core values, 238
linking core values to performance
    appraisals, 238
objectives and key results (OKRs),
    235–238
quarterly report on state of
    business, 240–241
rule of seven, 239–240
Wegman's "Ask Bob"
    initiative, 242
leadership metrics
    CEO ranking, 234
    employee satisfaction rating, 233
    leadership development success
        rate and failure rate
        (percent), 232
    percent of employees who can
        repeat verbatim the core
        philosophy, 234
    percent of key positions filled by
        right people, 231
    ranking among best places to
        work, 234
    talent acquisition success rate and
        failure rate (percent), 231
    talent retention rate (percent), 233

no right number of, 228
as not well understood or
extensively utilized, 229
ways of implementing as
impacting culture, 58–59
mechanisms and metrics. *See also*
execution mechanisms;
execution metrics; leadership
mechanisms; leadership
metrics; strategy mechanisms;
strategy metrics
introduction, 227–229
cash conversion cycle, 199
free cash flow, 129, 154–155, 246
implementation of, 31
as needed to drive foundational
pillars and related core
principles, 228–229
utilizing key metrics and
implementing
mechanisms, 140
metaphors. *See* climbing metaphors;
mountaineering metaphors
metrics, as well understood and
extensively utilized, 228–229
Microsoft
as example of execution
excellence, 164
as example of reimaging business
model, 113
as exceptional at building
strength and positioning
themselves to
dominate market and
competition, 68

exemplary purpose statement
of, 81
as having internal ventures
group, 191
Mondelez, 218
Motorola, as developer of Six
Sigma, 173
mountaineering metaphors, 115–116,
117, 118, 122, 128, 149, 152, 153,
154, 216, 244, 267–268. *See also*
climbing metaphors
Mulally, Alan, ix

N

Nadella, Satya, 130
Narayanan, V. G., 202
narrative (Amazon), as execution
mechanism, 222, 223, 241,
264–265
Nest, as Alphabet product group, 212
net CapEx-to-sales percentage, as
strategy metric, 249
Net Promoter Score on customer
satisfaction, as execution
metric, 258
Netflix
as example of scanning the
environment in real
time, 101
as example of winner, xv
new products to total revenues, as
strategy mechanism, 251
niche businesses, investing and
growing of, 190–191
Nordstrom, exemplary purpose
statement of, 82

Nucor
    examples of exceptional unique
        practices, 96–99
    pay for high performance, 263
    unique activities of, 94
number two, identifying or
        appointing a strong one, 46–47

O

objectives and key results (OKRs)
    as execution mechanism, 261–262
    as leadership mechanism,
        235–238
    as strategy mechanism, 250–251
onboarding program, developing
        intensive onboarding
        program, 30
one-company initiative, 105–107
online classes, as indispensable
        tool, 64
Only the Paranoid Survive (Grove),
        117–118
on-the-edge investments, exploration
        with, 138
operational excellence
overview, 204–205
    as principle of execution, xvi,
        204–214
    consistently delivering superior
        product, 206–207
    developing exceptional program
        management skills, 213
    development of engineering and
        technical capabilities,
        210–211

execution of product management
        strategy, 211–212
    implementation of standardized
        processes, 205–206
    implementation of variable cost
        model, 212–213
    managing inventory effectively,
        208–209
optimization of global supply chain,
        207–208
optimization of operational footprint,
        209–210
    rationalization of assets, 214
    utilization of sales, inventory, and
        operations planning, 206
    utilization of value engineering
        and design, 210
operational footprint, optimization of,
        209–210
opportunities, assigning your most
        talented people to your greatest
        ones, 39
organic growth, as compared to
        inorganic growth, 183–184
organizational structure
overview, 102–103
    as principle of strategy, xvi, 74,
        102–114
    as being designed around unique
        practices, 102
    building flat and responsive
        organization, 109–110
    building value-creating corporate
        center, 109, 110–111
    five effective practices to
        optimization of, 109–114

price/earnings ratio and expansion trend, as strategy metric, 249

prices, increasing prices to offset inflation, 200

pricing, as lever to build organic growth engine, 184

pricing strategies
focusing on, 196–197
as lever to build organic growth engine, 185

principles
of execution, xvi, 163–224
guiding principles, 82–83
of leadership, xvi, 1–70, 25–34
of strategy, xvi, 73–159

proactive leader, described, 13

proactiveness, as core personal characteristic, 3, 10, 13

processes
digital transformation of, 131
implementation of standardized processes, 205–206

product innovation, excelling at, 193–194

product line contribution margin, as execution metric, 256

product management strategy, execution of, 211–212

products, consistently delivering superior product, 206–207

program management, developing exceptional program management skills, 213

projects, investing in major projects with partner, 158

promotion, from within for senior management positions, 37

protecting the house, as strategy mechanism, 252

pulse surveys, use of, 40

purpose, defined, 79–80

purpose, values, and mission, as principle of strategy, xvi

purpose, values, and vision
as defining core philosophy, 55
as principle of strategy, 73, 77–92

purpose statement
development of, 80–81
exemplary ones, 81–82

Pyhrr, Pete, 218

Q

quarterly report on state of business, as leadership mechanism, 240–241

R

Reagan, Ronald, 180

real-time environmental scan
to detect and assess trends, 151
as essential lifeline, 127–129
as one of seven fundamental components to building a successful and high-impact learning organization, 61, 62

recognition of excellence, awards in, as leadership mechanism, 243

recruitment, from the outside for senior-level positions as high-risk, 28

red flag mechanisms, as strategy
mechanism, 253
references, validating of, 29
reporting structure, optimization of,
109, 112–113
repurposing products, as lever to build
organic growth engine, 186
response plan, developing an effective
one as essential lifeline, 131–132
retention, innovative approaches
to, 40
return on invested capital, as strategy
metric, 245
Ridley, Matt, 136
right people
described, 15
framework for right people in
right positions, 21–23
questions for each person who
is being considered for
critical position, 22–23
in the right positions, xvi, 14–15
risks, managing risks well, 216–217
Roman Legion, 66, 164–165
Roosevelt, Eleanor, 77
Roper Technologies
cash conversion cycle of, 199
cash return on investment
(CRI), 253
decentralized model of, 105
as example of execution
excellence, 164
as example of reimaging business
model, 113
as example of successfully
executing acquisitions, 187

examples of exceptional unique
practices, 95–96
unique practices of, 94
Rosenberg, Jonathan, 32, 142, 235,
239, 241
rule of seven (Google), as leadership
mechanism, 239–240

S

sales, inventory, and operations
planning (SIOP), use of,
206, 208
sales and distribution channels,
optimization of, 201–202
Sandberg, Sheryl, 41–42
SARS outbreak, as example of
shock, 148
scalability, unleashing the power
of, 190
scaling, as lever to build organic
growth engine, 184
scenario analysis, as integral part
of high-performance plan,
153–154
Schmidt, Eric, 32, 142, 235, 239, 241
70/20/10 rule (Google), as leadership
mechanism, 239
severe shocks, 119, 120
SG&A (selling, general, and
administrative), 218
SG&A expenses as percentage of sales,
as execution metric, 257
shared consciousness, defined, 69
Sharma, Robin S., 192
shocks
examples of, 148